AMERICA COOKS KOSHER

THE ALL-SEASON
ALL-REASON
KOSHER COOKBOOK

D1247060

The recipes in AMERICA COOKS KOSHER have been screened for compliance with Kosher dietary laws. However, if you have any doubts about the kashrut of any recipe, please consult your Rabbi.

When references are made to MARGARINE, the intent is that it is PAREVE MARGARINE. It is important to read labels carefully as some margarines are dairy.

All liqueurs require kosher certification.

Please also be aware that ingredients in recipes are subject to change due to availability.

This book or any portion thereof may not be reproduced in any form without the written permission from the publisher.

Copyright © 2004
by
Beth Tfiloh Congregation
and Beth Tfiloh Dahan Community School

ISBN: 0-9748255-0-6

1st Printing October 2004

For additional copies, please use the order form in the back of the book.

WIMMER
COOKBOOKS

A CONSOLIDATED GRAPHICS COMPANY

800.548.2537 wimmerco.com

TABLE OF CONTENTS

KOSHER FOR PASSOVER   WINE SUGGESTION

Jay Schlossberg-Cohen

Beth Tfiloh is the largest Modern Orthodox congregation in Baltimore, Maryland. It stands as a pillar in the local and international Jewish community and is an active center of communal life. Beth Tfiloh presently serves the spiritual, educational, cultural and social needs of 1300 member families from a wide range of backgrounds and levels of observance.

The Beth Tfiloh Dahan Community School, founded in 1942, is Baltimore's largest coeducational Jewish Day School with a growing population of over 1000 students. It is nationally renowned and has received numerous awards for excellence in education.

Beth Tfiloh Congregation
and
Beth Tfiloh Dahan Community School

3300 Old Court Road
Baltimore, Maryland 21208
410-486-1900

KASHRUT...THE AMERICAN DREAM?

For a Jew who wants to keep kosher in the 21st century, our country has become "the American Dream." I remember growing up in Jewish New York when there were only a handful of restaurants that were kosher. Now, there seem to be hundreds, serving everything from pizza to prime rib ... with sushi "to go." I remember as a child when the choices of available kosher wines were limited to Concord or Malaga. Now there is everything from Chardonnay to Gewürztraminer! As a child I remember taking a big ice cooler along on our family vacations so that we would have kosher food to eat. Now, just about every supermarket in every city in the country is filled with kosher products ranging from the traditional to the quintessential "American" foods. Even popular products such as Oreo Cookies and Campbell's vegetable soup have gone kosher! And if you don't want to bother shopping for food on vacation ... then you can just board a kosher cruise ship to everywhere from Barbados to the Baltic Sea! "God bless America!"

But while kosher food is readily available "out there," it is within our homes that the food we prepare has the most profound effect on future generations. Most of us have fond memories of the tastes and smells that emanated from our mothers' and grandmothers' kitchens. Their gefilte fish and cholent, their kugels and kreplach are so much a part of who and what we are today. So here's the challenge: it has often times been said that ours is the generation that gives our children everything ... everything but memories. What "kosher" memories are we giving our children? And here's the second challenge: many of the foods associated with the Jewish people—from chopped liver to chicken fat—are no longer considered healthy. Indeed, many of the ingredients that went into Jewish cooking—potatoes, noodles, flour, eggs, scraps of meat—were used because they were relatively inexpensive. In the 17th and 18th century, the vast majority of the Jews of Europe were poor, so their menus included high proportions of relatively inexpensive ingredients which were very filling.

But the Jews living in 21st century America are part of one of the most affluent Jewish communities in history. So here's the third challenge: how do we blend traditional Jewish tastes with modern ingredients and recipes? How do we bring together the old and the new? Beth Tfiloh, as a Modern Orthodox congregation, has dealt with this challenge in every aspect of our religious heritage; blending together the old and the new, the traditional and the contemporary, the modern and the Orthodox. We've done this in the synagogue and school. This cookbook attempts to do that in our kitchens and dining rooms as well. One popular commercial proclaims, "Nothing says loving like something from the oven!" We hope this cookbook will help spread the love of Jewish cooking and the Jewish heritage into countless American Jewish homes.

We are grateful to the many volunteers who have given their time and effort, their heart and soul, to this endeavor. For those who made this wonderful cookbook possible, we will use the ancient words of King Solomon: "Many women have done superbly, but you surpass them all!"

Rabbi Mitchell Wohlberg, Beth Tfiloh Congregation and
Dean, The Beth Tfiloh Dahan Community School

FROM AMIT'S PALETTE

Amit Yaffe is an Israeli-born artist now living in Baltimore with her husband and two sons. She studied Graphic Design at the WIZO-Hadassah Nerri Bloomfield School of Design in Haifa, Israel. We are honored to showcase her beautiful hand-painted artwork throughout *America Cooks Kosher*.

The book cover Amit has designed and illustrated represents this unique kosher cookbook where American culture is combined with Jewish heritage. Amit created an original watercolor tapestry which weaves together the American and Jewish food symbols into one perfect package. This patchwork quilt of symbolic foods subtly reminds us of our warm, familiar kitchen memories. The rich colors symbolize the richness of our intergenerational experiences.

Amit has included the foods and flowers many of us consider synonymous with American and Jewish cultures. Most notable are the "seven species" which, according to the Torah, represent the fruit and grains that the land of Israel is blessed with. They are wheat, grapes, pomegranates, figs, olives, dates and barley. The seven species surround the blue Star of David, a most notable symbol of the Jewish people. Amber waves of grain, golden wheat, farmers' corn and field daisies depict the landscape of America many of us remember learning about in grade school.

The challah, the traditional bread eaten on Shabbat, is shown opposite the fish, a symbolic food served on Rosh Hashanah. The fish also represents good luck in the Jewish tradition.

To complete the artist's representation of the blending of our cultures, Amit chose the familiar American red, white and blue bunting which also serves here as a chuppah, a Jewish wedding canopy. The chosen symbols marry together the traditional Jewish cooking of yesterday with the contemporary American kosher cooking of today.

We hope the beautiful artwork of this book makes it as pleasing to your eye as these recipes will be to your palate!

ABOUT "AMERICA COOKS KOSHER"

America Cooks Kosher" has been an exciting journey with the input of over 200 devoted and talented committee members, comprised of the school parents, congregants and friends of the Beth Tfiloh Synagogue and Beth Tfiloh Dahan Community School of Baltimore, Maryland. Unlike a cookbook written by *one* chef with *one* style, this book reflects many varied cooking styles and trends from Bubby's matzah ball soup and home-baked challah to the most up-to-date fusion foods. Our food editors and recipe contributors are talented chefs—each in their own right. Some bring to you their secret family recipes as handed down through the generations—directly from their tables to yours. Others give to you their most current and most beloved recipes ever!

We received an outpouring of more than 800 recipes to this project. All 800 were tested and tasted — a labor of love for many of our committee members. Every recipe submitted was truly a winner. Yet after much deliberation and careful examination, we believe that the 320 recipes featured in *America Cooks Kosher*, **"the chosen ones"**, are the **"best of the best"** bound up in this book just for you.

Whipping up this masterpiece with so many hardworking and talented people has been a rewarding experience for all of us. We fed off each other's innovative ideas, and thrived on each other's determination and drive. It has been our privilege to work with the many master chefs of this book, whether they added a ¼ teaspoon of help or a pound of effort. This book is what it is because of them. Please check pages 13 through 16 to applaud every author of this creation. They were each amazing! Thank you and yasher koach to everyone.

If we had one wish, it would be to jump off this page, meet with you personally and take you by the hand through this wonderful book. *America Cooks Kosher* is sprinkled with food trivia, Jewish stories, American food histories, cooking experiences, wine selections, kosher substitution information, Passover options, children's recipes, and so much more. Blank sidebars are there for you to jot down notes about each recipe while cooking to make it your own. This cookbook's intent is to be personal and user-friendly, no matter how sophisticated or unsophisticated you are in the kitchen, or how experienced or inexperienced you are with keeping kosher. It speaks to anyone and everyone who has a love of food and an appreciation of how food enhances your family's life.

We hope you and your family enjoy this book—we are very proud of it. Refer to it for your American celebrations, Jewish holidays and everyday dining. Each of these recipes and stories is a timeless treasury and a legacy to pass on to your future generations and dearest friends. We would be honored to know that this book was used as a major ingredient in your family's memories, traditions and happy occasions.

Thank you for selecting *America Cooks Kosher*.

Shellye Attman Gilden and Wendy Miller
America Cooks Kosher — Co-Chairs

THE MAIN INGREDIENT — THE LOVE OF FAMILY

"AMERICA COOKS KOSHER" is a celebration of our traditions, our faith and our families. It speaks to generations as it passes down cherished recipes and conjures up memories of holidays and special moments shared. And, so it occurred to me, as my daughter Shellye was actively involved in the creation of this book that was the perfect place to pay tribute to the memory of my dear mother, Ida Attman.

My mother preserved our home and drew our family close together through her love of food. As we gathered at the dining table, we not only feasted on her lovingly prepared dishes, we also shared stories, prayers and dwelled on the love of Yiddishkeit.

A tall and stately woman, my mother presented herself as a woman of regal bearing in both her manner and dress. She was the queen of our household and certainly of the kitchen, as she reigned over the table laden with her food passions during the Sabbaths and Yom Tovim.

My brothers and I spent many childhood days at her side as her loving hands guided us in the preparation of her delicacies. These times would become snapshots forever frozen in our minds of the sumptuous tastes and treasured traditions of our family's life. I can well remember to this day a home filled with enticing aromas. The warmth of the kitchen's activity would emanate throughout our entire household. The scents and sensations of my youth still recall special memories of the holidays and our family and guests as we gathered together around the table.

My mother's recipes and her recipe for a much admired and emulated life have become the pages of our family's history. These are the time-honored ingredients for living that my wife, Phyllis and I now pass along to the younger generations of our family. We remember that no matter what the dish, the love of family remains the main ingredient at all times.

Ida Attman's remarkable spirit of family is the reason for our dedication of this book. Through it we hope to draw people together, foster the love of Judaism and create a bond that will last for generations. Shalom.

Leonard J. Attman

This page is sponsored by
The Phyllis and Leonard Attman Charitable Foundation

Leonard Attman (10 years old), (left), Ida Attman, (center) Harry Attman (right) together on Baltimore and Charles Street in front of the former B&O Building across from today's Mechanic Theatre.

PRESENTING SPONSOR
THE PHYLLIS AND LEONARD ATTMAN CHARITABLE FOUNDATION

DIAMOND SPONSOR
THE ISAAC SAMUEL FAMILY AND THE ELITE SPICE FAMILY
IN MEMORY OF KATARINA (KATHY) SAMUEL
*Her heart and her home were open to all. Her cooking and love gave
physical and spiritual nourishment to her family and added spice to our lives.*

RUBY SPONSOR
Sylvia and Martin Tulkoff

SAPPHIRE SPONSOR
Myra and Bill Fox

GOLD SPONSORS
Chesapeake Communications Group Public Relations
FutureCare Health and Management Corporation
courtesy of the Attman, Gilden, Levitas, and Powers Families

SILVER SPONSORS
The Attman Family of Acme Paper and Supply Company, Inc.
Rosalie and Richard Alter and The Alter and Kershman Families
Randi, Brian, Jordana, Zoe, and Sofia Eisenberg
Shellye and Steve Gilden and Family
Lowell and Harriet Glazer Family Foundation
Carol and Sheldon Glusman
Kedem Royal Wine Corporation
Jeffrey, Wendy, Joshua, Adam, and Erin Miller
Brenda Brown Rever, Sara Brick Brown, Amanda Brown Lipitz
Rochlin, Settleman and Dobres, P.A.

BRONZE SPONSOR
Sue Singer

THE CHAI CLUB SPONSORS HONOR

My children, Samara and Arielle Ashpes *by Marcy Ashpes*
Phyllis and Leonard Attman's 50th Wedding Anniversary *by their children and grandchildren*
America Cooks Kosher Cookbook Committee *by Lysbeth Courtney*
Alexandra, Drew, and Mica *by Genine and Josh E. Fidler*
Rose Lazinsky's 95th Birthday *by her grandchildren and great grandchildren*
Leah and Talia Greenwald *by Randee and Benjamin Greenwald*
Lauren, Michael, and Andrew Hurwitz *by Linda and Steven Hurwitz*
Elaine Kuntz, my mother, who instilled the love of home and entertaining *by Nancy Siegel*
Our grandchildren *by Danielle and Saul Roskes*
Natalie Wilder and Rosalie Sellman *by Beth Sellman*
Our daughters, Arielle and Kira *by Dr. Ronald and Mrs. Scarlett Sherman*
My daughters, Lauren and Melanie Wilson and Deborah Margulis *by Jillian Wilson*

THE CHAI CLUB SPONSORS MEMORIALIZE

Parents, David and Dora Nelson *by Ruth N. Brooks*
Janette Hack *by Karen and Bill Glazer*
Samuel and Freda Guben *by Roslyn Guben*
Joseph W. Lazinsky *by Rose Lazinsky*
Roz Lesser, Grandmas Jennie and Mollie *by Loryn Sari Lesser*
Selma and Marvin Newman *by Wand Family*

THE CHAI CLUB SPONSORS

Maureen Davidov and DeVera Nachman
Robert and Shelley Kaye and Family
Dr. and Mrs. Victor Salama and Family
The Sheller Family
The Sochol Family: Lori, David, Ryan, Jason and Jessica
Henry P. Zetlin

THE CIRCLE OF FRIENDS SPONSORS HONOR

The birth of Sidney Ben Rabinowitz *by Henry and Brenda Belsky*
My father, Calvin Belsky *by Robin S. Belsky with love*
Mia, Avi, Liba, and Naomi Benus *by Sharon and Jacob Benus*
Wendy Miller - Mazel Tov on a job well done *by The Blanco Family*
Judy and Myrna Cardin Shabbat Dinners *by Jan and Andy Cardin*
Wendy Miller *by The Felton Family*
Shellye, *we love you... Aunt Myra and Uncle Danny Framm*
Rachael, Sarah, Sam, and Lance *by Leslie and Ron Goldberg*
David Jacob Gordon, 2004 Graduate *by Mr. and Mrs. Arthur Gordon and Family*
Seth Eric Goldstein and Alexandra Danielle Goldstein *by Harriet and Morton Hyatt*
Co-chair, Shellye Gilden-old friends are the best! *by Amy Berman Jackson*
Dr. Melissa Katz *by Ann Katz*
Albert Kishter's 90th Birthday *by Fannie and Albert Kishter*
Our children *by Reyna and Douglas Lederman*
Shellye Gilden and her dedication to Beth Tfiloh *by Barbara Leone*
Our grandchildren *by Marc and Elaine Lowen*
My mother, Rose Cohen a great cook *by Rachel Meisels*
Ian, Ricka, Roberta, and Jonathan *by Phyllis Neuman*
Shellye Attman Gilden; to Food...to Friends...L'chaim *by Debby Schwaber Petasky*
Shellye Gilden *by Pam and Jeffrey Platt*
Erika Rief's Bat Mitzvah *by Joanne and Marshall Rief*
Sydney, Abigail, and Andrew Reibman *by Dr. and Mrs. Stephen Rosenbaum*
Our grandchildren, Rachel, Harry, Julie, Jacob, and Noah *by Irene and Robert Russel*
Our granddaughters, Samara and Arielle *by Selma and Richard Rynd*
Joyce Greenwald *by Sherri Sacks*
Shellye Gilden *by The Saft Family*
Shellye Gilden *by Jack and Ellen Kahan Zager*

THE CIRCLE OF FRIENDS SPONSORS MEMORIALIZE

Seymour Attman *by Dr. Marc and Debbie Attman*
Sharon Roxin and Helen Granat *by Julie and David August*
Marci Glazer Crosby *by Cindy and Jack Bienenfeld*
Florence Liss *by Marcia Caplan*
Evelyn and Jack Deckelbaum *by Susan and Eric Fisher*
Mom, Florence Miller, and sisters who taught me to make gefilte fish *by Helen Gordon*
Milia and Bernie Hercenberg *by Steve and Elaine Hercenberg*
Robi Jungreis-Brager *by The Hollander Family*
Shirley Richman *by Andrea Hyatt*
Parents, Edith and Phillip Fruman *by Betty and Melvin M. Katz*
Edward S. Margolis *by Beverly Margolis*
Loving Dad and Pop-Pop, Claude Magat *by Dr. and Mrs. Scott Millison and Family*
Harold and Norma Naftaly *by The Naftaly Family*
Miriam Kossman *by Sue and Michael Paymer*
Harry Smulson and Samuel Rashbaum *by Beverly and Gerald Rashbaum*
My dear father, Isaac Hecht *by Eleanor H. Yuspa*

THE CIRCLE OF FRIENDS SPONSORS

Aaron's Gourmet Emporium, inc.
Debbi, Louis, Alisa, and Abigail Baer
Elayne Berg
Ellen and Sidney Cohen
Reta and Alfred Davis
Ellen and Stewart Falk
Betty J. and Melvin M. Katz
Linda Freud and Adam Freud Kruger
Hoffman and Company
Shelley Gitomer
Sonia and Stanley Goldberg
Jeanette Greenblatt
Jacob's Ladder
Marcia Leavey
Angela Munitz
Jessica Munitz
Betsy and Allen Robinson
Marcia and Alvin Sachs

CONTRIBUTIONS IN HONOR OF

Robert Brown *by Henry Brown*
Steven, Casey and Rachel Lichter *by Caren Lichter*
Wendy Miller and the Cookbook Committee
by Karen and Leon Wilkowsky

CONTRIBUTORS

Bob and Devorah Brooks
Jann L. Sidorov

CONTRIBUTIONS IN MEMORY OF

Ethel Meyerowitz *by Barbara Aarons*
Hillel Aarons *by Barbara Aarons*
Benjamin Schindler *by Stephanie and Bradley Barthlow*
Steven Gladstein *by Mr. and Mrs. Mel Gladstein*
Louna Lichaa *by Diane Seegull*
Mrs. Helen Walder *by Dr. Charles and Suzanne H. Walder*
Jerome Joel Wilen *by Jaqueline Wilen*

IN KIND SPONSORS

America Cooks Kosher wishes to thank all of the businesses and friends who volunteered countless hours and made this book possible through their participation and dedication. Words cannot express our appreciation for all of your expertise, time, generosity and support. Todah Rabbah!

Faye Adler, *DKS Design*
EKZ Graphic Design and Creative Services
Ned T. Himmelrich
Richard Kremen
Paul Lande, *Jacob's Ladder*
Miller and Associates Advertising
Jack Miller
Gwyn Walcoff, *Chesapeake Communications Group Public Relations*
Amit Yaffe, *cover artist*

*Steve Gilden, Rebecca and Marissa Neuman, Jon Gilden, Jayme and Courtney Wood.
Jeffrey Miller, Josh, Adam, and Erin Miller...
Our words of thanks and gratitude cannot begin to express our heartfelt love for all of your continuous support, encouragement, and patience for over two years as we co-chaired this enormous project. We love you, Shellye and Wendy*

A very special thank you to my parents, Phyllis and Leonard Attman for showing their love, support and belief in me by investing so generously in this project from the very beginning. Thank you, Mom and Dad.

Congratulations to everyone who participated in AMERICA COOKS KOSHER. Your incredible hard work, dedication, expertise, energy, time and talent have been important ingredients to insure the success of this project. This book is the culmination of the collective efforts of everyone listed here on the VOLUNTEER PAGES. Thank you for believing in this project along with us.

COOKBOOK EXECUTIVE COMMITTEE
Shellye Attman Gilden and Wendy Miller, Co-chairs

EDITORS

Julie August
Robin Belsky
Deborah-Jo Essrog
Debi Gallo
Shellye Attman Gilden
Leslie Goldberg
Randee Greenwald
Karen Hyman
Esther Lichtenberg
Loryn Lesser

Wendy Miller
Zipora Schorr
Beth Sellman
Lisa Shepherd
Sylvia Tulkoff
Gwyn Walcoff
Nina Wand
Laurie Weitz
Arlene Wolfe
Ida Zelaya

TYPING COORDINATOR
Sylvia Tulkoff

WORD PROCESSOR
Ida Zelaya

BUSINESS CONCEPTS
Paul Lande
Sue Singer

RECIPE ADVISORS
Julie August
Randi Roxin Eisenberg
Myra Fox
Wendy Miller

TESTERS AND TASTERS COORDINATORS
Maureen Davidov
DeVera Nachman

DATA CHAIR
Myra Fox
Laura Wolf

FOOD FACT RESEARCH
Loryn Lesser
Beth Sellman

FINANCIAL OFFICERS
Deborah-Jo Essrog
Karen Glazer

JEWISH HOLIDAY AND AMERICAN CELEBRATION MENUS
Wendy Miller

COVER AND ORIGINAL ART
Amit Yaffe

COOKBOOK STAFF
Leslie Goldberg
Karen Grabush

SPECIAL THANKS
Rabbi Mitchell Wohlberg and Mrs. Zipora Schorr for their creativity, talent and unending support.

Eve Kresin Steinberg for always being there to listen and help.

Joan Feldman and the entire Beth Tfiloh staff for their continued assistance and guidance.

RECIPE TYPISTS

Sylvia Tulkoff, *Chair*

Irene Amernick
Randee Greenwald
Stephanie Hefter
Sonia Maltinsky
Lori Sochol
Arlene Wolfe
Judy Woolfson
Ida Zelaya

RECIPE TESTERS AND TASTERS

Maureen Davidov and DeVera Nachman, *Co-chairs*

Esther Ann Adler
Ahuva Albrecht
Marcy Ashpes
Julie August
Frona Brown
Cherie Brownstein
Maria Clyde
Ellen Cohen
Melissa Cohen
Sandy Dobres
Randi Eisenberg
Deborah-Jo Essrog
Myra Fox
Shellye Gilden
Karen Glazer
Jeanette Greenblatt
Randee Greenwald
Ann Katz
Shelley Kaye
Marcia Leavey
Elaine Malinow
Sonia Maltinsky
Sheila Margolis
Rachel Meisels

Ellen Miller
Shirley Miller
Wendy Miller
Alyson Nachman
Rebecca Neuman
Paula Pearl
Ann Louise Perlow
Ellyn Polakoff
Josef Rosenblatt
Nancy Safferman
Naomi Samet
Beth Sellman
Nancy Siegel
Susan Sless
Fran Sonnenschein
Katie Spivak
Sylvia Tulkoff
Nadyne Turner
Nina Wand
Dora Waranch
Rachel Steinberg Warschawski
Arlene Wolfe
Ida Zelaya

Cookbook Committee Members

Arlene Abramson
Esther Ann Adler
Ahuva Albrecht
Rosalie Alter
Janice Altman
Irene Amernick
Marcy Ashpes
Phyllis Attman
Steven Attman
Julie August
Robin Belsky
Elayne Berg
Cheryl Berman
Devorah Brooks
Barbara Solomon Brown
Frona Brown
Cherie Brownstein
Jan Cardin
Rabbi Yaakov Chaitovsky
Roz Chazen
Maria Clyde
Ellen Cohen
Melissa Cohen
Odette Cohen
Wimmer Cookbooks
Rachel Dahan
Elka-Minna Dannenbaum
Maureen Davidov
Sandy Dobres
Randi Eisenberg
Deborah-Jo Essrog
Joan Feldman
Anita Fisher
Maria Fleischmann
Myra Fox
Faigie Friedman
Debi Gallo

Shellye Gilden
Karen Glazer
Carol Glusman
Barbara Goldberg
Jane Goldseker
Helen Gordon
Phyllis Gordon
Karen Grabush
Jeanette Greenblatt
Randee Greenwald
Esther Gross
Evelyn Gross
Ann Sue Grossman
Roz Guben
Stephanie Hefter
Judith Herman
Berly Hershkovitz
Harriett Heyman
Bob Hillman
Edward & Robyn Hoffman
Linda Hollander
Linda Hurwitz
Myrna Hurwitz
Karen Hyman
Ann Katz
Betty Katz
Shelley Kaye
Sharan and Mel Kushner
Hillel Kuttler
Paul S. Lande
Michele Lax
Marcia Leavey
Loryn Lesser
Dani Levin
Wende Levitas
Melinda Lewis
Esther Lichtenberg

Barbara Lichter
Rona Love
Elaine Lowen
Carole Luterman
Ellen Macks
Elaine H. Malinow
Sonia Maltinsky
Sheila Margolis
Roslyn Mazur
Rachel Meisels
Lois Miliman
Ellen Miller
Shirley Miller
Wendy Miller
David Mitnick
Marsha Modell
Alyson Nachman
DeVera Nachman
Rebecca Neuman
Jane Oshinsky
Sue Paymer
Paula Pearl
Ann Louise Perlow
Ellyn Polakoff
Raellen Polan Polakoff
Henne Rapkin
Brenda Brown Rever
Alison Roffe
Josef Rosenblatt
Alfred B. Rosenstein
Danielle Roskes
Barbara Roth
Selma Rynd
Marcia Sachs
Nancy Safferman
Dianne Salama
Naomi Samet

Barbara Samuelson
Erika Pardes Schon
Zipora Schorr
Beth Sellman
Lisa Sheperd
Irene Sherman
Beverly Siegel
Nancy Siegel
Diana Sue Singer
Susan Sless
Lori Sochol
Fran Sonnenschein
Katie Spivak
Shirley Stein
Eve Kresin Steinberg
Rosalind Taylor
Larry Trope
Sylvia Tulkoff
Nadyne Turner
Sandy Vogel
Gwyn Walcoff
Gary and Nina Wand
Aileen Waranch
Dora Waranch
Rachel Warschawski
Laurie Weitz
Rabbi Mitchell Wohlberg
Faith Wolf
Laura Wolf
Arlene Wolfe
Jayme Wood
Judy Woolfson
Amit Yaffe
Ida and Jim Zelaya

RECIPE CONTRIBUTORS

Thank you to everyone from far and wide who submitted their treasured recipes and personal stories to AMERICA COOKS KOSHER. This book's contents come directly from YOU. Perhaps you will find a little of yourself, your family or your friends as you read through it. Every recipe we received was a winner! We regret our inability to include every recipe submitted due to page limitation. On behalf of AMERICA COOKS KOSHER, thank you to everyone.

Basia Adler
Esther Ann Adler
Ahuva Albrecht
Eleanor Alpert
Leonard Attman
Lisa Attman
Patti Attman
Phyllis Attman
Ida Attman*
Julie August
Hilary Azreal
Linda Barron
Sharon Bennett
Elayne Berg
Cheryl Berman
Ina Berman
Beth Blanco
Barbara Blumberg
Gladys Blustein
Marilyn Brock
Goldie Brodie
Devorah Brooks
Alicia Broth
Barbara Solomon Brown
Frona Brown
Karen Brown
Chef Diane Bukatman
Yvonne Bull
Carolyn Reznik Camras
Shari Caplan
Jan Cardin
Myrna Cardin
Bernice W. Cohen
Ellen Cohen
Odette Cohen
Wimmer Cookbooks
Liz Courtney
Felicia Cutler
Estelle Cuttler
Rachel Dahan
Sally Davis
Gilda Donner
Myrna Duther
Kendel Ehrlich
Marcey Eisen
Randi Eisenberg
Chef Emilio
Esther Epstein
Ellen Falk
Irma Fishbein
Hanna & Luke Fisher
Sandy Fisher

Bess Fishman
Myra Fox
Anne Fox*
Pam Fradkin
Trudy Freedman
Debra J. Friedman
Faigie Friedman
Elaine Gershberg
Shellye Gilden
Leah Pleeter Girnon
Sally Gladstein
Harriet Glazer
Rachel Glazer
Barbara Goldberg
Mark Goldberg
Leah Goldseker
Helen Gordon
Phyllis Gordon
Joan Gottlieb
Gail Libov Grant
Barbara Green
Jeanette Greenblatt
Randee Greenwald
Esther Gross
Evelyn Gross
Ann Sue Grossman
Roz Guben
Joshua Gurewitsch
Miriam Hack
Faith Harrison
Wendy Hefter
Elaine Hercenberg
Berly Hershkovitz
Selma Hess
Harriett Heyman
Heidi Hiller
Bob Hillman
Ellen Himmelfarb
Linda Hollander
Cheri Hurwitz
Linda Hurwitz
Andrea Hyatt
Joyce Hyman
Ruth Kabernick
June Karlin
Ann Katz
Betty Katz
Julie Katz
Sylvia Katzel
Mona Kaufman
Shelley Kaye
Merle Kierson

Linda Klitenic
Lara Kowalsky
Janet Kramer
Yehudis Krigsman
Sharan and Mel Kushner
Hillel Kuttler
Dorothy Kwatinetz
Norman LaCholter
Neysa Lafferman
Vikki Lane
Rose Lazinsky
Marcia Leavey
Reyna Lederman
Barbara Leone
Karen Levin
Naomi Levin
Wende Levitas
Mira Mitrani Lichter
Rochelle Lipsitz
Suzanne Low
Elaine Lowen
Lillian Lowen
Carole Luterman
Ellen Macks
Sonia Maltinsky
Beverly Margolis
Sheila Margolis
Sherry Mauer
Lillian Mayer
Roslyn Mazur
Rachel Meisels
Wendy Miller
Gail Millison
Joan Morris
DeVera Nachman
Ami Nachomowitz
Robin Neuman
Brenda Nudelman
Brenda Pariser
Sue Paymer
Ruth Pear*
Paula Pearl
Riva B. Pheterson
Pam Platt
Raellen Polan Polakoff
Beverly Rashbaum
Joanne Rief Block
Ann C. Robinson
Betsy Robinson
Ilona Robinson
Harriet Rosen
Mrs. David Rosenblatt

Josef Rosenblatt
Danielle Roskes
Marcia Rubin
Irene Russel
Selma Rynd
Marcia Sachs
Sherri Sacks
Janet Safran
Dorothy S. Sager
Dianne Salama
Janice Salzman
Barbara Samuelson
Erika Pardes Schon
Zipora Schorr
Susan Schultz
Charlotte Schwartz
Elliott Schwartz
Stacy Schwartz
Diane Seegull
Beth Sellman
Ed Shaivitz
Roz Shenker
Irene Sherman
Marianne Shor
Nancy Siegel
Harriet Silverstein
Sylvia Sklar
Mary Jane Snyder
Penny L. Spark
Shirley Stein
Halaine Steinberg
Randy Sweren
Sylvia Tulkoff
Debbie Tyrangiel
Sandy Vogel
Suzanne Walder
Family, Walder
Dora Waranch
Sara Weinberg
Rosie K. Weiner
Jennifer S. Weiss
Ellen White
Paula Williams
Laura Wolf
Ellen Kahan Zager
Miecia Zaplatynski
Ida and Jim Zelaya
Murray & Rhoda Zeligman
Dianne Zweback

*Deceased

APPETIZERS
AND
BEVERAGES

APPETIZERS
AND
BEVERAGES

COUNT YOUR BLESSINGS WITH KASHRUT

Food plays a prominent role in Jewish tradition. The Bible is filled with stories that revolve around food in one way or another. Genesis opens with a story that features an apple—some say an etrog—in the dramatic portrayal of our first couple in which food played a pivotal role. As Genesis continues, we read about the angels who received a home-cooked meal when they came to tell Abraham and Sara they would have a son, Isaac. That same Isaac gave the birthright to his son Jacob after a meal of lentil soup was prepared for him. Moving to Exodus, our redemption from Egypt had at its centerpoint the Paschal lamb and matzah. Even the Land of Israel is referred to as a land flowing with milk and honey.

Why the obsession with food? The key is not in the food itself, but in the energy that is in the food—not just the physical energy, but also the spiritual energy that we believe is invested in food if we elevate it above the mundane. The blessings made before and after we eat put food in a totally different category for us—not just calories and carbs, but sparks for the soul. Food is life. It is a heavenly gift that we should celebrate together. Judaism is a religion that teaches enjoyment of this world, within proper parameters. In the case of food, those parameters are defined by Kashrut.

From generation to generation we gather to celebrate the unbroken union of family. As Jews we believe in the spirituality of that union, and the table as the place where it is nourished. With that in mind, we can understand a little better the concept of the table being like a *Mizbeach*, an altar on which we bring offerings to the Almighty. If Kashrut is a statement of our faith, and if our food, by being blessed, represents the sacred element in our lives, then the very act of mealtime is an affirmation of our spiritual connection and our ability to serve the Divine in our everyday actions.

How easily we can become elevated, and how rewarding it can be to eat a good meal. Just think how much more rewarding it is to prepare a good meal—one that is both pleasurable and kosher, one that is good for the body and for the soul. *America Cooks Kosher* captures that principle—with food that looks good, that tastes good, that is good—and at the same time helps us to *be good* by being kosher as well.

B'tayavon, Bon appetit, Enjoy.

**Zipora Schorr, Director of Education,
The Beth Tfiloh Dahan Community School**

All-American Baked Pizza Dip

Dairy

1 (8 ounce) package cream
cheese, softened

1 teaspoon Italian seasoning

1 (8 ounce) package shredded
mozzarella cheese, divided use

1¼ cups pizza or spaghetti sauce

Preheat oven to 350 degrees.

Beat cream cheese and Italian seasoning until well blended. Spread mixture over the bottom of a 9-inch pie plate.

Top with layers of 1 cup of the mozzarella cheese and pizza or spaghetti sauce; sprinkle with remaining mozzarella cheese.

Bake 15 to 20 minutes or until mixture is thoroughly heated and cheese is melted.

Serve with your favorite crackers.

Makes 3 cups

Mini Mushroom Rolls

Dairy

1 loaf white bread, crusts removed

1 (8 ounce) can mushrooms,
drained

4 tablespoons (½ stick) butter

3 tablespoons flour

¾ teaspoon salt

1 cup light cream

2 tablespoons chives

1 teaspoon lemon juice

Preheat oven to 400 degrees.

Flatten bread slices with a rolling pin. Cut each into 2 strips.

Mince mushrooms in a processor. Sauté mushrooms in butter for 5 to 10 minutes. Reduce heat and stir in flour. Add salt, cream, chives and lemon juice.

Increase heat to medium high and stir until a thick paste forms. Spread mixture over bread slices. Roll up bread and place on a baking sheet. (Can prepare rolls several days ahead and store in refrigerator.)

Bake 10 minutes.

Makes about 48 pieces

Oh-So Famous Spinach Artichoke Dip

Dairy

½ cup grated Romano cheese

1 large clove garlic

1 (10 ounce) package frozen chopped spinach, thawed and firmly squeezed dry

1 (6¼ ounce) jar artichokes, drained, patted dry

1 (8 ounce) container chive cream cheese

2 large eggs

1 cup shredded mozzarella or Italian mix cheese

Cook's Notes

Preheat oven to 375 degrees.

Put Romano cheese in a food processor with a metal blade. Turn motor on and drop garlic through feed tube to mince. Stop machine and add spinach, artichokes, cream cheese and eggs. Process until thoroughly blended; turn into a medium bowl. Fold in mozzarella. Transfer to a 2- or 3-cup baking dish.

Bake 20 to 25 minutes or until heated through. Serve hot with tortilla chips, sour cream and salsa.

Serves 16

Pecan Nutted Salmon Ball

Dairy

1 pound can salmon, skin and bones removed, drained and flaked

1 (8 ounce) package cream cheese, softened

1 tablespoon lemon juice

2 teaspoons grated onion

1½ teaspoons prepared white horseradish

¼ teaspoon salt

¼ teaspoon liquid smoke (optional)

½ cup chopped pecans

3 tablespoons snipped parsley

Combine all ingredients except pecans and parsley. Mix thoroughly and roll into a ball. Refrigerate overnight.

Combine pecans and parsley. Roll salmon ball in nut mixture and chill. Serve with crackers or vegetables.

Asparagus Wraps

Pareve

COOK'S NOTES

Frozen puff pastry squares, room temperature

Dijon mustard

About 1 pound fresh asparagus, bottoms trimmed

1 egg, beaten (optional)

Preheat oven to 375 degrees.

Cut each puff pastry square diagonally to form two triangles. (Diagram 1).

Cut each triangle into thirds. (Diagram 2).

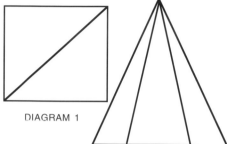

DIAGRAM 1

DIAGRAM 2

Generously spread mustard inside each strip.

Place 1 asparagus spear on each pastry triangle. Wrap asparagus in a spiral from top to bottom, covering most of asparagus spear but leaving the tips uncovered.

Place on a greased baking sheet. For extra shine, brush beaten egg lightly over dough.

Bake about 10 to 15 minutes or until dough is golden brown. Serve immediately.

Baked Spinach Pick-Ups

Dairy

Balls

2 packages (10 ounces) frozen chopped spinach, thawed and drained

2 cups seasoned breadcrumbs

1 cup Parmesan cheese (5 ounce wedge), grated, firmly packed

½ cup butter, melted

4 small green onions, chopped

3 large eggs, beaten

1 dash nutmeg, grated

Preheat oven to 350 degrees.

Combine all ingredients for balls in a large bowl and mix well. Shape into 1-inch balls. Cover and refrigerate or freeze until ready to bake.

Bake on ungreased baking sheet for 10 to 15 minutes. Serve with Mustard Sauce.

Mustard Sauce

½ cup dry mustard

½ cup white vinegar

¼ cup sugar

1 large egg yolk

Combine mustard and vinegar in small bowl. Let stand at room temperature for 4 hours.

Mix sugar and egg yolk in a saucepan. Add mustard mixture and cook and stir over low heat until thickened. Cover and chill. Serve sauce at room temperature.

Makes 70 pieces

COOK'S NOTES

"CHEEZY" CRISPS

Dairy

1 pound (4 sticks) margarine or
    butter, softened
1 pound sharp cheese, shredded

4 cups sifted flour
½ teaspoon cayenne pepper

Preheat oven to 425 degrees.

Combine margarine, cheese, flour and cayenne pepper into a dough. Shape dough into marbles or larger depending on what size cracker you want. Place on an ungreased pan and flatten with bottom of a glass. Bake about 9 to 10 minutes.

Let cool and serve at room temperature. Store in a tin container.

BRUSCHETTA WITH ARTICHOKE PESTO

Dairy

1 (14 ounce) can artichoke
    hearts, drained
Salt and pepper to taste
1 medium clove garlic, crushed
2 tablespoons Parmesan cheese

1 tablespoon lemon juice
3 tablespoons extra-virgin olive
    oil
1 loaf French bread, cut into
    1-inch thick slices and lightly
    toasted

To make pesto, combine artichoke hearts, salt and pepper, garlic, Parmesan, lemon juice, and olive oil in the bowl of a food processor. Purée until smooth and creamy. Cover and chill until needed; return to room temperature before proceeding. (This may be made 2 to 3 days in advance.)

Preheat oven to 400 degrees.

Spread 1 tablespoon of pesto atop each slice of bread. Place on a baking sheet and bake 10 minutes. Serve hot.

Makes 20 pieces

To complement the Bruschetta with Artichoke Pesto, we recommend Rashi Pinot Grigio, an enjoyable Italian white wine with a light citrus flavor and aromas of green apples.

"Egg"-Cellent Pâté

Dairy

21 hard-cooked eggs, chopped

¼ cup chopped pimiento

¾ cup chopped green bell pepper (optional)

¾ cup chopped celery

3 tablespoons chopped parsley

1 onion, grated (optional)

2 teaspoons salt

1 (8 ounce) package cream cheese

½ cup mayonnaise

3 tablespoons ketchup

Combine eggs, pimiento, bell pepper, celery, parsley, onion and salt.

Blend soft cream cheese, mayonnaise and ketchup and add to egg mixture.

Press mixture into a mold that has been coated with nonstick spray. Refrigerate overnight.

Recipe can be cut in half.

The egg commemorates the destruction of the Temple. It is traditionally eaten at the end of Yom Kippur, births and deaths, on Passover and all important life cycle moments and events.

To hard-boil eggs: Place eggs in tepid water to cover the eggs. Bring to boil exactly 12 minutes. Immediately immerse in pot of ice cubes and water. Peel.

Herb-Toasted Pita Crisps

Pareve

2 teaspoons dried thyme

1 tablespoon finely minced fresh parsley

2 teaspoons sesame seeds

¼ teaspoon kosher salt

¼ cup olive oil

3 (6 inch) round pita breads

Preheat oven to 350 degrees.

Stir the thyme, parsley, sesame seeds, salt and oil together in a small bowl.

Using kitchen shears, cut the pita breads in half, then cut each half into four triangles. Tear each triangle in half at the seam, and brush the rough sides generously with herb mixture. Place on a large baking sheet, herb side up.

Bake 12 to 15 minutes or until lightly browned and crisp. These will keep for 3 to 4 days in an airtight plastic bag.

Makes 48 pieces

Tuna Pâté

Dairy

1 package (14 grams) plain
    kosher gelatin

½ small onion

2 (6 ounce) cans tuna, drained

8 ounces less 1 tablespoon sour
    cream (can use reduced-fat
    sour cream)

8 ounces less 1 tablespoon
    regular mayonnaise

1 teaspoon spicy deli mustard

2 teaspoons fresh lemon juice

Put gelatin in a small cereal bowl. Add enough cold water to form a lump. Add enough boiling water to cover. Stir until completely dissolved; gelatin should be the consistency of syrup.

Put onion into a food processor and pulse until very fine. Add tuna, sour cream, mayonnaise, mustard and lemon juice. Pulse mixture until very smooth. Add gelatin and blend again. Pour into a greased small loaf pan or mold.

Chill for 3 hours or overnight. Take a sharp knife and go around edges to remove from mold. Serve as an hors d'oeuvre with French bread.

Layered Taco Dip

Dairy

1 (8 ounce) package cream
    cheese

1 (16 ounce) container sour
    cream

2 (1 ounce) packages taco
    seasoning

Chopped lettuce

Diced tomatoes

1 (8 ounce) package shredded
    sharp Cheddar

Chopped scallions

Blend together cream cheese, sour cream and taco seasonings until smooth. Spread over a large round plate. Layer with lettuce, tomatoes, cheese and scallions.

Serve with tortilla chips.

My Daughter's Sweet Mini Blinis

Dairy

2 egg yolks
½ cup sugar
2 (8 ounce) packages cream
    cheese, softened

1 (1 pound) loaf thin sliced
    bread
¾ cup (1½ sticks) butter, melted
Cinnamon sugar

Cream egg yolks, sugar and cream cheese. Cut crusts off bread and press thin. Cut each slice in half and spread with cream cheese mixture.

Roll up bread. Dip bread roll in butter, then cinnamon sugar. Place on baking sheet and freeze.

When ready to bake, preheat oven to 400 degrees. Bake frozen rolls for 15 minutes.

COOK'S NOTES

Garlic and Sun-Dried Tomato Spread

Dairy

½ cup low-fat cream cheese
½ cup cottage cheese, 1% milk
    fat
¼ cup sundried tomatoes,
    chopped

3 cloves garlic, minced
1 teaspoon basil
1 teaspoon rosemary, chopped

Combine all ingredients in a food processor. Blend until mixture is creamy.

Spread mixture on bagels or serve with fresh cut vegetables and crackers.

Serves 8

Early Jews believed garlic possessed aphrodisiac qualities, and according to a tradition mentioned in the Jerusalem Talmud, Ezra decreed that garlic be eaten on Friday evenings because it "promotes and arouses sexual desire."

Bartenura Moscato D'asti, a crisp and refreshing semi sweet favorite from Italy's renowned Asti region, is just perfect when served with the Garlic and Sun-Dried Tomato Spread appetizer. It features lingering pear, tangerine, nectar and melon flavors.

Also known as garbanzo beans, chickpeas have long been a staple in the Jewish diet. Wise women have long believed that eating chickpeas promotes fertility. It is also recommended that they be eaten on the Sabbath after the birth of a son.

CHUMMUS

Pareve

1 (20 ounce) can chickpeas, drained

½ cup olive oil

¼ cup lemon juice

2-3 cloves garlic, crushed

¼ teaspoon cumin

1 teaspoon dried parsley

Salt and pepper to taste

Place the chickpeas in a colander and rinse with cold water. Drain well.

Combine the drained chick peas, oil, lemon juice, garlic, cumin, parsley and salt and pepper in the bowl of a food processor or blender. Purée the mixture until smooth.

Transfer the chummus to a bowl and chill until needed. Will keep refrigerated for 2 to 3 days.

Serve with Herb-Toasted Pita Crisps (see page 23) or plain pita bread wedges.

LINDA'S EGGPLANT DIP

Pareve

½ cup chopped onion

1 medium fresh garlic clove, minced

1 red bell pepper, chopped fine

1½ teaspoons olive oil

1 (1 pound) eggplant

1 (14½ ounce) can chopped tomatoes

1 (4 ounce) can chopped mushrooms or ¼-pound fresh mushrooms, chopped

1 tablespoon capers

1 tablespoon fresh basil (1 teaspoon dried)

½ teaspoon cumin

½ teaspoon sugar

¼ teaspoon salt

Pepper to taste

1 tablespoon red wine vinegar

In a skillet, sauté onion, garlic and bell pepper in olive oil.

Slice eggplant in half lengthwise. Scoop out pulp and reserve, leaving outer shell intact to use as a boat for serving. Finely chop eggplant pulp and add to skillet along with tomatoes and mushrooms. Add capers, basil, cumin, sugar, salt, pepper and vinegar.

Simmer 10 minutes or until tender. Remove from heat and cool.

Serve at room temperature in hollowed out eggplant shell. Serve with Herb Toasted Pita Crisps (page 23).

Four Cheese Stuffed Mushrooms

Dairy

12 large mushrooms ("stuffers")
1 tablespoon olive oil
1 tablespoon onion, minced
½ teaspoon garlic, minced
½ teaspoon basil

¼ cup white wine
½ cup grated provolone
½ cup grated mozzarella
¼ cup grated Parmesan
¼ cup grated Romano

Preheat oven to 350 degrees.

Remove the stems from the mushrooms; mince stems and set aside.

Heat oil in a skillet. Add onions, garlic and minced mushroom stems. Cook over medium heat about 5 minutes or until soft. Add basil and wine. Simmer about 7 minutes or until almost dry. Cool slightly.

Blend in all cheeses. Fill mushroom caps with cheese mixture.

Place mushroom caps on a lightly greased baking pan. Bake 15 minutes or until lightly browned. Serve warm.

Makes 12

Kahlúa Pecan Baked Brie

Dairy

1 (15 ounce) Brie cheese
½ cup chopped pecans

2 tablespoons kosher Kahlúa* or any kosher coffee liqueur
1½ tablespoons brown sugar

Preheat oven to 350 degrees.

Remove rind from top of cheese as best you can. Place in an oven-safe dish.

Combine pecans, Kahlúa and brown sugar. Spread mixture over top of cheese.

Bake about 5 minutes or until soft. Serve with crackers.

COOK'S NOTES

Note: Be sure Kahlúa is marked with an Ⓤ symbol.

LAYERED PESTO CHEESECAKE

Dairy

1 tablespoon butter, softened

¼ cup fine dry breadcrumbs

½ cup plus 2 tablespoons freshly grated Parmesan cheese, divided use

2 (8 ounce) packages cream cheese, softened

1 cup ricotta cheese

¼ teaspoon salt

⅛ teaspoon cayenne

3 large eggs

½ cup pesto sauce

¼ cup pine nuts, plus extra for garnish

Fresh basil sprigs for garnish

Preheat oven to 325 degrees.

Rub butter over bottom and sides of an 8-inch springform pan. Mix breadcrumbs with 2 tablespoons grated cheese. Coat pan with crumb mixture.

Using an electric mixer, beat cream cheese, ricotta, remaining ½ cup Parmesan, salt and cayenne in a large bowl until light and fluffy. Add eggs, one at a time, beating well after each addition.

Transfer half of mixture to a medium bowl. Mix pesto into remaining half of mixture. Pour pesto mixture into prepared pan; smooth top. Carefully spoon plain mixture over pesto; gently smooth top. Sprinkle with pine nuts.

Bake about 45 minutes or until center no longer moves when pan is shaken. Transfer to a rack and cool completely. Cover tightly with plastic wrap and refrigerate overnight.

Run a small sharp knife around pan. When serving, put a few pine nuts and basil sprigs on top. Serve with crackers.

Wendy's Stuffed Grape Leaves

Pareve

1 (16 ounce) jar grape leaves, rinsed well under cold water

½ cup extra-virgin olive oil, divided use

1 large yellow onion, diced

1 medium-size clove garlic, minced

1 cup chopped fresh parsley

¾ cup raisins

⅓ cup pine nuts, toasted

1 cup canned plum tomatoes, drained and chopped

1 tablespoon dried mint

¼ cup lemon juice

1¾ cups water

Salt and pepper to taste

1 cup raw long-grain rice

Cook's Notes

Blanch grape leaves in boiling water for 2 to 3 minutes; drain in a colander.

Heat ¼ cup olive oil in a medium saucepan. Add onion and garlic and sauté over medium heat until onion is soft. Add the parsley, raisins, pine nuts, tomatoes, mint, lemon juice, water and salt and pepper. Bring to a boil.

Stir in rice and cover. Reduce heat and simmer 20 minutes without stirring. (The mixture will be somewhat wet.) Let cool.

Preheat oven to 350 degrees. Grease a large baking pan.

Spread drained leaves out on a flat surface. Place a heaping tablespoonful of rice stuffing in the middle of each leaf. Fold the sides in and roll up tightly, cigar-fashion.

Place rolled leaves on prepared pan, seam side down. Pack the leaves tightly in the pan. Drizzle with remaining ¼ cup olive oil. Cover and bake 30 to 35 minutes. Let cool and serve at room temperature. (These may be made 1 to 2 days in advance and refrigerated; return to room temperature to serve.)

Makes about 50, serves 12-16

LINDA'S TRADITIONAL MEAT KNISHES

Meat

2 pounds soup meat

2 onions, sliced

2 eggs

½ teaspoon black pepper

½ teaspoon salt

Scant ½ teaspoon Kitchen Bouquet

2 (1 pound) boxes frozen puff pastry dough

Boil meat and onions in water for 2 hours or until tender; drain. Grind meat and onions in a food processor. Add eggs, pepper, salt and Kitchen Bouquet and process.

Cut each dough sheet into 12 squares. Spoon a small amount of meat mixture into each square and fold into little purses.

These can be frozen raw until you are ready to bake and eat.

When ready to bake, preheat oven to 350 degrees.

Bake 45 minutes on a baking sheet.

Knishes are a pocket pastry originating from Russia filled with shredded or ground potato or beef. They were sold from pushcarts in New York in the early 1900's. In Russia and Eastern Europe, they were small in size. In New York, they became HUGE.

ASIAN CHICKEN WINGS

Meat

"These tasty caramelized wings are easy to prepare and are always a favorite when I entertain."

3 pounds chicken wings

2 tablespoons vegetable oil

Salt and pepper to taste

1 cup honey

½ cup soy sauce

½ clove garlic, chopped

2 tablespoons ketchup

Preheat oven to 375 degrees.

Place chicken wings in a dish. Pour oil over wings and sprinkle with salt and pepper.

Combine honey, soy sauce, garlic and ketchup and pour over wings.

Bake 1 hour or until chicken is cooked and sauce is caramelized.

Serves 6

BUBBIE'S ORIGINAL CHOPPED LIVER

Meat /

3 medium onions, chopped
¼ cup vegetable oil
1 pound fresh chicken livers,
    broiled lightly first

1½ tablespoons chicken fat
Salt and pepper to taste
3 hard-cooked eggs

Sauté onions in oil until brown. Add the livers and cook about 5 minutes or until they are firm. (You don't want to overcook; the livers will dry out and get tough.) Livers can be completely broiled to reduce amount of oil needed.

Chop the livers and onions in a food processor or with a manual chopper until a good consistency but not puréed. Add a tablespoon or a little more of chicken fat. Mix. Season with salt and pepper.

Chop the hard-cooked egg with food processor or chopper. Sprinkle on top of chopped liver.

THE BEST QUICK CHOPPED LIVER EVER

Meat

1 (12 ounce) carton frozen
    chopped liver spread, thawed
4 hard-cooked eggs, chopped, or
    4 hard-cooked egg whites,
    chopped

Salt and pepper to taste
½ teaspoon sherry
Parsley for garnish

Mix all ingredients except parsley. Serve in a beautiful bowl and sprinkle top with chopped parsley.

Serves about 6

COOK'S NOTES

YOU WON'T BELIEVE IT'S NOT CHOPPED LIVER – 4 WAYS

Pareve

NUMBER 1

1 large can baby peas, drained

2 large onions, chopped, sautéed in 3 tablespoons oil until well done

1 cup walnuts

Salt and pepper to taste

Put everything in a food processor and blend until the consistency of chopped liver.

NUMBER 2

"When I grew up in Israel, liver was extremely expensive so the pioneers as well as the first settlers served vegetarian chopped liver on holidays, which tasted and looked just like liver."

1 eggplant

½ cup vegetable oil

1 small chopped onion or 3 scallions

2 hard-cooked eggs

Salt and pepper to taste

Peel eggplant and slice into rings. Heat oil in frying pan. Add eggplant and fry until golden brown. Remove from pan into a bowl. Add onion, eggs and salt and pepper to bowl. Mash it all together.

Chill in the refrigerator for 2 hours. Serve over a slice of tomato as an appetizer.

Serves 4-5

(Continued on next page)

NUMBER 3

1 cup sliced mushrooms

1 cup chopped onions

3 tablespoons pareve margarine

3 hard-cooked eggs

¼ pound shelled walnuts

1 teaspoon salt

¼ teaspoon white pepper

COOK'S NOTES

In a large skillet, sauté mushrooms and onions in margarine until the onions are golden brown.

Pass the mushrooms, onions, hard-cooked eggs and walnuts through a food processor or chop very fine in a chopping bowl. Season with salt and pepper. Refrigerate to chill thoroughly.

Serves 6

NUMBER 4

6 large yellow onions, chopped

6 tablespoons margarine

1 (16 ounce) can peas, drained

4 hard-cooked egg whites

2 cups walnuts

1½ teaspoons pareve chicken
   stock mix

⅛ teaspoon salt

⅛ teaspoon pepper

¼ teaspoon ginger

Preheat oven to 350 degrees.

Sauté onions in margarine very slowly until caramelized.

Heat walnuts in oven for a few minutes until warm to the touch (this brings out the flavor).

Process all ingredients together in food processor.

Apricot Glazed Bologna "Casserole"

Meat

This "casserole" of cubed bologna in sauce, freezes very well. If you cook it from its frozen state, defrost and skim off fat.

This recipe is best if prepared several days ahead so the flavor mellows and the fat can be skimmed off.

Try serving this dish with different types of mustards; for example, horseradish mustard, Dijon mustard, honey mustard, deli mustard or traditional mustard.

1 large onion, chopped
2 cloves garlic, minced
2 tablespoons pareve margarine
1 (12 ounce) bottle chili sauce
1 (12 ounce) bottle water
   (use chili sauce bottle)

¼ (1 pound) box dark brown sugar
3 tablespoons white vinegar
Juice of ½ lemon
½ cup apricot preserves
3 kosher midget bolognas, cubed

Preheat oven to 350 degrees.

Sauté onion and garlic in margarine until onion is translucent.

Add chili sauce, water, brown sugar, vinegar, lemon juice and preserves. Simmer 20 minutes. Pour over the cubed bologna in a deep, covered casserole dish.

Bake, covered, for 1 hour, 30 minutes to 2 hours.

Serve with toothpicks.

Serves 6

Olive Tapenade on Pita

Pareve

Olive Tapenade

1 cup pitted ripe black olives, drained

1 medium clove garlic, crushed

Freshly ground pepper to taste

¼ cup extra-virgin olive oil

Put the olives, garlic, pepper, and olive oil in the bowl of a food processor and purée. Transfer to a container and chill until needed.

Return to room temperature before using. This will keep for 4 to 5 days in the refrigerator.

Makes about ¾ cup of Olive Tapenade

Baked Pita

4 (6 inch) pita rounds

Preheat oven to 400 degrees.

Place pita on a baking sheet. Spread each round with 2 to 3 tablespoons Olive Tapenade.

Bake 10 minutes. Cut each piece of pita into 6 wedges and serve.

Makes 24 wedges, serves 8

Cook's Notes

BLACK BEAN AND CORN SALSA

Pareve

This salsa is refreshing, delicious and great with tortilla chips.

16 ounces cooked black beans

16 ounces frozen or fresh white corn

½ cup fresh cilantro, chopped (optional)

¼ cup chopped green onion

¼ cup chopped red onion

⅓ cup lime juice

2 tablespoons vegetable oil

1 tablespoon ground cumin

1 garlic clove, chopped

1 chopped dried red pepper with seeds

1 cup ripe or canned diced tomatoes

Combine all ingredients except tomatoes. Marinate for 2 hours or more.

Add tomatoes and serve.

COLORFUL CORN SALSA

Pareve / Dairy

This is the best—so versatile. Serve as a side dish, as a salsa with chips, as a topping for fish, or as a topping over greens.

2 pounds frozen corn kernels, do not cook

1 (10 ounce) box frozen baby lima beans

1 small red onion, chopped

10 large green or black olives, sliced

1 small red bell pepper, diced

1 small green bell pepper, diced

3 tablespoons crushed, hot red pepper (from a jar – not flakes)

2 teaspoons oregano

3 tablespoons olive oil

¼ cup red wine or balsamic vinegar

6-8 ounces crumbled feta cheese (optional as a dairy dish)

Defrost corn and lima beans in a covered dish. When thawed, add remaining ingredients and mix well.

Allow flavors to blend for an hour while chilling in the refrigerator. Lasts for several days.

Serves 8 as a side dish and many more as a dip or topping

SPICY BEAN DIP

Pareve

10 ounce can red kidney beans, rinsed and drained

1-2 cloves garlic, crushed

1 tablespoon chili powder

½ teaspoon celery seed

¼ teaspoon cayenne pepper

Salt to taste

⅛ teaspoon black pepper

1 tablespoon dried parsley

2 tablespoons lemon juice

½ cup olive oil

Put all ingredients except olive oil in the bowl of a food processor. Purée until pasty. In a slow, steady stream, add olive oil while continuing to process, until thick and creamy.

May prepare 1 to 2 days in advance and refrigerate until needed. Bring to room temperature before serving.

Serve with tortilla chips or vegetables.

BAKED TRAIL MIX

Pareve / 🍪

10 ounces chopped walnuts

8 ounces date nuggets, chopped

4 ounces golden raisins

4 ounces dried cranberries

3 egg whites

1 teaspoon vanilla

Mix all ingredients. Line miniature cupcake pans with paper liners. Fill cups until almost full. Put in a cold oven. Turn on oven to 350 degrees. Bake for 15 to 18 minutes or until a little crunchy on top.

Serves 24-30

For variety, use other dried fruit

Add pareve chocolate chips for an option.

"CINN-FUL" PECANS

Pareve /

1 egg white	¾ teaspoon salt
1 tablespoon water	1 teaspoon cinnamon
1 cup sugar	1 pound pecans

Preheat oven to 200 degrees.

Beat egg white and water until frothy, not stiff. Stir in sugar, salt and cinnamon. Add pecans and stir until well covered.

Spread pecans on a large greased baking sheet. Bake 45 minutes, stirring every 15 minutes, or until dry and tasty.

Makes a terrific hostess gift or holiday gift!

SWEET DORM DELIGHT

Pareve / Dairy

A favorite for college students!

12 ounces chocolate chips (regular or pareve)	1 (16 ounce) box cinnamon flavor Chex cereal
½ cup peanut butter	1½ cups 10x powdered sugar
¼ cup butter or margarine	

Heat chocolate chips, peanut butter and butter or margarine for 1 minute in a microwave. Mix cereal and melted mixture in a large bowl. Spread on a foil-lined baking sheet to cool.

Sprinkle powdered sugar over mixture, then break into bite-size pieces. Store in a plastic bag.

Makes 9 cups

Apricot Brandy Slush

Pareve

Very refreshing. Great after a day on the beach.

4 tea bags
2 cups boiling water
7 cups cold water
2 cups sugar
1 (12 ounce) can orange juice concentrate, thawed

1 (12 ounce) can lemonade concentrate, thawed
2 cups apricot brandy
50/50 citrus soda, 7-Up or Sprite, chilled
Mint leaves or lemon slices for garnish

Steep tea bags in boiling water at least several hours or overnight.

In a large bowl, mix steeped tea with cold water, sugar, orange juice concentrate, lemonade concentrate and brandy. Stir well. Freeze in two ½-gallon containers.

To serve, fill each glass or mug half-way with slush. Fill the rest of the glass or mug with chilled soda.

Garnish with mint leaves or lemon slices.

Café Brûlot

Pareve

1 cinnamon stick
12 whole cloves
Peel of 1 orange
Peel of 1 lemon

6 sugar cubes
8 ounces brandy
8 ounces Curaçao
2 cups strong black coffee

In a chafing dish, put cinnamon, cloves, orange and lemon peels and sugar.

Add brandy and Curaçao and stir together.

Ignite brandy and gradually add coffee.

Serves 10-12

COOK'S NOTES

Bourbon Slush

Pareve

"I first served this recipe to Little League parents gathered at our house. Most of the boys were new to the game and the parents really didn't know each other, having only their sons on the team as a common factor. The slush, munched leisurely, was a tasty ice breaker!"

COOK'S NOTES

REGULAR RECIPE	DOUBLE RECIPE
2 teabags	2 family size teabags or 4 regular size
1 cup boiling water	2 cups boiling water
1 cup sugar	2 cups sugar
3½ cups cold water	7 cups cold water
6 ounce can orange juice, thawed	12 ounce can orange juice, thawed
¾ cup bourbon	1 cup bourbon (I choose not to double)
½ of 6 ounce can lemonade, thawed	6 ounce can of lemonade, thawed

Steep teabags in boiling water for 2 to 3 minutes. Squeeze teabags to remove all moisture and throw them away.

While teabags are steeping, pour the measured sugar into a container 2½ inches deep and 12 inches in diameter or one (two if recipe is doubled) plastic pitcher that can be tightly sealed and placed into the freezer.

Add the hot tea to the sugar and stir until dissolved. Add cold water, orange juice concentrate, bourbon and lemonade concentrate.

Freeze until ready to serve; slush may be prepared several days to a week ahead. Remove from freezer about 15 to 30 minutes before serving.

Serve drink mixture in small cups with a spoon to munch the icy mixture.

Slush may be partially thawed and frozen again for the next party. (Thaw completely, stir and then freeze a second time.)

Ed's Cosmopolitan

Pareve

1 ounce vodka

½ ounce Triple Sec liqueur

¼ lime, squeezed

1 ounce cranberry juice

Lime slice for garnish

Mix vodka, Triple Sec, lime juice and cranberry juice in a shaker with ice to cool. Pour into a martini glass, straining ice, and serve.

Garnish with a slice of lime.

COOK'S NOTES

Kahlúa Party Punch

Pareve

Great for holidays.

2 cups kosher Kahlúa

1 can (12 ounces) frozen apple juice concentrate

½ cup lemon juice

1-2 cups small chunks of ice

1 (750 ml) bottle sparkling apple juice

1 quart bottle club soda or lemon-lime soda

1 bottle (750 ml) dry champagne

Lemon and orange slices for garnish

Chill all ingredients.

Combine Kahlúa with undiluted apple juice concentrate and lemon juice. Pour mixture over small chunks of ice in a punch bowl.

Add sparkling apple juice and club soda or lemon-lime soda. Add champagne and stir gently.

Add lemon and orange slices for garnish.

Serves 30 (½-cup) servings, makes about 1 gallon

FROZEN HOT CHOCOLATE

Dairy

½ cup unsweetened Dutch processed cocoa

¾ cup sugar

2¾ cups low-fat milk (increase or decrease the richness of this concoction to your taste by replacing some or all of the low-fat milk with whole or nonfat milk)

In a small saucepan, combine the cocoa and sugar. Stir in just enough milk to form a smooth paste. Stir in all but 2 tablespoons of the remaining milk. Stir over low heat until mixture is warm and sugar is dissolved.

Pour into a shallow pan or ice cube trays, cover well and freeze for at least 6 hours or overnight. Mixture can be frozen for one week or more.

Break frozen mixture into chunks with a fork or table knife. Place chunks in a food processor bowl fitted with the steel blade. Process with the remaining 2 tablespoons milk until no lumps remain and mixture is thick and light in color.

Serve at once in frozen goblets as a spoon drink or scrape into a bowl, cover and refreeze for at least 8 hours or overnight. Scoop and serve frozen.

Variations:

Frozen Chocolate Malt: Add 2 tablespoons malt powder to cocoa mixture in Step 1.

Frozen Mocha or Chocolate Espresso Bean: Add 4 teaspoons instant espresso or coffee powder to cocoa mixture in Step 1. Or add 4 teaspoons freshly-ground espresso beans to the frozen mixture in Step 3.

Frozen Orange or Lemon Chocolate: Add ½ teaspoon freshly grated orange or lemon zest in Step 1.

Frozen Chocolate Mint: Add a scant ¼ teaspoon mint extract.

Serves 6-7

Hot Toddy for One or a Crowd

Pareve

Hot Toddy for One

2 ounces whiskey, rum or brandy

1 teaspoon honey or sugar

5-6 ounces boiling water

Lemon slice

Cinnamon stick

2-3 whole cloves

Put alcohol and honey or sugar in a cup and fill with boiling water.

Stir and garnish with lemon, cinnamon stick and cloves.

Serves 1

Hot Toddy for a Crowd

3 quarts water

12 ounces brandy, scotch,
   bourbon or whiskey

¼ cup honey or sugar, divided use

12 lemon twists

6 cinnamon sticks

5 whole cloves

Boil 3 quarts of water in a large pot.

For each serving, place 1 ounce liquor and 1 teaspoon honey or sugar into a mug and fill to the top with boiling water.

Twist a lemon peel above the liquid and drop it in.

Serves 12

Cranberry Citrus Warmer

Pareve

1 (32 ounce) bottle cranberry
   juice cocktail

2 cups orange juice

½ cup honey

½ cup lemon juice from
   concentrate

¼ cup lime juice from
   concentrate

3 whole cloves

2 cinnamon sticks

1 (32 ounce) bottle ginger ale

In a large saucepan or pot, combine all ingredients except ginger ale. Simmer over medium heat for about 15 minutes to blend flavors.

Remove spices with a spoon.

Just before serving, add ginger ale and heat through. Serve hot, garnish as desired.

COOK'S NOTES

TIO PEPE SANGRÍA

Pareve

1 (750 ml) bottle wine (a heavy red or white that is not too sweet)

½ cup Triple Sec

½ cup brandy

¾ cup sugar

1 apple, unpeeled and diced

1 orange, unpeeled and cut in wedges

1 lemon, unpeeled and quartered, then cut into smaller pieces

Mix all ingredients.

Serves 8

Generally, a sangría has at least two fruits. Choose from diced apples, lemons, oranges, grapes, peaches, cherries, melon slices, strawberries – there are plenty of choices, especially in the summer.

Instead of rum or brandy, try grenadine and sweet vermouth and substitute cranberry juice for the lemon or lime. Or use a peach-flavored brandy with a white Spanish wine and make sure the fruit includes fresh peaches.

WHITE ZINFANDEL SANGRÍA

Pareve

1 (750 ml) bottle chilled Zinfandel

½ cup peach schnapps

2 tablespoons orange liqueur

2 tablespoons sugar (optional)

2 cinnamon sticks, broken in half

1 lemon, sliced

1 orange, sliced

1 peach, sliced into wedges

1 (10 ounce) bottle club soda, chilled

Ice cubes

Mix all ingredients except club soda and ice in tall pitcher. Refrigerate at least 30 minutes to allow flavors to blend.

Mix in club soda.

Fill 6 wine glasses with ice cubes. Pour sangría over ice and serve.

Serves 6

BREADS
AND
SOUPS

BREADS
AND
SOUPS

A SPICE CALLED SABBATH

There is a wonderful little story in the Talmud about Rabbi Yehoshua ben Hananiah. When asked by the Roman Emperor "Why does the Sabbath dish have such a fragrant odor?" the rabbi replied, "We have a certain spice called *The Sabbath* which we put in it and which gives it the fragrant odor."

One can easily picture the Roman seeking to understand the secret of Jewish cooking, only to be told that it lies within Jewish observance. Jewish life and food have always been tightly bound together. From prayers thanking the Almighty for sharing the earth's food bounty, to stories of feasts and famines; from the complex ritual practices of Kashrut observance, to the ceremonies of the ancient Temple; and from the miraculous mannah of the desert, to the Sabbath and holiday meals enjoyed regularly by our own families, food plays a central role in Jewish life. In part this is because Judaism elevates the mundane everyday elements of existence and imbues them with holiness. Since food is so central to sustaining life, it is natural that food is such an important part of our religious practices and observances.

With this in mind, it is especially pleasing to share the secret of the fragrance of Baltimore Jewish cooking. If we had to explain what secret ingredient makes our food so special, we would say it's called "Beth Tfiloh." I am sure you will find this collection of recipes inspirational in creating your own savory aromas and sweet occasions. Enjoy!

Sandy Vogel, Director
The Beth Tfiloh Dahan Center for Jewish Learning

Traditional Challah

Pareve

Challah, the braided egg bread eaten on Shabbat and holidays, reminds us of manna because both challah and manna are perfect foods. We place 2 loaves of challah on our Shabbat and festival tables to remember that our ancestors received a double portion of manna on Friday so they wouldn't have to gather and carry food on the Sabbath.

For centuries, Jewish women in Eastern Europe baked ladders into their challahs for special occasions: for the meal just before Yom Kippur, so that their prayers for forgiveness could ascend to heaven, and for Shavout, to remember how Moses climbed all the way up Mount Sinai to receive the Torah.

All ingredients should be at room temperature

3 packages dry yeast (2 tablespoons plus ¾ teaspoon)

¾ cup sugar plus 2 teaspoons sugar, divided use

2 cups warm water

8 cups flour

⅔ cup oil

3 eggs

1 tablespoon salt

Egg wash (see below)

Poppy seeds or sesame seeds or cinnamon sugar (optional)

Egg wash

1 egg, beaten

1 teaspoon vanilla sugar (optional)

Combine yeast, 2 teaspoons sugar and water. Let sit until yeast foams, about 10 minutes.

Place flour, remaining ¾ cup sugar, oil and eggs in a large bowl of a mixer.

Add yeast mixture to flour mixture and knead with dough hook until well blended. Mix on low speed for 10 minutes. After 5 minutes of kneading, add salt. (Kneading may be done by hand.)

Put dough in a large bowl sprayed with cooking spray, lightly rub a little oil on top of dough. Cover with a dish towel and let rise in a warm, draft-free place until double in size, about 1 to 1½ hours.

Punch dough down and shape into loaves. Place on baking sheet sprayed with cooking spray. Let challah rise, covered, for about 1 hour or until doubled in size.

Preheat oven to 350 degrees.

Brush egg wash over challah. Sprinkle with sesame or poppy seeds or with cinnamon sugar, if desired.

Bake in center of oven for 30 minutes or until brown on top. Cool on wire racks.

Makes 2 large or 3 medium loaves

The Bible (Leviticus 2:13) commands, "On all your meal-offerings shall you sprinkle salt," and the Talmud (Menachot 20a, b) extended the requirement to all sacrifices. Before challah is eaten, it is traditionally dipped into salt as a reminder of the salt used on the sacrificial altar of the Holy Temple.

Salt is a preservative, and since sacrifices were not always eaten immediately by the Priest or the offerer, it was necessary to use salt to retard food spoilage.

Salt in general was important throughout biblical and later times. Treaties were sealed with salt. The Bible (Numbers 18:19) speaks of "an everlasting covenant of salt." The Talmud says, "The world can get along without pepper, but it cannot get along without salt."

BREAD MACHINE SWEET CHALLAH

Pareve

In Jewish tradition, no food is more important than bread. In Deuteronomy 8:8, bread is mentioned before all other foods. It is for this reason that when the blessing over the bread (Hamotzi) is recited at the beginning of the meal, it covers all foods to be eaten during the course of the meal.

2¼ teaspoons yeast (for bread machine)

8-10 tablespoons sugar

1-1½ teaspoons salt

4 cups bread flour

2 eggs

¼ cup canola oil

¾ cup water

Consult bread machine manual as to what order ingredients should be added. Add ingredients according to directions. Put on dough cycle.

When cycle is over, it is time to braid the challah. After braiding, cover with either a towel or plastic wrap. Put in a warm area (like in a microwave with the light on) for 3 to 4 hours or until double in size.

Preheat oven to 325 degrees.

Bake 20 to 30 minutes; do not let the bread get dark. Remove and cool on a rack or it will get soggy on the bottom.

This recipe can be halved for a 1 pound loaf.

Makes 2 loaves

COOK'S NOTES

BRAIDING CHALLAH
6 STRAND INSTRUCTIONS

This method, though not difficult, requires some practice. Try practicing using colored string. It's worth the work and makes a gorgeous challah!

Divide the dough into 6 equal balls.

To make the braids, use little or no flour. If the dough sticks use a very light dusting. Using the palms of your hands, roll each ball into ropes approximately 12" long, thick in the center and tapered to a point on each end.

Set aside, covered, and allow to rest for a few minutes.

Form two 3-strand braids.

Line up the 6 strands and pinch the ends together (Figure 1)

Figure 1

Bring strand #6 from the right end over strand #1 and up to the left (Figure 2).

Bring strand #1 from the left up to the top right (Figure 3). You now have a four-legged "creature" with the arms crossed over each other.

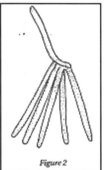

Figure 2

Figure 3

Keeping the "legs" spread apart in pairs, the left "arm" (as you face it) comes down into the center between the "legs" (Figure 4).

Bring the outer right "leg" over and up to form a new top left "arm" (Figure 5).

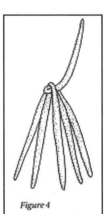

Figure 4

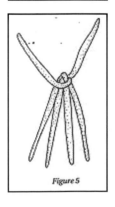

Figure 5

(Continued on next page)

In many passages throughout the Bible, the significance of bread is indicated. Whenever a guest is invited for a meal, bread is served (Genesis 18:5).

In present-day Israel, the mayor of Jerusalem often greets distinguished visitors at the entrance to the city with an offering of bread and salt. Today, it is a common Jewish practice to bring a gift of bread and salt when visiting someone in their new home.

BRAIDING CHALLAH – 6 STRAND INSTRUCTIONS *(Continued)*

The top right "arm" comes down between the "legs" (Figure 6).

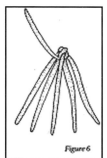

Figure 6

Repeat the pattern. The left outer "leg" comes up to form the new right "arm" and the left "arm" comes down to the center. The right "leg" comes up to form the left "arm", and the right "arm" comes down to the center.

Continue by alternating: Left "leg" up to become right "arm", left "arm" down to the center. Right "leg" up to become left "arm", right "arm" down to the center. Always keep hold of the last strand you moved so you remember your location in the pattern. Keep the "legs" spread in pairs so that the "arms" can easily be brought down the center (Figure 6).

When braiding, if you become disoriented, remember that "arms" come down, "legs" come up. If you make an error, open the braid and begin again.

Finish by pinching the ends closed.

COOK'S NOTES

ALL-AMERICAN DROP BISCUITS

Dairy

2 cups flour

1 tablespoon baking powder

2 teaspoons sugar

½ teaspoon cream of tartar

⅛ teaspoon salt

½ cup butter

1 cup milk

Preheat oven to 450 degrees.

In a bowl, stir together flour, baking powder, sugar, cream of tartar, and salt. Cut in butter until mixture resembles coarse crumbs.

Make a well in the center and add milk. Stir until dough clings together. Drop dough from a tablespoon onto a greased baking sheet. Bake 10 to 12 minutes.

Makes 10-12 biscuits

An American classic, developed by the colonists, that took the place of bread.

AMY'S CRANBERRY QUICK-BREAD

Dairy / Pareve

2 cups sifted flour

1 cup sugar

1 teaspoon salt

½ teaspoon baking powder

½ teaspoon baking soda

¼ cup shortening or butter or margarine

1 teaspoon grated orange peel

¾ cup orange juice

1 egg, well-beaten

1½ cups (or more) fresh cranberries, chopped, or ⅔ cup chopped and ⅔ cup whole

½ cup nuts (optional)

Preheat oven to 350 degrees.

Sift together flour, sugar, salt, baking powder and baking soda. Cut in shortening.

Combine orange peel, juice and egg. Add to dry ingredients and mix until moistened. Add berries and nuts.

Turn into a greased 9x5x3-inch pan. Bake 1 hour.

Kendel S. Ehrlich

Dear Beth Tfiloh:

Thank you for this opportunity to share a recipe for Pineapple Bread that I inherited from my mother. Pineapple Bread was a real favorite in my house growing up; I can remember my siblings and I getting excited whenever my mom made it for us. It's also a quick and tasty addition to any holiday spread.

I hope all who buy *America Cooks Kosher* will enjoy this recipe as much as I have over the years. Best of luck with this project!

Warmest regards,

Kendel S. Ehrlich

Government House
Annapolis, Maryland 21401

PINEAPPLE BREAD FROM THE GOVERNOR'S KITCHEN

Dairy

From Kendel Ehrlich, Governor Ehrlich's wife, Maryland's First Lady

4 eggs, slightly beaten
1 cup sugar
¼ cup butter
2 tablespoons flour

1 (20 ounce) can crushed
   pineapple with juice
2 slices white bread, cubed

Preheat oven to 350 degrees.

Combine eggs, sugar, butter, flour and pineapple. Mix in bread cubes. Pour into 1½-quart greased casserole dish. Bake for 1 hour until brown and bubbling.

Native Americans used pumpkin as a staple in their diets centuries before the pilgrims landed. When other settlers arrived, they saw the pumpkins grown by the Native Americans. Pumpkin soon became a staple in their diets, too.

Morton, Illinois, is the self-proclaimed "Pumpkin Capital of the World," where Libby has its pumpkin industry and plant.

PUMPKIN BREAD

Pareve

My mother has been making this recipe for 25 years. It is always a big hit, especially for Thanksgiving.

3 cups flour	1 teaspoon salt
2 cups sugar	½ teaspoon double acting baking powder
2 teaspoons baking soda	
1 teaspoon ground cloves (optional)	1 (15 ounce) can pumpkin
1 teaspoon ground cinnamon	⅔ cup vegetable oil
1 teaspoon nutmeg	3 eggs, slightly beaten
	Raisins (optional)

Preheat oven to 350 degrees.

In a large bowl with a fork, mix flour, sugar, baking soda, cloves, cinnamon, nutmeg, salt and baking powder. Add pumpkin, oil, eggs and raisins and mix well until blended.

Divide batter between 2 greased 9x5x3-inch loaf pans. Bake 1 hour or until a toothpick inserted into center comes out clean. Let cool.

POPPY SEED BREAD

Dairy

2½ cups flour	1 cup sugar
¼ cup poppy seeds	3½ teaspoons baking powder
1 teaspoon salt	1¼ cups milk
⅓ cup oil	1 egg
1 teaspoon vanilla	

Preheat oven to 350 degrees. Grease bottom only of two 9x5x3-inch loaf pans.

Mix all ingredients. Beat for 30 seconds and pour into prepared loaf pans.

Bake 50 to 55 minutes or until a toothpick inserted in center comes out clean. Cool slightly. Loosen sides of loaf from pan and remove from pan. Cool completely before slicing.

To store, wrap and refrigerate no longer than one week.

Banana Bread

Pareve

"My grandchildren love this banana bread. Put some peanut butter on the bread, cut into little squares, serve with a glass of milk and you have a nutritious meal."

¾ cup sugar

1½ cups mashed bananas (3 large)

½ cup vegetable oil

2 eggs

2 cups flour

1 teaspoon baking soda

½ teaspoon baking powder

½ teaspoon salt

2 teaspoons vanilla

½ cup chopped nuts (optional)

Preheat oven to 325 degrees.

Mix sugar, bananas, oil, vanilla and eggs in a large bowl with a wooden spoon.

Add flour, baking soda, baking powder and salt and mix until just blended. Do not overmix. Fold in nuts.

Pour batter into a greased 9x5x3-inch loaf pan. Bake 60 to 70 minutes or until a toothpick inserted in center comes out clean.

Serves 8-12

½ cup chocolate chips, raisins or dried cranberries can be added for variety.

Large-scale banana traffic began in 1870 from Jamaica to Boston by schooner. Today, Americans eat more bananas than any other fruit.

Hint: Overripe bananas are good to use when baking. Save in freezer in a zip lock bag and use when needed.

Hint: To ripen bananas, put in a brown paper bag and check daily.

In Jewish tradition, the apple is noted for its healing power as well as its sweetness. Apples were often sent as gifts to people in ill health. The curative power of the apple is associated with its sweetness. The Hebrew word for apple, tapuach, is derived from the word nafach, meaning "exhale" or "emit a sweet scent."

CINNAMON APPLE MUFFINS

Dairy

1½ cups all-purpose flour
½ cup sugar
1½ teaspoons baking powder
1 teaspoon cinnamon
½ cup skim milk

5 tablespoons (⅓ cup) butter or margarine, melted
1 large egg, beaten
1 cup chopped apple
½ cup chopped nuts or raisins

Preheat oven to 375 degrees. Line a 12-cup muffin tin with paper baking cups

Combine flour, sugar, baking powder and cinnamon. Add milk, butter, egg, apple and nuts or raisins. Stir until flour is moistened. Spoon batter into a 12-cup muffin pan.

Bake 18 to 23 minutes or until lightly browned. Let stand 5 minutes and remove from pan.

Makes 1 dozen muffins

COCONUT MUFFINS

Dairy

8 tablespoons (1 stick) butter, melted
1 cup sugar
2 eggs, lightly beaten
1 cup milk
1 teaspoon coconut extract

2 cups all-purpose flour
2 teaspoons baking powder
Pinch of salt
1 cup sweetened shredded coconut

Preheat oven to 375 degrees. Line a 12-cup muffin tin with paper baking cups.

In a large mixing bowl, stir together butter, sugar, eggs, milk, and coconut extract until well blended.

Sift together flour, baking powder, and salt. Add dry ingredients to batter, stirring just until mixture is combined. Fold in coconut. Spoon batter evenly into the muffin tins.

Bake 20 minutes. Remove muffins to racks to cool completely.

Makes 12 muffins

Good Morning Muffins

Dairy / Pareve

8 tablespoons (1 stick) butter or margarine, softened

¾ cup granulated sugar

¼ cup dark brown sugar, packed

2 eggs

1 cup all-purpose flour

2 teaspoons baking soda

¼ teaspoon salt

1½ teaspoons cinnamon

Pinch of cloves

Pinch of nutmeg

½ cup sweetened, shredded coconut

½ cup chopped walnuts

¾ cup coarsely grated carrots

¾ cup coarsely grated unpeeled zucchini

⅓ cup raisins

Preheat oven to 350 degrees. Line a 12-cup muffin tin with paper baking cups.

In a large mixing bowl, cream butter and sugars until fluffy. Add eggs and mix well.

In a separate bowl, sift together the flour, baking soda, salt, cinnamon, cloves and nutmeg. Add dry ingredients to the creamed mixture, stirring until combined.

Gently stir in coconut, nuts, carrot, zucchini and raisins.

Spoon batter into muffin tins, filling each ¾ full. Bake 20 minutes. Remove muffins to racks to cool completely.

Makes 12 muffins

COOK'S NOTES

BERRY-BAKED FRENCH TOAST

Dairy

12-15 (1-inch thick) slices challah or French bread, cut in chunks

1 cup fresh blueberries or other berries (if frozen, drain well)

16 ounces cream cheese, cubed

12 eggs

½ cup maple syrup

2 cups skim milk, or more

1 teaspoon vanilla

Mix bread with fruit and cream cheese. Mix eggs, syrup, milk and vanilla and pour over bread mixture. Chill overnight.

When ready to bake, preheat oven to 350 degrees.

Bake, covered, for 30 minutes. Uncover and bake 30 minutes longer.

OUTRAGEOUS BAKED FRENCH TOAST

Dairy

8 eggs

2 cups half & half

1 cup whole milk

1 teaspoon vanilla

¼ teaspoon cinnamon

¼ teaspoon nutmeg

Dash of salt

1½ loaves of Italian bread

TOPPING

1¼ cups sweet butter

1¼ cups pecans

1¼ cups brown sugar

2½ teaspoons light corn syrup

Mix eggs, half & half, milk and vanilla together with an electric mixer. Stir in cinnamon, nutmeg and salt by hand.

Slice bread about 1 inch thick. Soak each slice in egg mixture and place in a baking dish. Pour any remaining liquid over the bread. Soak overnight.

When ready to bake, preheat oven to 350 degrees.

Combine all topping ingredients and sprinkle over French toast.

Bake 40 minutes.

Morning Meadows Farm Baked Oatmeal

Dairy

"We stayed at a Bed & Breakfast farm. The kids got to go to the chicken house to get eggs in the morning. The proprietor served us this recipe. It's great on a cold autumn morning."

½ cup oil

2 beaten eggs

1 cup sugar

1 teaspoon vanilla

3 cups instant oatmeal

2 teaspoons baking soda

1 teaspoon salt

1 cup milk

Cinnamon and sugar for topping

Preheat oven to 350 degrees.

Combine oil, eggs, sugar and vanilla. Add the oatmeal, baking soda, salt and milk.

Pour into an 8x8-inch glass baking dish. Sprinkle cinnamon and sugar on top.

Bake for 30 to 35 minutes.

Serve without milk.

Serves 8

Pineapple Bread Pudding

Dairy / Pareve

1 cup sugar

½ cup (1 stick) butter or
   margarine, softened

4 eggs

6 slices challah (crusted or not),
   cubed

1 (20 ounce) can crushed
   pineapple, undrained

Preheat oven to 350 degrees.

Beat sugar and butter with a mixer. Add eggs, one at a time. Add challah. Add crushed pineapple with juice.

Bake in a 1½-quart casserole dish for 1 hour.

Serves 6-8

COFFEE CAN PUMPKIN BREAD

Pareve

½ cup applesauce

½ cup sugar

½ cup brown sugar

2 eggs, beaten

1 cup canned pumpkin

1½ cups flour

½ teaspoon salt

1 teaspoon pumpkin pie spice

1 teaspoon baking soda

Walnuts

Pecans

Raisins

Preheat oven to 350 degrees.

Blend applesauce and both sugars. Stir in eggs and pumpkin. Add flour, salt, pumpkin pie spice and baking soda. Mix in nuts and raisins.

Pour batter into greased and floured 2 pound coffee can. Bake about 1 hour.

OVERNIGHT STICKY BUNS

Dairy

¼ cup chopped pecans or nuts of choice

½ cup raisins

1 (24 count) package frozen white dinner rolls

1 teaspoon cinnamon

½ (3 ounce) package butterscotch pudding (not instant)

8 tablespoons (1 stick) butter or margarine

½ cup brown sugar, firmly packed

Sprinkle nuts and raisins in bottom of greased Bundt pan. Layer rolls on top. Sprinkle with cinnamon and dry pudding mix.

Melt butter and stir in brown sugar. Pour over rolls. Cover lightly with plastic wrap and towel. Let rise overnight on counter top. Do not refrigerate.

In the morning or when you are ready, preheat oven to 350 degrees. Uncover rolls and bake 30 minutes. Cool 5 minutes and invert onto a serving dish. Remove pan and serve immediately.

AHUVA'S ACORN SQUASH SOUP

Meat / Pareve /

4-5 pounds acorn squash or
    butternut squash

1-2 sweet potatoes

1 onion

1 celery root, leaves reserved for
    garnish

2 tablespoons vegetable oil

2 tablespoons chicken bouillon
    powder (or pareve vegetable
    soup powder mix)

Salt and pepper to taste

Dill to taste

Peel and cut squash, potatoes, onion and celery root into cubes.

In a large pot, heat oil. Add onions and sauté. Add celery root, then squash and sweet potatoes. Stir well and add bouillon and salt and pepper.

Cover with water, bring to a boil and simmer for 45 minutes.

Remove vegetables and purée in a blender or food processor. Transfer puréed vegetables to another pot. Slowly add soup liquid until desired consistency is achieved.

Garnish with dill and celery leaves.

Serves 10

A fresh acorn squash is green on the outside and orange on the inside.

To make peeling easier: Score the squash first. Then, microwave on high for about 4 minutes. Cut into quarters, scoop pulp and cube.

Matzah Balls
Meat / 🟫

"This recipe was handed down to me by my mother who got it from her Hagerstown, Maryland cousin about 50 years ago."

4 eggs, beaten
½ cup seltzer
⅓ cup vegetable oil (preferably canola)

1 teaspoon salt
Dash of pepper
1 cup matzah meal
Prepared clear chicken soup

Combine eggs with seltzer, oil, salt and pepper. Mix. Add matzah meal and stir. Let stand or refrigerate for at least 20 minutes. Bring soup to a boil. Form dough into small balls and drop into boiling soup. Cover and cook for 20 minutes over low heat. Enjoy!

Try adding any one of the following for variety:

2 tablespoons finely-chopped parsley
Pinch of powdered ginger
Pinch of ground nutmeg
½ teaspoon garlic powder

Serves about 6

Born as a Passover specialty, matzah balls became so well-liked that they are now eaten throughout the year.

Matzah Ball Floaters

Meat /

4 eggs

⅓ cup cold water

2 teaspoons salt

¼ teaspoon pepper

1 teaspoon nutmeg

6 tablespoons melted chicken fat

1¼ cups matzah meal

2 quarts water, lightly salted

Beat eggs. Add ⅓ cup cold water, salt, pepper, nutmeg and melted chicken fat. Blend well. Stir in matzah meal. Mixture should be stiff, but not too solid. Place in refrigerator for at least 3 hours or leave overnight.

In a large deep saucepan, bring 2 quarts of lightly salted water to a rapid boil. Remove matzah meal mixture from refrigerator and form into balls about 1¼ inches round. Gently put matzah balls into boiling water and boil slowly for 20 minutes, until fluffy and tender. Remove, drain and set aside in refrigerator until needed.

About 15 minutes before serving, add matzah balls to a clear chicken soup and simmer. Do not boil or leave them in the soup for too long as they absorb liquid and you will be left with very little soup.

Makes 24 matzah balls

COOK'S NOTES

BUBBIE NELLYE'S
TRADITIONAL CHICKEN SOUP
Meat /

Depending on how flavorful of a broth you want, use more or less carrots, parsley, celery, dill and onions.

2-3 stalks celery with tops
1 large onion
2 parsnips whole
6-8 carrots
1-1½ bunches fresh dill
1-1½ bunches fresh parsley

1 chicken (pullet), skin removed, cut into quarters
1 bag chicken bones
10 cups water
Salt and pepper to taste

Cut up celery, onion, parsnips and carrots and put into a huge pot along with dill, parsley, chicken, bones and 10 cups water. Bring to a boil, reduce heat and cook for about 2 to 3 hours. Add salt and pepper to taste.

Strain cooked soup through a colander into a fresh pot or containers. Cut chicken into pieces and return to soup along with cooked carrots.

• Chicken Soup is traditionally served as a wedding party soup as well as on Shabbat.

• In the "Old Days," chicken soup was called, "Golden Broth."

• Add a pinch of saffron to give chicken soup a golden hue.

• Chicken soup has long been considered a "cure-all," or "Jewish Penicillin." Its medicinal properties have been backed by scientific research!

• Try adding any of the following to the soup: matzah balls, noodles (lokshen), extra carrots or soup nuts.

Erika's Carrot Root Vegetable Soup

Pareve / 

"Vegetarian soups are my specialty, and this one reheats or freezes well."

2 large or 5 small onions, coarsely chopped

4-5 tablespoons vegetable oil, or as needed

20 carrots, peeled and coarsely chopped

Vegetarian soup stock mix

5 parsnips, peeled and chopped

1 turnip, peeled and chopped

Salt and pepper to taste

Dash of nutmeg to taste (optional)

Dill for garnish

Sauté onions in hot oil until tender and transparent, stirring often. When nearly done, stir in chopped carrots, and continue to cook for about 5 minutes. Add water to cover plus about 2 inches. Add stock mix. Stir in parsnips and turnips. Bring to a boil, then simmer about 40 minutes until all vegetables are tender.

Using an immersion blender, purée to desired consistency. (I prefer to leave the soup a bit chunky.) Season with salt and pepper and nutmeg, if desired.

Garnish each bowl with a sprig of dill.

This vegetable mixture can be used to make a "golden" chicken soup. Just reduce the quantities (use 7 carrots, etc.), purée very smooth, and add to chicken stock. (I recommend chilling the stock, skimming off the fat the next day, and then adding the vegetables.) Great for Shabbat and Pesach.

COOK'S NOTES

ALL-AMERICAN CORN CHOWDER

Pareve

3 tablespoons olive oil, butter or margarine

3 medium yellow onions, chopped

5 carrots, sliced

5 celery stalks, sliced

6 cups fresh corn kernels (can use frozen, not canned)

3 cups pareve chicken broth or vegetable stock

¾ teaspoon salt

½ teaspoon freshly ground black pepper

1 large red bell pepper, seeded and chopped

3 tablespoons chopped fresh dill

Heat oil in large pot. When hot, add onions, carrots and celery. Cook 10 to 12 minutes or until just tender, stirring frequently. Add corn and cook 2 more minutes.

Remove 4 cups of vegetables to a food processor (or use an immersion blender in the original pot and purée about half of the vegetables). Purée mixture and return to pot.

Add broth, salt and pepper and bring to boil. As soon as soup boils, add bell peppers and simmer for 2 minutes. Add dill and adjust seasonings as needed. Serve hot.

Asparagus Soup

Pareve /

1 stick (or less) pareve
  margarine

2 large onions

8 cloves garlic, chopped

6 cups pareve chicken stock

3 pounds asparagus

1 cup parsley, chopped

3 to 4 large carrots, cut into
  pieces

1 tablespoon dried tarragon

1 teaspoon salt (optional)

½ teaspoon pepper (optional)

Melt margarine in large pot over low heat. Add onions and garlic. Cook until wilted, about 20 minutes. Add stock and heat to a boil.

Trim ends of asparagus and cut into 1-inch pieces. Reserve tips. Add bottom pieces of asparagus, parsley, carrots, tarragon, salt and pepper to stock. Reduce heat to medium and simmer, covered, for 50 minutes.

Remove from heat and let cool. Place in a food processor in batches and purée. Return soup to pot. Add asparagus tips and simmer 10 more minutes. Enjoy!

Serves about 8-10

For a healthy alternative, substitute light olive oil for margarine when sautéing vegetables.

Asparagus has been cited as an aphrodisiac.

Asparagus was cultivated in the Old World at least 2,000 years ago.

EASY DELICIOUS POTATO ONION SOUP

Meat / Pareve /

"My family loves this soup; you'll enjoy it, too!"

1 bunch green onions (scallions)
2 medium onions
3 potatoes
3 tablespoons margarine or oil

1 quart chicken stock (or vegetable stock-1 teaspoon of mix to 1 cup of hot water)
Pepper to taste

Cut green onions, separating white bottoms from green tops. Slice bottoms as well as tops, but reserve tops to use as a garnish. Slice onions into small pieces. Cut potatoes into smaller pieces, the size you might use to pan-fry.

Melt the margarine in a soup pot. Add onions and white part of scallions. Cook until softened, do not brown. Add potatoes and chicken or vegetable stock. Season with pepper. Bring to a boil. Reduce heat and simmer 30 to 40 minutes, stirring frequently.

Purée soup until smooth. Adjust seasoning as needed using pepper and/or instant soup mix.

Ladle soup into bowls and garnish with green onions or scallions.

Leek and Potato Soup

Meat / Pareve /

2 tablespoons oil

1 onion, diced

4-5 leeks, diced (about 2½ cups)

4 potatoes (about 1 pound), peeled and sliced

1 carrot, grated

1 sprig fresh parsley

1 sprig fresh dill

4 cups pareve chicken or vegetable stock (homemade or canned)

Salt and freshly ground pepper to taste

1 tablespoon minced fresh chives and parsley

Heat oil in 4-quart soup pot. Add onion and leeks. Cook about 5 minutes or until vegetables are glazed but not browned. Add potatoes, carrot, parsley, dill and stock. Cover and cook 35 to 40 minutes.

It is preferable to purée the mixture through a food mill. If you use a food processor, pulse it off and on. Sometimes potatoes acquire a pasty texture when they are beaten too long in the processor.

Taste and adjust seasoning as needed. Return soup to pot and heat. Serve with a sprinkling of chives and parsley.

Be careful when adding salt to this soup. Homemade stock will probably require salt, whereas canned broth will not.

Cleaning Leeks

1. Rinse the leeks under running water to get rid of any large clumps of dirt.

2. Cut off the green leafy part just above where it starts to fan from the body of the leek.

3. Cut the body of the leek in half lengthwise, starting about ½ inch from the root; DO NOT cut through the root.

4. Rotate the leek ¼ turn and make another lengthwise cut; the leek should now be cut into quarters, but still joined at the root.

5. Fan out the "leaves" of the leek (the white part) and wash well under cold running water.

6. Cut off root.

FABULOUS FLORIDA FISH CHOWDER

Pareve

Recipe is from a fabulous waterfront restaurant in Longboat Key, Florida.

2 celery stalks, diced

1 onion, diced

2-3 carrots, diced

2 tablespoons olive oil

3-3½ pounds of salmon or
   grouper

16 cups vegetable broth

1 (28 ounce) can diced tomatoes

1 bay leaf

1 tablespoon dried thyme

1 tablespoon dried oregano

Salt and pepper to taste

1 box orzo

Steam or sauté celery, onions and carrots in olive oil, to your taste. The chef recommends steaming.

Poach fish and cut into chunks. Set aside.

In large stockpot combine cooked vegetables, vegetable broth, tomatoes, bay leaf, thyme, oregano, and salt and pepper. Cook over medium heat for about 30 minutes.

Add fish. Lower heat and simmer 30 minutes.

Cook orzo as directed on box in a separate saucepan. Serve soup over orzo.

Serves 12

CHOWDER VS. SOUP:

Chowder is thick soup, typically made with fish, potatoes and onions.

Kosher vegetable broth is available in cans, boxes of liquid or in powdered form.

FRENCH ONION SOUP

Dairy

The secret of a successful French onion soup is cooking the onions long and slow to allow their natural sugars to caramelize. This gives the soup its characteristic depth of flavor and rich mahogany color.

2 tablespoons unsalted butter

2 tablespoons olive oil

5 medium onions, thinly sliced

Pinch of dried thyme

2 tablespoons dry sherry or
   cognac

3½ cups "vegetarian" beef stock

½-1 teaspoon salt

¼-½ teaspoon ground black
   pepper

8-24 slices French bread, toasted
   if fresh

1½ cups grated Gruyère, Swiss
   or Jarlsberg cheese

Heat butter and oil in a soup pot over medium-low heat until the butter is melted. Add onions and stir to coat. Stir in thyme. Cook over medium heat for about 15 minutes, stirring occasionally and keeping a vigilant eye on the onions so they do not scorch. As soon as onions start to brown, reduce heat to medium-low, cover, and continue to cook about 40 minutes, stirring more often, until onions are a rich brown color.

Stir in sherry. Increase heat to high and cook, stirring constantly, until all the sherry has cooked off. Add vegetarian beef stock and bring to a boil. Reduce heat and simmer, partially covered, for 20 minutes. Season with salt and pepper.

Place 8 oven-proof soup bowls or crocks on a baking sheet. Ladle hot soup into bowls and top each serving with 1 to 3 slices of French bread. Sprinkle each bowl with 3 tablespoons grated cheese.

Broil or bake at 450 degrees until cheese is melted and starting to brown. Serve immediately.

Serves 8

Don't cry over chopped onions: Instead, light a candle before slicing or chopping them. The heat from the candle flame burns off some of the noxious fumes and carries the rest away from your work-space, taking the sting out of a normally tearful task.

BREADS AND SOUPS

Barley is one of the seven species of Israel. It is a grain that is indigenous to the Promised Land.

MUSHROOM BARLEY BEEF SOUP

Meat

1½ pounds mushrooms, sliced

4 medium carrots, chopped

3 celery stalks, thinly sliced

5 garlic cloves, chopped

3 pounds crosspiece (lean) of beef cut into cubes

8 cups water

8 cups beef broth (or pareve beef-flavored broth)

2 large parsnips, peeled and chopped

2 red peppers, chopped and seeded

5 carrots, peeled and sliced

1½ cups pearl barley

2 ounce package dried mushrooms

1 (28 ounce) can crushed tomatoes with added purée

Salt and pepper to taste

Spray bottom of an 8-quart pot with nonstick cooking spray. Add onions and mushrooms and gently sauté 10 minutes. Add all other remaining ingredients.

Cook for 2½ hours.

Freezes beautifully!

ITALIAN BEAN SOUP

Meat

2 cups sliced carrots or 1 package baby carrots

1 onion

Lots of celery

½ cup olive oil

1 (8 ounce) can tomato sauce

1 (10½ ounce) can condensed chicken broth

2 tablespoons crushed garlic

Seasonings to taste: oregano, basil and thyme

1 (16 ounce) package of frozen string beans

2-3 (16 ounce) cans beans in different colors (for example: chickpeas, kidney beans, black beans)

Chop carrots, onion and celery in a blender. In a large pot gently sauté chopped vegetables in olive.

Add tomato sauce, broth, garlic, seasonings and beans. Add enough water to cover.

Cook slowly over medium-low heat for about 1 hour. Add more water as needed while cooking.

LENTIL SOUP

Meat / Pareve

¼ cup olive oil

1 large clove garlic, crushed

2 large yellow onions, chopped

2 large carrots, peeled and chopped

1 large stalk celery, chopped

1 bay leaf

1 teaspoon dried thyme

½ teaspoon dried marjoram

Salt and freshly ground pepper to taste

1 (28 ounce) can Italian plum tomatoes with their juice

5 cups chicken broth (or pareve vegetable stock)

1 cup dry brown lentils, rinsed and picked through, discarding any dirt

Heat olive oil in a large stockpot. Add garlic, onions, carrots, and celery and sauté over medium heat until vegetables are soft, about 10 to 15 minutes.

Add seasonings and tomatoes, breaking them into pieces. Stir in chicken or vegetable broth and lentils.

Bring soup to a boil, cover, lower heat, and simmer until lentils are tender, about 40 minutes. Serve piping hot.

Serves 6-8

It is a Jewish custom to eat lentil soup during Parshat Toldot when it is read in the synagogue, usually in the month of November. Lentils were the most important legumes in the Middle East of ancient times. Jacob's stew was probably made of Egyptian lentils, which are red. Esau was willing to sell his birthright for a pot of red lentils, so it must have been a fabulous soup!

Multi-Bean Soup

Pareve

⅓ cup dried black turtle beans or
    kidney beans

⅓ cup dried pink beans

⅓ cup dried baby limas

⅓ cup dried navy beans

⅓ cup dried pinto beans

⅓ cup dried lentils

⅓ cup dried split peas

⅓ cup barley

2 tablespoons oil

2 stalks celery, minced

1 carrot, minced

2 medium onions, minced

3 cloves garlic, minced

1 (28 ounce) can tomatoes

8 cups water

½ teaspoon dried thyme

1 teaspoon chili powder

¾ teaspoon salt

Scant ½ teaspoon pepper

1 tablespoon vinegar - put in at
    very end, you can use any
    kind

Bring about 1½ quarts water to a boil in a 3-quart pot. Add beans, lentils, split peas and barley. Cook 1 minute. Turn off heat, cover and soak for 1 hour.

Heat oil in a fairly large pot. Add celery, carrot, onion and garlic and sauté several minutes. Process tomatoes in a food processor. Add them and their juices, water, thyme, chili powder, salt and pepper to the pot. Drain and rinse soaked beans and mix them in.

Bring to a boil, reduce heat and simmer about 1½ hours. Remove about 2 cups of beans and purée in the food processor. Return beans to pot and add vinegar. Simmer about another ½ hour. Add one or two cups of water for desired consistency.

It is always best to wash dried beans before cooking. Rinse under cold running water discarding any stones, dirt or debris.

It is also best to soak dried beans in water overnight before cooking. This will make them soft and tastier. If time is a factor, cook beans until boiling. Turn off heat and let cool for 1-2 hours. Lentils and peas do not need to be soaked.

Wild Mushroom Soup with Sherry

*Meat / Pareve**

"My friends lick their bowls when I serve this soup. My children even like it, which is unusual, given it is loaded with mushrooms!"

8 tablespoons margarine or oil, divided use

2 cups sliced celery

1 cup sliced shallots

¾ cups chopped onion

3 garlic cloves, minced

3 cups (6 ounces) fresh shiitake mushrooms, sliced and stemmed

3 cups (6 ounces) cremini mushrooms, sliced

3 cups (4½ ounces) oyster mushrooms

½ cup dry white wine

½ cup dry sherry

¼ cup all-purpose flour

***8 cups chicken stock, canned low-salt broth, or mix**

Salt and pepper to taste

When shopping for fresh mushrooms, if you can't find one kind or the other, just make up the difference with what you can find. It will still be delicious.

- *To store mushrooms, pack unwashed mushrooms loosely and uncovered in plastic container. They will keep for 7 days in refrigerator.*

- *To clean mushrooms simply wipe them with a damp cloth.*

Melt or heat 6 tablespoons margarine, butter or oil in large pot over medium-high heat. Add celery, shallots, onion and garlic and sauté until onion is translucent, about 8 minutes. Add mushrooms and sauté until beginning to soften, about 4 minutes.

Add white wine and sherry. Boil until liquid is reduced to glaze, about 6 minutes.

Mix remaining 2 tablespoons margarine, butter or oil and flour in a small bowl until smooth paste forms. Add flour paste to mushroom mixture in pot; stir until mixture melts and coats the vegetables. Gradually mix in stock. Be careful not to add too quickly, as the flour mixture will clump. Bring to a boil, stirring frequently. Reduce heat to medium-low and simmer until mushrooms are tender, stirring often, about 10 minutes. Season with salt and pepper.

Purée soup in a blender or in pot using a hand-held immersion blender until smooth.

Can be made a day ahead. Just chill then reheat over medium-low heat before serving.

*To make this a Pareve soup, substitute pareve powdered chicken soup mix for chicken stock. You can also substitute boxed "no-chicken broth" liquid or vegetable stock and make according to directions.

Serves 8 to 10

SHIITAKE MUSHROOM BARLEY SOUP

Meat / Pareve

2 tablespoons margarine

1 large sweet onion

1 large garlic clove, peeled and minced

8 ounces shiitake mushrooms, stems removed and thinly sliced

1 tablespoon tamari or soy sauce

6 cups vegetable stock or chicken stock

½ cup pearl barley, rinsed and drained

¼ cup medium-dry sherry, not cooking sherry

Kosher salt and pepper to taste

Melt margarine in a large soup pot over medium-high heat. Add onion and garlic and sauté until very lightly colored, about 5 minutes. Stir in mushrooms and sauté, stirring frequently until completely softened and cooked down, 8 to 10 minutes. Add tamari and sauté for another minute.

Stir in stock and barley, bring to a gentle boil, and reduce heat. Simmer, partially covered, over medium heat just until the barley is tender, 25 to 30 minutes. Add the sherry, stir and warm for a couple minutes. Season with salt and pepper, to taste. Serve hot.

This soup can be made ahead of time but barley will continue to absorb the liquid. You may need to thin the soup with additional stock and adjust seasoning.

PEASANT PEA SOUP

Pareve

16 ounce split peas

6 tablespoons canola oil

2 onions, diced

8 cloves garlic, minced

2 quarts water

2 large carrots, diced

2 white potatoes, diced and placed in just enough water to cover

3 tablespoons pareve chicken soup powder

1 tablespoon Hawayij (Yemenite spice)

½ teaspoon turmeric

Salt to taste

¼ to 1 bunch cilantro, chopped, or to taste

Add water to split peas with enough water to cover plus an extra cup or two. Soak peas in water overnight. Drain.

In a pan, heat oil. Sauté onion and garlic until lightly browned. Add 2 quarts water, drained split peas, carrots and potatoes and their water. Cook 40 minutes, uncovered. Add soup powder, Hawayij, turmeric and salt to taste. Mix well. Add cilantro. Can be made ahead of time.

Note: If serving just like this, make sure dicing and chopping is done uniformly. If you would prefer, this soup can also be puréed in a blender, food processor or by hand-held immersion blender. Both ways are delicious!

HAWAYIJ

2 tablespoons black pepper

1 tablespoon caraway seed

1 teaspoon cardamom seed

1 teaspoon saffron

2 teaspoons turmeric

Pound in mortar, stir well, and store in sealed container.

If you can't find Hawayij, you can make it as described below or just use pepper, cardamom powder, and caraway powder.

RED PEPPER SOUP

Meat / Pareve

3 carrots, peeled

3 shallots, peeled

1 clove garlic, peeled

1 pear, peeled and quartered

8 red bell peppers, divided use

1 tablespoon olive oil

4 tablespoons (½ stick) unsalted margarine

1 quart chicken stock or vegetable stock

1 tablespoon crushed dried red pepper (consider going very light on this)

Dash of cayenne pepper

Salt and black pepper to taste

Sprigs of fresh tarragon, to taste

Thinly slice carrots, shallots, garlic, pear and 6 red peppers.

Heat oil and margarine in a large skillet and sauté sliced vegetables and pear over medium-low heat until tender, about 8 to 10 minutes.

Add stock, dried red pepper, cayenne pepper, and salt and black pepper. Bring to a boil and simmer, covered, for 25 to 30 minutes.

While soup is cooking, roast remaining 2 red peppers directly on gas flame or under broiler, rotating them with tongs until completely charred. Put roasted peppers in a paper bag for 5 minutes to sweat. Wash off blackened skin under cold running water and remove seeds. Drain on paper towel.

Purée soup in a food processor, blender or in pot using a hand-held immersion blender, adding one of the roasted red peppers. Pour puréed soup back into pan and reheat over low flame.

Julienne remaining red pepper into fine strips and add to soup.

Garnish with tarragon and serve with French bread.

An immersion blender is a hand-held appliance which allows you to blend food (especially soups) directly in the pot you are cooking in. They can also be used for whipping up cream or egg whites for meringues. It is a handy helper to have in your kitchen!

SPRING VEGETABLE SOUP

Dairy / Pareve

"My children go crazy for this soup! It's dairy, but can easily be made pareve."

2 tablespoons butter or pareve
    margarine

2 leeks, cleaned and chopped

1 small onion, chopped

6 cups hot water

2 potatoes, peeled and thinly
    sliced

2 carrots, peeled and thinly
    sliced

2 teaspoons salt

¼ cup uncooked rice

8 stalks asparagus, cut into
    ½-inch pieces

½ pound spinach washed well
    and chopped

1 cup light sour cream or Tofutti
    sour cream

COOK'S NOTES

Melt butter in a large soup pot. Add leeks and onion. Simmer over low heat until tender, about 5 minutes.

Add hot water, potatoes, carrots and salt. Bring to a boil. Reduce heat. Simmer 15 minutes. Add rice and asparagus. Simmer 25 minutes. Add spinach and simmer 10 minutes.

Stir in sour cream. Bring to a boil.

Note: Flavor improves if soup is chilled overnight. Heat through before serving.

Serves 6-8

ZUCCHINI DILL SOUP

Meat / Pareve / Dairy /

"My family begs me to make this soup. It is extremely easy, healthy and delicious. Enjoy!"

2 tablespoons oil or margarine
   or butter

1¼ pounds zucchini, thinly
   sliced

1 large onion, chopped

4 garlic cloves, chopped
   (add more if you like garlic)

¼ cup chopped fresh dill
   (use more or less, depending
   on how much you like dill)

4 cups canned chicken broth or
   vegetable soup mix

Heat or melt oil or margarine in large pot over medium-high heat. Add zucchini, onions, garlic and dill. Sauté until tender, about 10 minutes.

Add broth and bring to a simmer for 10 minutes. You can cook longer; this won't hurt the soup.

Purée soup in either a blender or using the hand held immersion blender. Season with salt and pepper. Can be made a day in advance. Chill, then bring to a simmer when ready to serve. Good hot or cold.

Serves 6

Zucchini is a summer squash of a variety that has green skin and shaped somewhat like a cucumber. Be sure the zucchinis are firm and heavy for their size; they should not be bruised or discolored. Store in refrigerator, as they tend to spoil easily.

GAZPACHO

Pareve

2 cups finely chopped tomatoes

1 cup finely chopped cucumber

1 cup finely chopped celery

1 cup finely chopped green bell
   pepper

½ cup finely chopped onion

4 teaspoons snipped parsley

2 teaspoons chives

1 teaspoon Worcestershire sauce

2 small cloves garlic, minced

2-4 teaspoons tarragon wine
   vinegar

2-4 tablespoons olive oil

4 cups tomato juice

½ chili pepper

Salt and pepper

Combine all ingredients in stainless steel or glass bowl.

COLD TOMATO-THYME SOUP

Meat / Pareve /

5 tablespoons olive oil
(preferably extra-virgin)

2 cups finely chopped onions

¾ cup finely chopped carrots

2½ teaspoons finely chopped
garlic

1 bay leaf

3 pounds ripe tomatoes, seeded
and chopped-yielding about
5 cups (can skin in boiling
water before chopping)

3 cups canned low-salt chicken
broth or vegetable soup
bouillon

3 tablespoons finely chopped
fresh thyme or 1 tablespoon
dried

Heat 4 tablespoons oil in heavy large pot over medium heat. Add
onions, carrots, finely chopped garlic and bay leaf. Cover; cook until
carrots are tender, stirring occasionally, about 10 minutes. Add
tomatoes. Cover; cook until tomatoes release juices, about 10 minutes.
Uncover; cook until juices evaporate, stirring often, about 20 minutes.

Add broth and chopped thyme. Partially cover pot and simmer about
10 minutes longer or until mixture is reduced to 6 cups, stirring
occasionally.

Cool soup slightly. Discard bay leaf. Purée half of soup in blender or
use immersion blender. Stir into soup in pot. Season with salt and
pepper. Chill uncovered until cold, then cover. (Can be made 1 day
ahead. Keep chilled.)

Serves 6

COOK'S NOTES

COLD STRAWBERRY SOUP

Pareve /

A cool refreshing summer soup, perfect for Shabbat lunch appetizer or bridal shower hors d'oeuvres.

2 pints firm strawberries or
   1 (16 ounce) bag of frozen
   strawberries. (I prefer frozen)
1¼ cups orange juice

½ cup sugar
1 (20 ounce) can of crushed
   pineapple (do not drain)

   Combine all of the above ingredients in the container of a blender. Process until smooth. Serve chilled.

COLD DILL AND CUCUMBER SOUP

This soup is very refreshing in the summer! Enjoy!

Meat / Pareve /

1 bunch of scallions
2 tablespoons margarine
4 cups diced peeled cucumbers
   (3-5, cut in half, scrape seeds
   out)

4 cups chicken stock or
   vegetable stock
2 tablespoons chopped fresh dill
1 large potato, peeled and sliced
½ teaspoon salt
1 tablespoon lemon juice

   In saucepan, sauté scallions in margarine until soft. Add cucumbers, chicken stock, dill, potato, salt and lemon juice. Simmer until potato is tender.

   Purée soup, 1 cup at a time. Return puréed soup to pot and heat.

   Chill and serve cold. Garnish with extra cucumber and fresh dill.

Ajo Blanco Con Uvas
(White Garlic Soup with Grapes)

Dairy / Pareve

This is a typical Spanish cold soup that can be served as an appetizer with crusty bread for dipping.

½ **pound stale bread, crusts removed**

½ **pound slivered almonds**

3 **cloves garlic**

5 **ounces extra-virgin olive oil**

5 **tablespoons white wine vinegar**

2 **teaspoons salt**

4¼ **cups water**

5¼ **ounces muscatel grapes, seedless, or any red seedless grapes**

Soak stale bread in some water until softened. Squeeze out water and put in a blender or processor with almonds and garlic. Blend to a smooth paste, adding a little water if necessary.

With motor running, add oil in slow stream, then vinegar and salt. Beat in some of the 4¼ cups water, then pour the mixture into a tureen, wooden bowl or pitcher and add remaining water.

Taste for seasoning, adding more salt or vinegar, if needed. The soup should be fairly tangy.

Serve immediately or chill.

Stir before serving into bowls containing grapes.

This white gazpacho, typical of Malaga, Spain, is usually made with ground almonds. This would traditionally be made by crushing them to a paste in a brass mortar. The process leaves them grainy, so the soup can be sieved, if desired.

Chopped apple or melon can be substituted for the grapes.

CHILLED TWO-MELON SOUP

Pareve /

A nice cool soup to serve for Shabbat lunch in the summer when melons are their ripest.

½ large honeydew melon, cut into 1-inch chunks

3 tablespoons fresh lime juice

½ teaspoon white pepper

1 small cantaloupe, cut into 1-inch chunks

1 tablespoon sugar

1 tablespoon orange juice

Fresh mint for garnish

In a food processor or blender, combine melon, lime juice and pepper; blend until smooth. Ladle into a bowl, cover and refrigerate at least 1 hour.

Clean processor bowl and add cantaloupe, sugar and juice. Process until smooth. Cover and refrigerate 1 hour.

When ready to serve, ladle about ½ cup of each soup into bowl, pouring at the same time. Gently swirl with a knife to create a pretty design.

Garnish with mint.

Serves 4

SALADS
AND
DRESSINGS

SALADS
AND
DRESSINGS

KEEPING THE FAITH

The word "kosher" has taken on a whole new meaning in our society. Today it is a generic, almost colloquial term meaning that a person or a situation is "OK", or on the up and up. The real translation of the word kosher applies to something that is fit or proper—such as that which is considered allowable to eat from a Jewish perspective. Well, if that is the case, then perhaps we should recognize that keeping kosher is not just a way to eat, but also a way to live.

In a global sense, my Kashrut observance signifies my constant identification as a Jew. Wherever I am, at home, at work or even on vacation, I choose to not shelve my Judaism. I do not simply suspend it for a while because of the inconvenience of not finding kosher food. Some people have asked me on occasion ..."Can I keep kosher at home but while I am out, as they say, 'eat out'?" The answer, at least, from my perspective, is that keeping kosher at home is a great thing to do. It is a remarkable step toward insuring that the home embodies a strong sense of Jewish identity.

So for all who haven't considered the Jewish practice of keeping kosher, perhaps now with this wonderful cookbook you will begin the journey to sanctify your home and those around you by going kosher. Hopefully it won't stop at the entrance of your home. It will extend beyond to where you work, study or play. Like Nike says, "Just do it." Making the commitment will have an immeasurable impact on your life for years to come.

Rabbi Gershon Sonnenschein,
Beth Tfiloh Congregation

Israeli Salad

Pareve /

4-5 small cucumbers (pickle variety), cubed

2-3 small tomatoes, cubed

1 small red pepper, cubed (optional)

3-4 leaves romaine lettuce, chopped (optional)

4 green onions, chopped

¼ cup fresh parsley, chopped

½-1 lemon, squeezed

3-4 tablespoons extra-virgin olive oil

Salt and pepper

Garlic powder

Combine all ingredients; adjust seasoning to taste. Depending on seasonings, vegetables will taste differently and therefore need adjustments.

Little Italy Salad

Dairy /

¼ teaspoon salt

1 garlic clove

½ hard-cooked egg

1 teaspoon pepper

1 teaspoon oregano

½ teaspoon lemon juice

Pinch of sugar

¼ cup red wine vinegar

¼ cup olive oil

1 head iceberg lettuce, torn

1 tomato, cut into wedges

1 red onion, thinly sliced

¾ cup Parmesan cheese

Mash together salt, garlic and egg in the bottom of a large salad bowl. Add in pepper, oregano, lemon juice, sugar, vinegar and oil.

Add lettuce, tomato and onion to bowl and toss until coated.

Sprinkle with Parmesan cheese and toss again. Enjoy!

CRUNCHY ROMAINE TOSS

Pareve

1 cup walnuts, chopped

1 (3 ounce) package Ramen
   noodles, uncooked, broken
   up, discard flavor packet

4 tablespoons (½ stick)
   margarine

1 bunch broccoli, coarsely
   chopped

1 head romaine lettuce, broken
   into pieces

4 green onions, chopped

1 cup Sweet and Sour Dressing
   (see recipe)

Brown walnuts and noodles in margarine. Cool on paper towels.

After sautéing, add 1 tablespoon dark brown sugar to walnut-noodle mixture.

Combine noodles and walnuts with broccoli, romaine, and onions.

Pour dressing on top and toss to coat well.

SWEET AND SOUR DRESSING

½ cup vegetable oil

¼ cup sugar

¼ cup red wine vinegar

1 tablespoon soy sauce

¼ teaspoon salt

Dash of black pepper

Whisk together all dressing ingredients. Can be made in advance and refrigerated.

Salad vegetables can be prepared ahead of time and kept separately in the refrigerator.

Wash romaine lettuce, wrap in paper towels and store in a plastic storage bag.

SALADS AND DRESSINGS

To make this salad a main meal, add any of the following:

12 ounces grilled chicken, seared tuna, smoked turkey breast, sliced beef or grilled salmon. You can use leftover chicken, turkey breast or beef to save time.

SPRING GREENS WITH PEARS

Pareve

¼ cup red wine vinegar

2 tablespoons pear nectar

1 clove garlic, finely minced

1 teaspoon Dijon mustard

½ teaspoon salt

½ teaspoon white pepper

½ cup olive oil

5 ounces baby lettuce

1 each red and green pears, cored, sliced

¼ cup coarsely chopped pecans, toasted

Pour vinegar and nectar into a small jar. Add garlic, mustard, salt and pepper; blend well. Gradually add olive oil, stirring rapidly until dressing mixture is emulsified. Can be mixed in food processor.

Place greens in a large bowl, coat lightly with dressing, tossing gently. Divide among 4 chilled plates.

Fan pears over greens and sprinkle with pecans. Pass extra dressing.

Serves 4

MIXED GREEN SALAD WITH NECTARINES

Pareve

12-14 cups assorted salad greens (red leaf, romaine, iceberg, etc)

2 nectarines, sliced into wedges

⅓ cup walnut meats, toasted

Choose at least three salad greens, using Boston or red leaf as a base and adding 2 other types for their color and flavor.

Wash the greens, pat dry, and pile them into a large salad bowl. Adorn the greenery with nectarines and toasted walnuts.

In winter, substitute apples or pears for nectarines.

Pour the vinaigrette over the greenery and toss well to coat evenly. Serve immediately.

BALSAMIC VINAIGRETTE

⅔ cup olive oil

2 tablespoons balsamic vinegar

¼ cup orange juice

1 tablespoon Dijon mustard

1 clove garlic, smashed

¼ teaspoon salt

Freshly ground black pepper to taste

Beat together vinaigrette ingredients in a bowl.

Serves 6

Mandarin Tossed Salad

Pareve

½ cup slivered almonds

1 teaspoon margarine

1 tablespoon sugar

1 head leaf lettuce, torn

½ red onion, sliced

2 (11 ounce) cans Mandarin oranges

Sauté almonds in margarine with sugar. Combine almonds with lettuce, onion and oranges in a bowl. Add vinaigrette and toss. Adjust amount of dressing or lettuce used as desired.

Sweet and Sour Vinaigrette

½ cup vegetable oil

¼ cup apple cider vinegar or tarragon wine vinegar

¼ cup sugar

½ teaspoon salt

¼ teaspoon pepper

½ teaspoon hot sauce

¼ teaspoon celery seeds

Combine all vinaigrette ingredients.

Spinach Salad with Strawberry Vinaigrette

Pareve

2½ cups quartered strawberries, divided use

2 tablespoons rice vinegar

2 teaspoons brown sugar

2 teaspoons olive oil

¼ teaspoon salt

⅛ teaspoon pepper

1½ cups thinly sliced peaches

2 tablespoons shallots, sliced thinly

1 (10 ounce) package fresh spinach, torn

Place 1 cup strawberries, vinegar, brown sugar, oil, salt and pepper in a blender; process until smooth.

In a large bowl combine remaining 1½ cups strawberries, peaches, shallots and spinach. Toss gently.

Drizzle dressing over spinach. Toss well.

COOK'S NOTES

STRAWBERRY BRIE SALAD

Dairy

1½ cups sliced almonds
¾ cup sugar
2 heads romaine lettuce, torn

1 (8 ounce) Brie cheese, cut into
½-inch pieces
2 pints strawberries, sliced

Combine the almonds and sugar in a saucepan. Cook over medium heat for 10 minutes or until the sugar begins to melt and the almonds turn light brown, stirring constantly. Cook for 2 to 3 minutes longer, stirring constantly. Spread on a sheet of foil. Let stand until cool. Break into bite-size pieces.

Mix the romaine, cheese, strawberries and almonds in a salad bowl. Drizzle with the Poppy Seed Dressing and toss to coat.

POPPY SEED DRESSING

½ cup salad oil
½ cup sugar
½ cup apple cider vinegar

1½ teaspoons poppy seeds
1 teaspoon dry mustard
¾ teaspoon minced onion

Combine the salad oil, sugar, cider vinegar, poppy seeds, dry mustard and onion in a jar with a tight fitting lid. Cover the jar and shake to mix.

Dressing may be prepared 1 day in advance and stored, covered, in the refrigerator.

Serves 8

For any recipe, almonds can be prepared a day ahead of time and stored in an airtight container.

SPINACH & MANDARIN ORANGE SALAD

Pareve

"We have a very large family. This has become a standard salad at many get-togethers. Simple but so yummy. Both my sister-in-law and I make this often."

12 ounces fresh spinach, washed, thick stems removed

1 (11 ounce) can Mandarin oranges, drained (or double, to taste)

½ cup slivered almonds, toasted (see note)

Heap spinach leaves in large bowl. Top with oranges and nuts.

Pour vinaigrette over the salad, toss well and serve.

HONEY-MUSTARD VINAIGRETTE

1 teaspoon dry mustard

⅛ teaspoon black pepper

1 tablespoon honey

2 tablespoons cider vinegar

½ cup vegetable oil

Salt to taste

In a small bowl, whisk together all vinaigrette ingredients.

To toast nuts: Spread almonds on a baking sheet and bake at 350 degrees for about 5 minutes. Keep an eye on nuts and turn as needed. May be done very easily in toaster oven.

Variations of this salad:

- *Substitute 1 head of any lettuce such as bib, Boston, green leaf or romaine.*

- *Substitute pine nuts for almonds.*

- *Add dried cranberries.*

SALAD WITH FRESH HERBS AND FRICO

Dairy /

Mixed salad greens
½ bunch or more flat leaf parsley
Fresh chives, basil and/or oregano

Chopped tomatoes or sliced cucumber (optional)
Oil and lemon or oil and vinegar dressing
Grated Parmesan cheese

Put the salad greens into a large bowl. Trim coarse ends off the parsley and fresh herbs. Cut long pieces in half, leave short pieces whole. Mix in with the salad greens. If desired, add tomatoes or cucumbers. Toss with dressing. Scatter crisp frico on top.

To make frico, preheat oven to 350 degrees.

Line a baking sheet with a piece of parchment paper. Sprinkle with grated Parmesan cheese (the powdery kind, not the shredded type). Sprinkle the cheese neatly into little oval or round shapes, with a bit of space in between. Use a bit less than 1 tablespoon for each. Bake until cheese is melted and lightly browned, usually 5 or 6 minutes. Remove the frico from the baking paper with a metal spatula. Lay out straight onto a rack or curve them over a slender rolling pin. Cool.

Frico, baked flat Parmesan cheese rounds (or strips) became popular in the United States in the 1980's.

Roasted Sweet Red Pepper Vinaigrette

Pareve

This is fabulous for green salads, over salmon and/or vegetables. It will keep in the refrigerator for weeks!

1 tablespoon Dijon mustard

1 cup roasted, peeled and chopped red peppers (see note)

1 tablespoon chopped shallots

2 tablespoons chopped fresh garlic or more to taste

⅓ cup red wine vinegar

¼ cup water

5 tablespoons brown sugar

Kosher salt and pepper to taste

½ cup canola oil

Mix all ingredients in a food processor and emulsify.

To roast red peppers… broil in oven, turning frequently, until charred evenly. Place in brown paper bag for 10 minutes. Then peel skin.

Green Bean and Orzo Salad

Pareve

½ pound green beans, trimmed

1 cup orzo

1 large tomato, chopped

1½ tablespoons chopped fresh dill

Salt and black pepper

¼ cup olive oil

2 tablespoons red wine vinegar

Steam green beans until just tender. Drain and rinse under cold water.

Meanwhile, cook orzo according to package directions. Drain and rinse under cold water.

In a large bowl, mix the tomato, dill, salt and pepper, oil and vinegar. Cut the cooled beans into ½-inch pieces and add to salad mixture. Add the orzo and toss well.

Refrigerate overnight for best taste.

CHEF DIANE'S PERSIAN ORZO SALAD WITH APRICOTS AND ALMONDS

Pareve

1 pound orzo
½ cup orange juice
4 tablespoons rice wine vinegar
2 tablespoons honey
1 tablespoon celery seeds
1 teaspoon dried tarragon

1½ cups dried Turkish apricots, snipped
½ cup dried currants
1 cup slivered almonds, toasted
Salt and pepper to taste

Cook orzo until al dente. Rinse with cold water, drain and set aside.

In a small mixing bowl, combine orange juice, rice wine vinegar, honey, celery seeds and tarragon.

In a medium mixing bowl, combine cooked orzo, apricots, currants and almonds. Toss with dressing and season with salt and pepper. Allow to stand at least 30 minutes before serving to allow flavors to meld.

Serves 10-12

RANDI'S POPPY SEED PEAR VINAIGRETTE

Pareve

1 large shallot
2 large garlic cloves
1 (16 ounce) can pears, drained
½ cup rice wine vinegar
1 cup canola oil

1 tablespoon poppy seeds
½-1 cup dark brown sugar (to taste)
Kosher salt and pepper to taste

Combine all ingredients in a food processor until completely emulsified, at least 1 to 2 minutes.

ORANGE WILD RICE SALAD

Pareve

1 cup dry wild rice

3 cups water

Salt to taste

1 (11 ounce) can Mandarin
oranges, drained

¼ cup pine nuts, toasted

⅓ cup thinly sliced scallions

⅓ cup dried cherries or dried
cranberries

⅓ cup orange juice

1 teaspoon grated orange peel

¾ cup coarsely chopped Italian
parsley

2 tablespoons balsamic vinegar

2 tablespoons extra-virgin olive
oil

Black pepper to taste

COOK'S NOTES

Rinse the rice well under cold water and drain. In a large saucepan,
bring the water and salt to a boil. Add the rice, cover, lower the heat
and simmer gently for 35 to 40 minutes. Drain well and transfer rice to
a large bowl. Add the oranges, pine nuts and scallions to the rice.

In a small bowl, mix the cherries and orange juice and let sit for
5 minutes. Whisk in orange peel, parsley, vinegar and olive oil. Season
with salt and pepper.

Pour the dressing over the rice salad and mix gently so as not to
break up the oranges. Serve at once or chill for later use.

This may be made 24 hours in advance and refrigerated; return to
room temperature to serve.

Serves 6

SALADS AND DRESSINGS

The Sephardic Jews were credited for importing tomatoes from South America in the early 1500's.

COLD PASTA SALAD

Dairy

1 pound penne or raditori pasta (can use a mixture of green and white)

1 small bunch fresh basil, stems discarded

2 teaspoons minced garlic in oil

2 tablespoons olive oil

½ pound sun-dried tomatoes without oil, chopped

2 large ripe tomatoes, seeded and chopped

12 ounces fresh mozzarella cheese, cut into small bite-size chunks

Pine nuts (optional)

Salt and pepper

Cook pasta in boiling water until almost done. Drain and rinse with cool water. Set aside and let dry in a large bowl.

In a food processor chop basil, garlic and olive oil. Add basil mixture to pasta and toss to coat. Mix in sun-dried tomatoes, fresh tomatoes, mozzarella and nuts. Season with salt and pepper to taste.

Best served at room temperature, but can be refrigerated.

MARINATED PEA SALAD

Pareve

3 large cans baby peas, drained

1 cup chopped onion

¾ cup chopped bell peppers (color of choice)

½ cup chopped celery

Combine drained peas, onion, peppers and celery in a bowl. Add dressing and mix. Refrigerate at least 24 hours, stirring once or twice while in the refrigerator.

Salad will keep in refrigerator for several days.

TARRAGON DRESSING

¾ cup sugar

½ cup oil

½ cup Tarragon Vinegar

1 teaspoon salt

½ teaspoon paprika

½ teaspoon pepper

Combine all dressing ingredients.

Serves 10-12

COLD GREEN BEAN SALAD

Dairy

1½ pounds green beans, whole, tips removed

1 small red onion, coarsely chopped

½ cup Lemon Vinaigrette (see recipe below)

¼ pound feta cheese

½ cup coarsely chopped walnuts

Lemon Garlic Vinaigrette: Simply add 2 cloves crushed garlic to the Lemon Vinaigrette recipe.

Plunge the beans into boiling salted water. Cook for 3 minutes. Drain and refresh with cold water. Drain the beans again.

Toss the beans with the red onion and Lemon Vinaigrette. Using a slotted spoon, move the bean mixture to a shallow bowl.

Crumble feta cheese over the beans and sprinkle with chopped walnuts. Serve chilled.

LEMON VINAIGRETTE

3 tablespoons lemon juice

3 tablespoon white wine vinegar

1 tablespoon Dijon mustard

Freshly ground pepper to taste

½ teaspoon sugar

¼ teaspoon salt

1 cup light vegetable or olive oil

Whisk together all vinaigrette ingredients except the oil until well blended. Add the oil gradually, whisking until incorporated.

Makes about 1½ cups vinaigrette

ALL-AMERICAN COLE SLAW

Pareve

4 cups shredded cabbage

1 green bell pepper, finely chopped

2 tablespoons sugar

1 teaspoon salt

1 teaspoon celery seed

Dash of black pepper

2 tablespoons white vinegar

1 teaspoon mustard

½ cup mayonnaise

Combine cabbage, bell pepper, sugar, salt, celery seed and black pepper in a large bowl.

In separate bowl, mix vinegar, mustard and mayonnaise. Add to cabbage mixture and toss to coat.

Broccoli Surprise Salad

Pareve

Salad

4 cups fresh broccoli, coarsely chopped

½ cup raisins

½ cup chopped onion

½ cup peanuts

Dressing

¾ cup mayonnaise, regular or light

3 tablespoons vinegar

¼ cup sugar

Combine broccoli, raisins, onion and peanuts in a bowl. Chill.

Combine mayonnaise, vinegar and sugar, blending well.

Add dressing to salad 1 to 2 hours before serving and keep refrigerated.

Serves 6-8

Cold Wild Rice Salad

Pareve

3 cups cooked and drained wild rice

1 cup chopped green bell pepper

1 cup chopped red bell pepper

1 cup chopped scallions (both green and white parts)

½ cup pine nuts, toasted in a dry skillet

½ cup sliced water chestnuts

¾ cup olive oil

¼ cup lemon juice

Salt and pepper to taste

Combine cooked rice, green and red bell peppers, scallions, pine nuts and water chestnuts and set aside.

Mix the olive oil and lemon juice and gradually add to the rice mixture. Season with generous amounts of salt and pepper. Serve at room temperature.

Serves 6-8

Substitute 1½ cups snow peas for the bell peppers. Be sure to add snow peas at the last minute, since they will lose their bright green color if left to sit in the dressing.

Cook's Notes

Corn Salad with Vidalia Onions

Pareve

Salad

Kernels from 6 ears of fresh
    corn or 3 cups frozen kernels

1 large Vidalia onion, chopped

2 medium zucchini, cubed

1 bunch scallions, chopped

1 red bell pepper, chopped

1 green bell pepper, chopped

½ cup minced fresh parsley

2 teaspoons mustard seed

Dressing

1 clove garlic, minced

Salt and pepper to taste

2 teaspoons Dijon mustard

1 teaspoon ground cumin

2 teaspoons sugar

1 teaspoon hot sauce

⅓ cup cider vinegar

⅔ cup olive or vegetable oil

Cook corn kernels in boiling salted water for 3 minutes. Drain thoroughly.

When cooled, toss corn with the onions, zucchini, scallions, both bell peppers, parsley and mustard. Set aside.

Whisk together all dressing ingredients.

Gradually add the dressing to the salad until the mixture is adequately coated.

Prepare a few hours in advance so flavors can blend.

Serves 6

COOK'S NOTES

SALADS AND DRESSINGS

HERRING SALAD

Pareve /

1 (8 ounce) jar herring in wine sauce, drained and cut into ½-inch slices

2 medium potatoes, cooked, peeled and diced (about 3 cups)

2 medium onions, minced (optional)

1 medium-size tart apple, peeled and diced

1 cup diced cooked beets

¾ cup finely chopped dill pickles

¼ cup red wine vinegar

2 tablespoons sugar

2 tablespoons water

⅛ teaspoon black pepper

1 hard-cooked egg, sliced

Pecan pieces (optional)

Lettuce leaves

Shredded carrots for garnish

Combine herring, potatoes, onions, apples, beets and pickle in large bowl.

Combine vinegar, sugar, water and pepper in a separate bowl and mix well. Pour dressing mixture over salad and toss gently. Cover. Refrigerate at least 4 hours, toss once.

Add egg and nuts when ready to serve.

To serve, mound salad on lettuce leaves. Garnish with carrots.

HALIBUT SALAD

Pareve

3-4 pounds fresh or frozen halibut

Dash of salt and pepper

½ cup vinegar

3 garlic cloves, crushed

1 pint mayonnaise

½ cup India relish

1 pint chili sauce

1 tablespoon mustard

1 small chopped onion

Place fish, salt and pepper, vinegar and garlic in a saucepan. Add enough water to cover. Cook over low heat until slightly tender. Cool and break into chunks.

Add mayonnaise, relish, chili sauce, mustard and onions. Refrigerate.

CREATIVE CURRIED CHICKEN SALAD
Meat

This is a "schittarine" recipe as far as amounts used but it shouldn't be much harder to make than tuna fish salad! Delicious!!

Leftover cooked chicken, chopped
   (soup chicken is best)

Mayonnaise

Chopped onions (optional)

Green or yellow bell pepper

Raisins

Chopped fresh celery

Chopped Granny Smith apple

Curry powder

Tarragon

Salt and pepper to taste

Put chopped chicken in a bowl. Add mayonnaise to taste. Add onions, bell peppers, raisins, celery and apple to taste. Add more mayonnaise as needed.

Top off with a generous amount of curry powder and tarragon. Season with salt and pepper. Mix together and serve.

To add a little crunch to this salad, fry leftover chicken skins in a pan (skins make their own fat) until crispy. Add "cracklins" to the salad.

"Schittarine" is a Yiddish expression that means to "throw in" a little of this and a little of that, to make the dish taste exactly how you want it. A "schittarine recipe" is a "judgement recipe" as far as amounts of ingredients are concerned.

Fried chicken skins are also known as "gribbiness" in Yiddish.

Oriental Steak Salad

Meat

Cook's Notes

Steak Mixture

3 cups broiled or grilled steak (done rare to medium-rare), julienned

1 large red bell pepper, cut into ½-inch chunks

⅔ cup sliced water chestnuts

2 scallions, finely chopped

Sesame-Soy Vinaigrette

½ cup vegetable oil

2 tablespoons white wine vinegar

1 teaspoon Dijon mustard

1 clove garlic, smashed

1 tablespoon soy sauce

Freshly ground pepper to taste

1 teaspoon sesame oil

2 tablespoons sesame seeds, toasted in a 350 degree oven until golden, about 5 minutes

Shredded lettuce, any kind

Combine beef, red pepper, water chestnuts, and scallions in a mixing bowl.

In a separate bowl whisk together the oil, vinegar, mustard, garlic, soy, pepper, sesame oil, and sesame seeds until blended.

Pour half of the vinaigrette over the steak mixture and toss well. The steak salad mixture may be made to this stage several hours in advance and refrigerated. Return to room temperature to serve.

Arrange the salad atop a bed of shredded lettuce, pouring the remaining dressing over all. Serve.

Serves 4

PAM'S CHINESE CHICKEN SALAD
Meat

"Pam brings this tasty salad on our boat every summer and all our guests gobble it up! It lasts the entire weekend and for midnight snacks if no one finishes it earlier. What a winner!"

SESAME CHICKEN

½ cup apricot or plum jam

½ cup Dijon or French mustard

3-4 boned chicken breasts

2-4 tablespoons untoasted sesame seeds

DRESSING

¼ cup sugar

½ teaspoon white pepper

1 teaspoon salt

1 cup oil

6 tablespoons rice vinegar

SALAD

1 head cabbage

2 tablespoons oil

½ cup sliced almonds

¼ cup sesame seeds

8 green onions, sliced

2 (3 ounce) packages Ramen noodles, broken up

1 (11 ounce) can Mandarin oranges

Preheat oven to 350 degrees.

Mix jam with mustard and spread on chicken. Coat chicken with 2 to 4 tablespoons sesame seeds and place in a baking dish. Bake, uncovered, for 45 to 60 minutes or until golden brown. Cut chicken into pieces.

Combine all dressing ingredients; set aside.

To prepare salad, finely chop cabbage using a food processor. Heat oil in a skillet . Add almonds and ¼ cup sesame seeds and toss, cooking until slightly brown; cool. Combine cabbage, toasted almonds and sesame seeds, green onions, broken noodles and Mandarin oranges in a bowl.

Add dressing and chopped chicken to salad and toss. Chill.

Serves 4-6

COOK'S NOTES

Carmel Vineyards Selected Emerald-Riesling, an Israeli wine, semi sweet, with tropical fruity flavors is the perfect complement to Pam's Chinese Chicken Salad.

SALADS AND DRESSINGS

AUTHENTIC SALADE NIÇOISE

Pareve

½ cup olive oil

3 tablespoons white wine vinegar

1 teaspoon salt, divided use

½ teaspoon pepper, divided use

1 teaspoon Dijon mustard

2 (6 ounce) fresh tuna filets

1 pound small thin-skinned potatoes, cooked, peeled, halved and sliced ⅜-inch thick

1 tablespoon chopped green onions

¼ cup dry white wine

1 head Boston lettuce, washed, crisped

¼ pound thin green beans, blanched, chilled

2-3 medium tomatoes, cut into wedges

2-3 hard-cooked eggs, quartered

½ cup Kalamata, Niçoise, or ripe olives

2 ounce rolled anchovy filets

2 tablespoons capers

3 tablespoons minced parsley

In a small bowl, whisk together oil, vinegar, ½ teaspoon salt, ¼ teaspoon pepper and mustard. Pour ¼ cup dressing over tuna in a shallow dish. Cover and marinate in refrigerator 2 hours, turning once.

In a large bowl, combine hot potatoes, green onions, remaining salt and pepper and wine. Toss gently. Add 3 tablespoons dressing and toss again. Cover and refrigerate.

Remove fish from marinade. Broil or grill 3 inches from heat, 4 minutes on each side, until fish begins to flake, basting occasionally with marinade. Cut each filet into 2 or 3 servings.

Line a platter with lettuce. Arrange potatoes, green beans, tomatoes, eggs, yolk side up, olives and tuna in separate mounds. Top tuna with anchovies and capers. Sprinkle potato salad with parsley. Drizzle with dressing. Serve remaining dressing on the side.

Serves 4-6

Discard any leftover marinade from the raw tuna.

May substitute canned tuna.

Segal's Special Reserve Chardonnay partners well with our Authentic Salade Niçoise. Enjoy the pineapple and lemon aromas in this fresh, fruity Israeli wine. It displays a crisp flavor and a long, pleasant finish which makes this wine a real delight.

ENTRÉES AND SAUCES
POULTRY, MEATS, FISH, TOFU

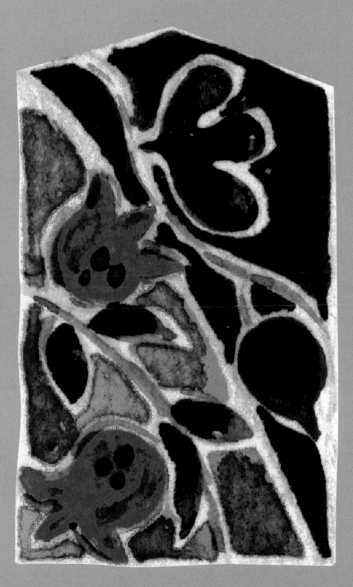

ENTRÉES AND SAUCES

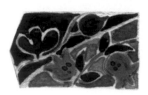

ENHANCE YOUR MEAL WITH A GLASS OF WINE

Wine was made to be paired with food, and when a fine wine is paired with the right dish, the naturally occurring flavor components found in each complement one another and create a graceful symphony of mouthwatering flavors.

In terms of the sacramental status of wine, it is true that among all foods and beverages, wine plays a prominent and frequent role in Jewish religious observance. And, one of the leading Jewish sages in history, Maimonides, writes in the Mishneh Torah that the consumption of wine at the beginning of a meal helps facilitate the digestion of food.

In today's world there are no specific rules for choosing the perfect wine. In general, white wines enhance the flavor of fish and poultry dishes and red wines complement dark meats. When preparing fish or poultry with lemon juice or other highly acidic ingredients, one may wish to serve a wine with bright acidity as well, such as a Sauvignon Blanc or a Chenin Blanc. If spicy meat dishes are preferred, then a slightly spicy Zinfandel or Rioja variety of wine would pair nicely. For desserts, such as pastries and fruit, a naturally sweet Late Harvest Chenin Blanc or Late Harvest White Riesling would match well. When in doubt, ask your local wine retailer for assistance in selecting the right wine for the dish you are preparing. In no time, you'll join the ranks of countless individuals who have begun to explore the burgeoning world of fine kosher wine throughout the week by pairing wine with meals.

Good luck on your quest and L'Chaim!

Eitan Segal, Kedem Wine Corporation

Baked Orange Chicken

Meat

¼ cup flour, or more
Salt and pepper
3 pounds chicken, cut up
2 tablespoons oil
¼ cup chopped green onions

¼ cup chopped onion
1 cup orange juice
½ cup chili sauce
1 teaspoon dry mustard
2 tablespoons soy sauce

Preheat oven to 350 degrees.

Combine flour, salt and pepper in a bowl. Coat chicken in flour mixture and bake until coating is browned.

Sauté both onions in oil until softened. Transfer onions to a mixing bowl. Add orange juice, chili sauce, mustard and soy sauce. Pour sauce over browned chicken. Bake, covered, for 30 minutes. Uncover and bake 10 minutes longer to caramelize coating.

Quick and Easy Catalina Chicken

Meat

2 packages white meat chicken
   on the bone
Chopped carrots
Chopped white potatoes
Chopped sweet potatoes
   (optional)

1 (1 ounce) package dry onion
   soup mix
1 (16 ounce) jar of Spicy or
   Saucy French salad dressing
1 (16 ounce) can whole
   cranberries or whole
   cranberry sauce

Preheat oven to 350 degrees.

Wash chicken well and put into a large roasting pan. Add carrots and white and sweet potatoes. In a mixing bowl, combine onion soup mix, salad dressing and cranberries. Pour mixture over the chicken.

Bake, covered, for 1 hour, 30 minutes.

BOUILLABAISSE OF CHICKEN

Meat

3 tablespoons olive oil

2-3 leeks, sliced (white and part of green)

1 medium onion, finely sliced

4 cloves garlic, minced

6-8 plum tomatoes, coarsely chopped

2 tablespoons tomato paste

½ teaspoon dried thyme

½ teaspoon dried basil

Pinch of fennel seed

Pinch of saffron (optional)

5½ cups chicken stock

½ cup dry white wine

Salt and pepper to taste

6-8 sprigs parsley

1 bay leaf

1 (3 inch) piece orange peel

2 pounds boneless, skinless chicken breast

In a deep large skillet or a medium soup pot, heat the oil. Add leeks, onions and garlic and sauté until partly cooked but not brown.

Remove from heat and add tomatoes, tomato paste, thyme, basil, fennel seed, saffron, chicken stock, wine, salt and pepper. Tie the parsley sprigs, bay leaf and orange peel with kitchen string into a bouquet garni and add to the pot.

Bring the mixture to a boil, lower the heat slightly and simmer about 30 minutes, using a "strong simmer" or a "gentle boil" so that the mixture reduces by nearly a third in the 30 minutes. Remove the bouquet garni.

Cut chicken into small strips or chunks. Put into the pot and simmer just until chicken is done, usually 20 to 25 minutes.

Serve each portion in a rimmed wide soup plate, perhaps with a large spoonful of plain cooked rice or orzo toward one side of the soup plate. Provide both forks and soup spoons.

COOK'S NOTES

Baron Herzog Chenin Blanc, focused and crisp, with intense passion fruit and citrus flavors finishes this outstanding Bouillabaisse of Chicken creation with a touch of sweetness.

ENTRÉES—POULTRY

Charcoaled Marinated Chicken Breasts

Meat

6 boneless chicken breasts,
   halved
6 garlic cloves, crushed
1½ teaspoons salt
½ cup brown sugar
3 tablespoons grainy mustard

¼ cup cider vinegar
Juice of 1 lime
Juice of ½ large lemon
6 tablespoons olive oil
Pepper to taste

Put the chicken in a shallow bowl. Mix the garlic, salt, sugar, mustard, vinegar and juices. Blend well. Whisk in the oil and add pepper. Pour over the chicken, cover and refrigerate overnight, turning once.

Remove from the refrigerator an hour before you are ready to cook and let come to room temperature.

Grill the breasts for approximately 4 minutes per side, or until done. You can also do this under the broiler for the same amount of time.

Chef Bukatman's
Orange Hazelnut Chicken

Meat

1 cup dried breadcrumbs

½ cup chopped toasted hazelnuts

½ teaspoon dried thyme

½ teaspoon salt

1 teaspoon black pepper

Parsley

3 tablespoons pareve margarine

½ cup orange juice concentrate, thawed

4-6 boneless, skinless chicken breasts

Orange slices for garnish

Preheat oven to 350 degrees.

On a sheet of aluminum foil, combine breadcrumbs, nuts, thyme, salt, pepper and parsley.

In a small skillet, melt margarine with orange juice concentrate. Remove from heat.

Dip chicken breasts, one piece at a time, into margarine mixture, then roll in crumb mixture. Transfer chicken to an 8x12-inch glass baking dish sprayed with cooking spray. Pour any leftover juice mixture over chicken.

Bake, uncovered, until chicken is golden and crisp and is no longer pink in the center, about 35 minutes. Transfer to a serving plate and garnish with orange slices.

Serves 4

If using chicken pieces with bone, increase baking time to 1 hour.

CHICKEN BREAST WELLINGTON WITH PORT WINE SAUCE

Meat

8 (5 to 6 ounce) skinless chicken cutlets

Seasoned salt and seasoned pepper

1 (6 ounce) package long grain and wild rice (not instant)

2 eggs, separated

1 package puff pastry sheets (in freezer section)

1 tablespoon water

2 (10 ounce) jars red currant jelly

1 tablespoon Dijon mustard

3 tablespoons Port wine

¼ cup lemon juice

Preheat oven to 375 degrees. Sprinkle chicken with salt and pepper. Cook rice according to directions. Cool.

Beat egg whites until soft peaks form. Fold into rice mixture.

Work pastry sheets, one at a time, until pliable and roll out to about 10x 14-inch. Place 4 chicken breasts in center of each pastry sheet. Spoon rice mixture over chicken breasts. Bring dough over stuffed breast forming 2 loaves and moisten edges with water to seal. Use excess pieces of pastry for decorations.

Place seam side down on a baking sheet that has been sprayed with cooking spray.

Mix egg yolks with water and brush over loaves. Bake, uncovered, for 40 to 45 minutes. If dough browns too quickly, cover loosely with foil.

Heat currant jelly in sauce pan. Stir in mustard, wine and lemon juice. Remove loaves from oven. Slice each into 4 separate slices and serve with warm wine sauce.

Serves 8

Chickens came to America with Columbus and the later settlers. Then, chicken became the focal point in many an American Sunday dinner.

CHICKEN MEDITERRANEAN

Meat

Flour for dredging

Salt and pepper to taste

4 boneless, skinless chicken breasts, halved

3 tablespoons margarine

3 tablespoons olive oil

1 large clove garlic, minced

¼ cup diced shallots

1 teaspoon dried oregano

¾ cup coarsely chopped sun-dried tomatoes

⅔ cup ripe black olives

2 tablespoons capers

2 tablespoons lemon juice

1 cup Port wine

COOK'S NOTES

Season flour with salt and pepper; dredge chicken in the flour mixture.

Heat margarine and olive oil in a large skillet. Add the garlic and shallots and sauté over medium heat until the shallots are translucent, about 2 minutes.

Add the chicken and sprinkle with the oregano. Turn the heat to high and sauté 3 to 4 minutes per side until golden. Then add tomatoes, olives, capers, lemon juice and wine and simmer 3 to 4 minutes until the sauce thickens and reduces to half its volume. Baste the chicken with the pan juices.

Serve at once or let cool and refrigerate overnight. Return to room temperature; cover and reheat in a 350 degree oven for 20 minutes until hot.

Serves 6 to 8

Carmel Vineyards Selected White Zinfandel, a semi-dry Israeli wine with cotton candy aroma and crisp acidity, is an ideal match for Mediterranean food.

CHICKEN WITH FIGS

Meat

2 (2½ to 3 pound) chickens, each cut into eighths

6 large cloves garlic, finely minced

2 tablespoons dried thyme

1 tablespoon ground cumin

1 teaspoon ground ginger

1 teaspoon salt

½ cup red wine vinegar

½ cup olive oil

4 teaspoons green peppercorns (packed in water), drained

1 cup black olives

1½ cups dried apricots

1 cup dried small figs or large fig pieces

¼ cup brown sugar

½ cup red wine

1 cup large pecan pieces

Zest of 2 lemons

One day before serving, combine chicken, garlic, thyme, cumin, ginger, salt, vinegar, oil, peppercorns, olives, apricots and figs in a large bowl. Marinate, covered, in refrigerator overnight. Remove the bowl from the refrigerator 1 hour before cooking.

Preheat oven to 350 degrees.

Arrange the chicken in a single layer in a large shallow baking pan. Spoon the marinade mixture evenly over the chicken. Sprinkle with the sugar and pour the red wine between the pieces.

Cover the pan with foil and bake 20 minutes. Remove the foil and bake, basting frequently with pan juices, until the juices run clear when a thigh is pierced with a sharp skewer, 40 to 50 minutes.

Using a fork and slotted spoon, transfer the chicken, olives and dried fruit to a large serving platter. Drizzle with a few large spoonfuls of the pan juices and sprinkle with the pecans and lemon zest. Pass the remaining pan juices in a sauceboat.

Serves 6

We recommend Baron Herzog Chardonnay with this wonderful dish. Pear, apple and chamomile notes characterize this tangy, citrus-flavored wine.

CRANBERRY CHICKEN

Meat

4 boneless, skinless chicken breasts

Flour

Salt and pepper

1 egg, beaten

Olive oil

3 shallots, minced

1 (16 ounce) can whole cranberry sauce

3 tablespoons soy sauce

1 tablespoon garlic powder

½ cup dry white wine

2 tablespoons Worcestershire sauce

3 tablespoons margarine

COOK'S NOTES

Preheat oven to 350 degrees.

Pound chicken breasts until thin. Season flour with salt and pepper. Dip chicken in egg, then in seasoned flour. Shake off excess flour. Brown in olive oil, undercooking to allow for reheating; set aside.

Brown shallots slowly in a saucepan in olive oil until caramelized. Add cranberry sauce, soy sauce, garlic powder, wine and Worcestershire sauce over medium-low heat for 10 minutes. Finish with margarine. In large baking dish, combine chicken and wine sauce.

Bake 30 to 40 minutes or until hot.

"Make sure you use 1 sauce recipe per 4 chicken breasts. I often make it the night before so all I have to do is pop it in the oven before I'm ready to eat."

Serves 4

PHYLLIS' ORANGE CHICKEN

Meat /

"This is a one step meal. You can put it together in five minutes and it tastes like it was a ton of work. It is a family favorite. I have given out the recipe and everyone loves it."

4 chicken breasts on the bone

2 large sweet potatoes

½ package of small cut carrots or peel 1 (2 pound) package of carrots

1 small can of frozen orange juice

Preheat oven to 350 degrees. Place chicken, potatoes, and carrots in a roasting pan. Mix orange juice with 1 can of water and pour on top of chicken and vegetables. Bake 1 to 1½ hours, covered.

Can double recipe if needed.

HONEY ORANGE CHICKEN

Meat

1 cup fine dry breadcrumbs

1 tablespoon grated orange zest

1 teaspoon salt

¼ teaspoon pepper

3-4 pounds chicken, cut up, skin can be removed without altering taste

½ cup orange juice

½ cup chicken broth

¼ cup pareve margarine

½ cup honey

Preheat oven to 350 degrees.

Combine breadcrumbs, zest, salt and pepper. Dip chicken pieces in orange juice, then roll in crumb mixture. Arrange chicken, skin side up, in a greased shallow pan.

Bake 30 minutes.

Combine broth, margarine and honey in a saucepan. Heat until margarine is melted. Pour over chicken and bake 30 additional minutes, basting occasionally.

Serves 4

ISRAELI CHICKEN

Meat

2 tablespoons cumin

1 tablespoon sweet paprika

¼-½ teaspoon hot paprika or
cayenne pepper (optional)

1½ teaspoons ground turmeric
(optional)

¾ teaspoon freshly ground
pepper

½-¾ teaspoon salt

4 pounds chicken thighs, or
whatever chicken parts you
like

4 pounds boiling or red potatoes,
scrubbed-peeled or unpeeled-
your choice

1 tablespoon olive oil or oil
spray

4-8 cloves of garlic (depending
on how much garlic you like)

1½ pounds onions, halved and
sliced

COOK'S NOTES

Preheat oven to 400 degrees.

Mix cumin, both paprikas, turmeric, pepper and salt in a bowl. Coat chicken pieces with spice mixture, rubbing spices onto chicken to coat well.

Peel potatoes or leave unpeeled. Slice potatoes about ½-inch thick. Add potatoes to a roasting pan that has been greased with 1 tablespoon olive oil or cooking spray. Sprinkle with additional salt and pepper and toss to coat. Lay potatoes flat in pan and sprinkle with chopped garlic.

Place coated chicken pieces on top of potatoes. Top the chicken with onion slices.

Cover tightly with foil and bake 1 hour to 1 hour, 30 minutes or until chicken and potatoes are tender. Before serving, uncover chicken and place under broiler about 4 inches from heat source and broil about 5 minutes or until browned, but not burned.

Serves 8

*Moscato di Carmel
with its sweet, bubbly,
pineapple, melon and
guava flavors, and a
cool, clean finish, pairs
well with Israeli
Chicken.*

Israeli Coffee Chicken

Meat

¾ cup brewed coffee

⅓ cup ketchup

3 tablespoons reduced-sodium soy sauce or tamari

2 tablespoons fresh lemon juice

2 tablespoons red wine vinegar (for more flavor, try half balsamic vinegar)

2 tablespoons olive oil

2 tablespoons brown sugar

1 whole chicken, cut into eighths, or 8 pieces of skin-on chicken parts (about 3½ pounds)

Preheat oven to 350 degrees.

Combine all ingredients, except chicken, in a medium saucepan. Bring to a boil. Reduce heat and simmer gently for 5 minutes or until slightly reduced.

In the meantime, place chicken, skin side up, in a shallow baking dish. Pour sauce over chicken. Bake, uncovered, for 1 hour, basting every 15 minutes.

Serve over rice.

Serves 3-4

Lemon Chicken with Pine Nuts

Meat /

¼ cup pine nuts

1 tablespoon olive oil

6 boneless, skinless chicken breasts

1½ cups dry white wine

1½ tablespoons lemon juice

Preheat oven to 400 degrees.

Toast pine nuts in oven until lightly browned. Put aside until ready to serve.

Heat olive oil in a large skillet. Add chicken breasts and sauté about 5 minutes or until golden brown. Turn and cook on the other side until golden brown and cooked through.

Transfer chicken to a platter. Pour out and discard any fat from the pan, but do not wipe it out. Add wine and lemon juice to the pan and bring to a boil. Reduce heat and simmer on low for 6 to 8 minutes. Pour sauce over chicken and sprinkle with pine nuts.

Cook's Notes

Baron Herzog Rosé of Cabernet Sauvignon is a bright, fresh and fruity wine, with a soft feel and excellent balance. It goes perfectly with your Lemon Chicken and Pine Nuts.

LIME GRILLED CHICKEN

Meat

2 tablespoons lime juice

1 tablespoon vegetable oil

¼ teaspoon cayenne pepper

4 cloves garlic, minced

4 chicken breasts

Black Bean Sauce (recipe below)

Diced red pepper, red onion and cilantro for garnish

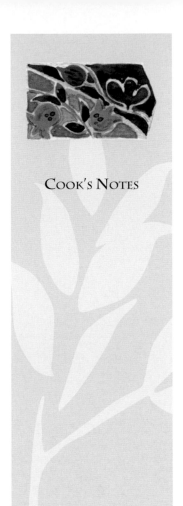

Place all ingredients in a plastic bag and marinate, turning occasionally for 8 hours.

Prepare sauce while grill is heating.

Grill chicken until done. Top chicken with sauce and garnish as desired. Serve with Spanish rice or couscous.

BLACK BEAN SAUCE

1 cup cooked black beans, rinsed and drained

½ cup orange juice

2 tablespoons balsamic vinegar

¼ teaspoon salt

2 cloves garlic, minced

Dash of pepper

Blend all sauce ingredients in a food processor. Heat sauce briefly in a pan.

CHICKEN MARSALA

Meat

6-8 boneless chicken breasts

2 eggs, beaten

Italian breadcrumbs

4 tablespoons (½ stick) pareve margarine

Garlic powder or chopped fresh garlic

2 cups water

Parsley flakes or chopped fresh parsley

2 cups water

4 chicken bouillon cubes

2 tablespoons flour

½ cup marsala wine

1 lemon, thinly sliced

Sliced mushrooms (optional)

Preheat oven to 350 degrees.

Dip chicken in eggs, coat with crumbs and sauté in olive oil. Transfer to a casserole baking dish and set aside. Reserve sauté pan.

Melt margarine in a saucepan. Add garlic and parsley to taste. Bring to boil over low heat. Remove from heat and sift in flour; set aside.

Bring 2 cups water with bouillon cubes to a boil. Add margarine mixture to bouillon. Stir in wine. Pour mixture over chicken.

Put lemon slices on chicken. Bake, uncovered, for 35 minutes.

Sauté mushrooms in sauté pan after chicken. Add mushrooms to sauce after baking.

Baron Herzog Syrah with its distinct berry and blackberry fruit notes, highlighted by subtle oak and intriguing complexity is our recommendation to pair with your Chicken Marsala.

PEACHY PERSIAN CHICKEN

Meat

A delicious peachy chicken recipe. Perfect for Sukkot.

3 tablespoons flour

½ teaspoon oregano

1 teaspoon salt

⅛ teaspoon pepper

3 pounds boneless, skinless
  chicken breasts, thinly sliced

1 large onion, chopped

Oil for sautéing

1 clove garlic, minced

1 cup minced fresh celery

¾ cup shredded carrots

8 ounces tomato sauce

16 ounces canned peaches,
  drained, reserve juice

1¾ tablespoons brown sugar

1 tablespoon dry tarragon
  leaves, crushed

1½ teaspoons chili powder

Preheat oven to 350 degrees.

Combine flour, oregano, salt and pepper in a plastic bag. Shake flour mixture with chicken pieces in bag to thoroughly coat. Brown chicken on both sides in a pan with some oil. Pat dry and place in a single layer in a 13x9x2-inch baking dish; set aside.

Sauté onions, garlic, celery and carrots in oil for about 10 minutes until just soft.

In a small saucepan, combine tomato sauce, peach juice, brown sugar, tarragon and chili powder. Heat, stirring often to just boiling. Combine with sautéed vegetables. Pour sauce over chicken.

Bake, uncovered, for 35 minutes. Add peaches, either thinly sliced or cut into chunks, baste with some sauce and bake 10 minutes longer.

Serves 4-6

Roasted Sabra Chicken

Meat

Cook's Notes

Good for Rosh Hashanah.

1 (7 pound) roasting chicken
1 orange, quartered
1 small onion, quartered

Salt and freshly ground pepper
  to taste
2 teaspoons dried rosemary
½ cup water

Glaze

1 tablespoon unsalted pareve
  margarine (optional)
3 tablespoons grainy Dijon
  mustard

3 tablespoons honey
1 tablespoon apricot jam
3 tablespoons Sabra or other
  fine orange liqueur

Preheat oven to 400 degrees.

Rinse the chicken inside and out and pat dry. Squeeze the juice of the orange quarters over the bird, inside and out. Place the orange and onion inside the bird and tie the legs together with kitchen string.

Sprinkle salt and pepper all over the outside of the bird, then sprinkle with rosemary. Place bird, breast side up, in a roasting pan and pour the water into the pan.

Roast 20 minutes. Reduce the heat to 350 degrees and roast for 1 hour.

While the bird is roasting, prepare the glaze. Heat margarine, mustard, honey and jam in a small saucepan until smooth and hot to the touch. Remove from the heat and stir in liqueur. Spoon glaze over the chicken and bake until the bird is golden brown and the meat is tender, about 40 minutes longer.

Serves 4-6

SALLY'S CHINESE CHICKEN AND RICE

Meat

2 fryer chickens, cut up

4 tablespoons (½ stick) pareve margarine, melted

2 cups celery, chopped

1 (6 ounce) can mushroom pieces, liquid reserved

1 (8 ounce) can water chestnuts, liquid reserved

½ cup slivered almonds

2 cups water

2 (1 ounce) packages instant onion soup

¼ cup soy sauce

Toasted almonds for garnish

2 cups long grain cooked rice

COOK'S NOTES

Preheat oven to 350 degrees.

Dip chicken in melted margarine. Put rice in a roasting pan. Sprinkle with celery, mushroom, water chestnuts and almonds.

Combine 2 cups water and onion soup mix. Arrange chicken pieces over vegetables. Combine reserved mushroom and water chestnut liquids, soy sauce and onion soup. Pour over chicken and rice.

Bake, uncovered, for 1 hour.

Serves 8

Sesame Chicken

Meat

4 boneless breasts, sliced	2-4 tablespoons canola oil
⅓ cup flour	½ cup white wine
Salt and pepper	½ cup peach jelly
1 teaspoon paprika	1 tablespoon Dijon mustard
2 tablespoons toasted sesame seeds	1 tablespoon honey
	¼ teaspoon garlic powder

Combine chicken with flour, salt and pepper, paprika and sesame seeds in a plastic bag. Shake and set aside.

In a large skillet, heat oil until hot. Add chicken. Sauté until done and golden brown. Remove to a warm platter.

Deglaze pan with wine, scraping bits and mixing well. Add jelly, mustard, honey and garlic powder. Cook 5 minutes.

Add chicken to pan and mix. Heat 3 to 5 minutes longer. Serve over rice with green beans.

I usually double sauce ingredients because my kids like extra sauce on their rice.

Toast sesame seeds on a tray in a toaster oven - watch carefully – they toast quickly. Cool before putting in bag.

Serves 4

We recommend Baron Herzog's White Zinfandel–semi-dry with a crisp texture and aromas of apple, strawberry and cotton candy to complement your Sesame Chicken dish.

TALKING TURKEY ABOUT TURKEY

For most families, disagreements over turkey usually fall into simple categories like who gets the drumstick, can I eat the skin or the lumpiness of the gravy. But, it may surprise many Jews to know that "talking turkey" is really more complicated than one might expect. The Kashrut (kosher status) of turkey is a little known but fascinating question of Jewish Law.

For certain types of animals, the Torah provides specific examples and criteria. To be kosher, for instance, land mammals must chew their cud and have split hooves. Just to be sure, the text also lists those animals like the pig and the camel that you might mistakenly believe to be kosher because they have one of these characteristics and not the other. Kosher fish are not listed by name, but must have fins and scales. Therefore, if you were to encounter a new species of fish or mammal, you could usually tell by simple examination whether or not the species is kosher.

Given the vagaries of the biblical language and ancient ornithology, how can we be absolutely sure that a particular bird is not in fact a member of one of the non-kosher families? Our ancient sages decreed that only birds for which there was a mesorah (an unbroken, reliable tradition) could be considered kosher, and any new birds subsequently discovered would be considered off limits.

Fast-forward to the 1500s, as the turkey, which was native to the Americas, was first brought back to Europe by the early explorers of the New World. Would this new bird, never before seen by Europeans, and for which there was no reliable *mesorah*, be accepted as kosher? Incredibly, turkey seems to have made a virtually seamless, no questions asked, entry into the kosher kitchens of Europe. Although the process by which this acceptance came about is unclear, there is absolutely no question today that turkey is kosher. That's a good thing, too, because according to the National Turkey Federation, Israel leads the world in turkey consumption, at a whopping 28.8 pounds per capita, considerably more than the world's second largest consumer—the United States of America, at 17.5 pounds per capita.

Enjoy your kosher turkey and please...don't fight too much over who gets the drumsticks!

Rabbi Yaakov Chaitovsky

FLAVORFUL GINGER TURKEY BREAST

Meat

1 (6 to 9 pound) turkey breast with skin and bone

¼ cup chopped shallots

¼ cup chopped fresh ginger

¼ cup fresh finely chopped garlic

¼ cup brown sugar

¼ cup soy sauce

⅓ cup vegetable oil

1 bunch fresh cilantro, leaves chopped

¼ cup frozen orange juice concentrate

Paprika

Place turkey breast in a large bowl. Whisk together shallots, ginger, garlic, sugar, soy sauce, oil, cilantro and orange juice concentrate. Pour mixture over turkey. Marinate 2 to 3 hours or overnight.

When ready to bake, preheat oven to 250 degrees.

Sprinkle top of turkey breast with paprika, for color. Slow cook, covered, for 3 to 4 hours or until internal temperature reaches 160 degrees.

Serves 10-12

Did you know...
The turkey was almost our National Bird?
In a vote in Congress, the bald eagle won out over the turkey as our national bird.
Had this not happened, we all would be eating bald eagle for Thanksgiving dinner!

Barbecued Turkey with Maple-Mustard Glaze

Meat

First the turkey is soaked overnight in a brine to improve flavor and ensure moist meat. (Be sure to use a pot large enough to hold both the brine and the turkey.) The smokiness of the turkey is offset beautifully by the tangy, sweet glaze, which incorporates two quintessential Napa Valley ingredients: wine and mustard.

Can use chicken and cook for less time.

Turkey

6 quarts water

2 large onions, quartered

1 cup coarse salt

1 cup chopped fresh ginger

¾ cup golden brown sugar

4 large bay leaves

4 whole star anise (optional)

12 whole black peppercorns, crushed

1 (13 to 14 pound) turkey, giblets discarded

2 large oranges, cut into wedges

¼ cup olive oil

2 tablespoons sesame oil

Glaze

¾ cup pure maple syrup

½ cup dry white wine

⅓ cup Dijon mustard

2 tablespoons pareve margarine (optional)

Combine water, onions, salt, ginger, sugar, bay leaves, star anise and peppercorns in very large pot. Bring mixture to simmer, stirring until salt and sugar dissolve. Cool brine completely.

Rinse turkey inside and out. Place turkey in brine, pressing to submerge. Refrigerate overnight, turning turkey twice.

Preheat grill (charcoal, electric, or gas). Remove turkey from brine; discard brine. Pat turkey dry with paper towels. Place orange wedges in main cavity. Mix olive oil and sesame oil in small bowl. Brush over turkey.

Arrange breast side up on grill, centering above empty broiler pan. Cover and cook about 3 hours or until thermometer inserted into thickest part of thigh registers 160 degrees. If using a charcoal grill, add 6 briquettes to barbecue every 30 minutes.

For glaze, bring all ingredients to a simmer in a heavy, medium-size saucepan. Once turkey reaches 160 degrees, brush glaze over turkey. Cover and cook about 1 hour longer or until thermometer reaches 180 degrees. Transfer turkey to a platter. Tent with foil and let stand 30 minutes.

Serves 8

123

DUCK WITH ORANGES AND OLIVES

Meat /

2 (5½ pound) ducks, cut into quarters

2 tablespoons oil, preferably olive

6 cloves garlic, minced

2 onions, chopped

1 cup dry sherry

1 quart duck or chicken broth

Juice and zest of 2 oranges

4 bay leaves

4 sprigs thyme

1 teaspoon salt

½ teaspoon black pepper

8 ounces pitted green olives

2 pounds potatoes, peeled, cubed or diced

Preheat oven to 400 degrees.

Rinse duck, remove excess fat and pat dry. Use wings and back for stock.

In a large skillet, heat oil over medium heat. Sauté duck on both sides until golden brown, about 10 minutes. Remove legs and thighs to a platter, cover duck breast and set aside.

Drain fat, leaving a few tablespoons in skillet. Sauté garlic and onions until tender. Add sherry, scraping up browned bits, add broth, orange juice, bay leaves, thyme, salt and pepper.

Return legs and thighs to skillet. Cover and simmer 1 hour.

Add olives and potatoes and cook 20 minutes or until potatoes are tender.

Roast duck breast for 20 minutes to heat through and crisp. On each plate, place one leg or thigh with some sauce, potatoes and olives around it. Fan some breast slices on top. Garnish with orange zest.

Serves 8

COOK'S NOTES

Joseph Zakon Red Muscatini is our choice to accent this delicious dish. This Italian wine is delightfully fresh, effervescent, and semi sweet, with outstanding fruity aromas and flavors.

London Fruit Chutney

Pareve

This chutney goes well with any of your poultry dishes.

1 (20 ounce) can unsweetened pineapple chunks

2 cups sugar

1 (1 pound) bag fresh or frozen cranberries

1 cup golden raisins

½ teaspoon cinnamon

¼ teaspoon ginger

¼ teaspoon allspice (optional)

1 cup walnuts, coarsely chopped

Drain juice from pineapple chunks and combine juice with sugar, cranberries, raisins, cinnamon, ginger and allspice in a saucepan.

Simmer 15 minutes or until cranberries are tender. Add pineapple chunks and walnuts and transfer to a serving bowl. Refrigerate until chilled.

This chutney can be frozen. It's delicious!

Apple-Cranberry Sauce

Pareve

Great for Thanksgiving! It's also a wonderful addition to a turkey meal all year long.

2 cups orange juice

1¾ cups sugar

1 (12 ounce) bag cranberries

2 apples, cored, peeled and cut into chunks

½ teaspoon pumpkin pie spice

½ teaspoon apple pie spice

In a saucepan combine orange juice and sugar. Heat to boiling and cook 5 minutes.

Stir in cranberries and apples. Boil another 5 minutes. Add both spices and cool.

Refrigerate before serving.

BAKED CRANBERRY CONSERVE

Pareve /

Delicious and easy. Great for Thanksgiving!

1 (12 ounce) bag fresh
    cranberries
1 cup packed light brown sugar
1 cup walnut or pecan halves,
    lightly toasted and coarsely
    chopped

1 tablespoon fresh lemon juice
1 cup orange, ginger or
    grapefruit marmalade

Preheat the oven to 350 degrees.

Toss the cranberries and brown sugar together and spoon them into a medium baking dish with a lid.

Bake, covered, for 1 hour, stirring after 30 minutes.

Stir in the walnuts or pecans, lemon juice and marmalade. Bake, uncovered, for 15 minutes.

Serve warm or at room temperature; do not serve cold. Store any leftover conserve in the refrigerator for up to 2 weeks.

Makes about 3½ cups

Bob's Three Fruit Salsa

Pareve /

"This tropical salsa, which is a cinch to make in fifteen minutes, transforms broiled fish or chicken into an exotic dish. I serve it over grilled tuna, grilled chicken breasts or any pan-fried fish."

1 cup finely chopped cantaloupe

1 cup finely chopped mango

1 cup sliced strawberries

½ cup finely chopped, peeled cucumber (you can seed cucumber if you prefer)

½ cup finely chopped green bell pepper

½ cup finely chopped red onion

1½ tablespoons chopped fresh mint

1 tablespoon chopped fresh basil

2 tablespoons fresh lime juice

2 tablespoons finely chopped, seeded jalapeño pepper, or to taste

1 tablespoon honey

¼ teaspoon salt

Combine all ingredients, toss well. Serve with a slotted spoon over fish or chicken.

"Don't be afraid to experiment and change recipe to taste. Feel free to substitute your favorite fruits. I have used all kinds of melons, pineapple and even peaches."

Pesach Stuffed Brisket of Beef

Meat /

Broccoli-Mushroom Stuffing

3 tablespoons margarine or
  chicken fat

2 cloves garlic, minced

1 large onion, chopped

½ pound mushrooms, chopped

10 ounces frozen chopped
  broccoli, thawed

1½ cups matzah farfel

1 whole egg

1 egg yolk

1 teaspoon salt or to taste

1 teaspoon dried basil

Freshly ground pepper to taste

Brisket

2 (5 pound) first cut briskets

Salt and pepper

Paprika

2 onions, quartered

3 carrots, peeled and cut into
  2-inch pieces

1 cup beef broth

1½ cups dry red wine

1 tablespoon potato starch
  mixed with 1 tablespoon
  water, if desired

To make stuffing, melt margarine in a skillet. Add garlic and onion and sauté until soft. Add mushrooms and sauté until most of the liquid has evaporated. Transfer to a bowl and cool slightly. Stir broccoli and farfel into sautéed vegetables. Mix egg and egg yolk in small bowl and add to broccoli mixture. Stir in salt, basil and pepper. Set aside.

For brisket, cut fat off meat. Make a pocket in the brisket by cutting horizontally though the center of the meat, leaving a ¾-inch uncut border on three sides. Loosely push stuffing into pocket; do not overstuff. Skewer closed with turkey lacers or a trussing needle. Press on top of meat to distribute stuffing evenly. Sprinkle both sides of meat with salt and pepper and paprika.

Preheat oven to 275 degrees.

Place brisket in a roaster or Dutch oven. Add onions and carrots. Pour broth and wine over top. Cover and bake for 3½ to 4½ hours, basting occasionally, until meat is tender when pierced with a fork.

(Continued on next page)

Remove from oven and place meat in a dish. Remove skewers. Place a damp towel directly on the meat to keep the top from drying out. Strain pan juices and refrigerate separately.

(The meat and sauce may be refrigerated up to 2 days or frozen. Defrost in refrigerator overnight.)

Before serving, preheat oven to 350 degrees.

Remove fat from sauce. Cut meat into slices about ½-inch thick and arrange overlapping in roasting pan. Pour sauce over meat, cover and bake 20 minutes or until heated through. Using a large spatula, carefully transfer meat to a platter.

If desired, thicken pan juices by stirring in dissolved potato starch and water. Place over moderate heat and whisk until sauce comes to a boil. Spoon a small amount of sauce over the meat and pass the rest.

Sweet & Sour Brisket

Meat /

"This one is delicious. I like to double the recipe for sauce, BUT I don't add more sugar because it is plenty sweet. You can serve this on top of cooked FINE noodles...delicious."

1½ cups ketchup
1 cup ginger ale
1 (1 ounce) package onion soup mix

½-1 cup brown sugar
¼ cup red wine
2 onions, sliced
1 first cut brisket

Preheat oven to 325 to 350 degrees.

Mix together ketchup, ginger ale, soup mix, brown sugar and red wine.

Spread onions on the bottom of a baking pan. Place brisket on top and pour ketchup mixture over brisket. Cover pan with foil.

Bake 4 hours.

SAVORY BRISKET

Meat

⅓ cup balsamic vinegar

¼ cup olive oil

2 teaspoons salt, plus extra to taste

½ teaspoon pepper

2 teaspoons soy sauce

2 onions, chopped

½ teaspoon garlic powder (optional)

2 teaspoons sugar

1 carrot, thinly sliced (optional)

1 (5 pound) first cut brisket

Paprika

Mix vinegar, olive oil, 2 teaspoons salt, pepper, soy sauce, onions, garlic powder, sugar and carrot in a shallow roasting pan. Sprinkle the brisket with a little salt and paprika and place in pan. Turn brisket to cover with marinade. Cover pan with aluminum foil and refrigerate overnight, turning occasionally to absorb marinade flavors. (If brisket is larger, double the marinade.)

When ready to cook, preheat oven to 350 degrees.

Place pan in oven, being sure foil is tightly covering the pan. Roast 3 to 3½ hours or until tender.

Slice brisket crosswise and serve.

Baron Herzog Zinfandel— spicy, smoky wine with plum and pepper notes and vibrant food-friendly acidity fares well with Savory Brisket.

Freddie's Lazy Texas Brisket with Tangy Sauce

Meat

2 cloves garlic, minced

1 (4 to 5 pound) beef brisket, trimmed

2 tablespoons chili powder

2 teaspoons paprika

1 tablespoon salt

1 teaspoon cumin

½ teaspoon sage

1 teaspoon sugar

1 teaspoon oregano

½ teaspoon cayenne pepper

½ teaspoon black pepper

Preheat oven to 200 degrees. Rub garlic into brisket. Combine chili powder, paprika, salt, cumin, sage, sugar, oregano, cayenne pepper and black pepper and rub into all surfaces of meat.

Wrap brisket in a large piece of heavy-duty aluminum foil and seal all edges tightly so no juices can escape. Place in a baking pan and roast 8 hours. When done, drain juices, slice against the grain and serve with Tangy Sauce.

Tangy Sauce

1 cup apple jelly

¾ cup ketchup

2 tablespoons white vinegar

1½ tablespoons chili powder

2 teaspoons prepared mustard

Mix all sauce ingredients together in a small saucepan. Simmer 3 to 5 minutes. Serve with sliced Freddie's Lazy Texas Brisket.

Cook's Notes

Entrées—Meats

GARLIC-INFUSED BRISKET

Meat /

2-3 large onions, sliced
Season-all
Freshly ground pepper
Matzah meal or flour

10-12 cloves of garlic, sliced, divided use
1 (10 to 15 pound) whole cut brisket
1-1¾ cups water

Preheat oven to 350 degrees.

Place onions in the bottom of a large roasting pan. Sprinkle with Season-all, ground pepper and matzah meal. Scatter about 4 cloves worth of garlic slices on top.

Make holes in brisket on all sides with a knife and insert remaining garlic slices in holes. Sprinkle both sides with pepper, Season-all and matzah meal. Roast, fatty side up and uncovered, for 45 to 60 minutes or until slightly browned.

Add ¼ cup water, turn onto other side, and brown this side for 45 minutes. Add an additional 1 to 1½ cups of water. Cover and cook until tender, about 3 to 4 hours, depending on size of brisket.

Cool before slicing. Can remove onions and drippings, if desired, to purée for a gravy.

Valero Syrah is our choice of wine to serve with your Garlic-Infused Brisket. This Argentinean wine exudes mouthwatering plum pudding and spice aromas, and it is crammed with boysenberry, plum and blackberry fruit flavors.

GRANDMA BESSIE'S TRADITIONAL BEEF TZIMMES

Meat /

4 onions, chopped

Vegetable oil

4 pounds flanken

Salt and pepper

8 sweet potatoes, peeled and cut in chunks

2 (1 pound) bags carrots, peeled and sliced

1 pound pitted prunes

1 (10 ounce) bag mixed dried fruit

½ (1 pound) box brown sugar

Grated fresh ginger

Couple dribbles of honey

1-2 lemons, thinly sliced

6 Matzah Balls (see recipe on page 60)

Sauté onions in vegetable oil. Sear meat in onions and season with salt and pepper. Cook, covered, for 30 minutes on low heat. Check after 15 minutes.

Preheat oven to 350 degrees.

Transfer onions and meat to a large roasting pan. Add potatoes, carrots, prunes, dried fruit, sugar, ginger, honey and lemon slices.

Roast 2 hours, basting every 30 minutes. Add matzah balls.

"Gadempt" is a Yiddush word that means "pan fry and then steam for as long as you want." Something could be steamed from ½ hours to 6 hours or more on the lowest heat setting.

Tzimmes is the Yiddish word for "fuss." Because it takes time to make tzimmes, the word came to mean "making a big fuss over something."

AHUVA'S CHOLENT

Meat

Serve with mint jelly.

Ahuva suggests that before Shabbat, make sure there is enough water to last through the night. Cholent should not be soupy.

3 or 4 onions

4 potatoes

1 package cholent mix (beans and barley)

Paprika to taste

1 tablespoon onion soup mix or powdered chicken soup

1 teaspoon salt

Pepper to taste

2-3 cloves garlic

¼-½ teaspoon Yemenite spice (Hawayij - see recipe below)

1 tablespoon honey (optional)

Beef Kaleky (whole—do not cut)

Chicken legs and thighs (optional)

Sauté onions. Line a crockpot with plastic liner. Place sautéed onions on bottom of crockpot. Add potatoes, cholent mix, paprika, soup mix, salt, pepper, garlic, Hawayij spice and honey. Place beef and chicken on top. Fill crockpot with enough water to cover meat.

Cook on high for 6 hours, then reduce heat to low and continue to cook overnight.

HAWAYIJ

2 tablespoons black pepper

1 tablespoon caraway seeds

1 teaspoon cardamon seed

1 teaspoon saffron

2 teaspoons turmeric

Combine all spices.

Serves 6-8

AMERICAN BEEF STEW

Meat

2 pounds chuck, cut in 1-inch cubes

Garlic powder to taste

Salt and pepper to taste

5 medium onions, sliced

7 medium potatoes, cut in chunks

4 small carrots, or more if desired

1 cup peas, drained

2 tablespoons flour

6 tablespoons ketchup

1 tablespoon Worcestershire sauce

¼ cup soy sauce or to taste

Season meat with garlic powder and salt and pepper, cover with water and cook in a heavy Dutch oven for about 1 hour, 30 minutes. Add onions, potatoes, carrots and peas and cook about 35 minutes longer.

Thicken the gravy that has formed while cooking with flour.

Mix in ketchup, Worcestershire sauce and soy sauce.

If you want to freeze this, do not add potatoes.

LONDON BROIL

Meat

1 (2 pound) London broil

¾ cup oil

3 tablespoons honey

2 tablespoons vinegar

¼ cup soy sauce

1½ teaspoons ginger

1 clove garlic, pressed

Slash meat with a knife a few times. Combine oil, honey, vinegar, soy sauce, ginger and garlic in a container. Add meat and marinate at least overnight – flavor improves with time. This meat can be marinated for up to 4 days, which tenderizes the meat and enhances the flavors.

Grill about 8 to 10 minutes on each side. Slice against the grain.

COOK'S NOTES

Wine with Beef Stew? But of course! Try Barkan Reserve Merlot, an Israeli wine with great structure and finesse, joined by a chorus of jam, tea, and mineral flavors highlighted with subtle bittersweet chocolate notes.

Weinstock Cellar Select Napa Cabernet Sauvignon — Full bodied with rich blackberry, anise and oak flavors, this Napa, California wine pairs astoundingly well with London Broil.

TOP OF THE RIB ROAST

Meat

COOK'S NOTES

1 tablespoon mustard

1 tablespoon garlic

1 tablespoon oregano

1 tablespoon basil

1 (5 pound) top of rib roast

1 small onion, sliced

1 (6 to 12 ounce) package
    mushrooms, sliced

2 tablespoons olive oil

1 (8 ounce) can tomato sauce

8 ounce red wine

1 (8 ounce) package baby carrots

2 large (thin skin) potatoes, cut
    in 1-inch cubes or 6 small red
    potatoes

Preheat oven to 350 degrees.

Mix mustard, garlic, oregano and basil together and rub over both sides of the roast.

Sauté onions and mushrooms in olive oil in a Dutch oven over medium to low heat until onions appear glazed. Add seasoned roast in the same pan and sauté until slightly browned on both sides.

Pour a mixture of tomato sauce and wine over the roast. Cover and roast in oven for 30 minutes per pound. Place carrots and potatoes around the roast (in the gravy) mid-way through cooking time. Cover and return to oven.

Remove roast about 30 minutes before completed time and allow to cool down before slicing. Slice the cooled roast against the grain.

Cool the gravy in the refrigerator allowing the fat to solidify quickly. If serving the next day, the entire cooled roast can go into the refrigerator. Skim the cold fat off the top of the gravy before replacing roast slices back in the pan.

Return the covered pot roast to a 325 degree oven to complete cooking. Do not overcook or it will get dry and stringy.

Add nuts and dried fruit as desired if NOT using garlic, oregano and basil.

For your prized Top of the Rib Roast we recommend Herzog Special Edition Chalk Hill-Warnecke Vineyard Cabernet Sauvignon. This Herzog wine is from the prestigious Chalk Hill region of California's Sonoma County. It is incredibly rich, full-bodied and viscous, and it displays hints of dark chocolate.

ROAST BARBECUE

Meat

"This is very popular with my family and friends and freezes very well."

3 pounds shoulder roast or chuck

2 tablespoons shortening

1 large onion, chopped

2 tablespoons lemon juice

¾ cup water

½ cup chopped celery

2 cups ketchup

3 tablespoons Worcestershire sauce

2 tablespoons brown sugar

1 tablespoon prepared mustard

2 tablespoons chili powder or to taste

Salt and pepper to taste

Trim meat and brown in shortening in a Dutch oven. Add all remaining ingredients.

Bring to boil. Reduce heat to low and cook 2 to 3 hours or until roast is tender enough for you to shred or pull meat apart. Continue cooking to blend all flavors.

Serve on rolls.

Serves 12

CHINESE BEEF RIBS

Meat

6 cloves garlic

1 tablespoon salt

1 cup honey

½ cup soy sauce

2 cups chicken stock made with 2 bouillon cubes

½ cup ketchup

4 pounds beef ribs

Mash garlic and mix with salt, honey, soy sauce, chicken stock and ketchup. Refrigerate and marinate ribs in garlic mixture overnight, turning or basting occasionally. Ribs can be frozen at this point.

When ready to cook, bring ribs to room temperature.

Preheat oven to 450 degrees.

Put ribs and marinade in a roasting pan. Bake 10 minutes. Reduce heat to 325 degrees and bake 60 to 80 minutes, basting frequently.

Ramon Cardova Rioja is a great complement to these Chinese Beef Ribs. This spicy and fruity Spanish wine boasts dark berry, oak and nutmeg aromas which lead into a delicious spicy and fruity flavor.

ENTRÉES—MEATS

GLAZED CORNED BEEF

Meat

Corned beef, whole cut

2 cabbages, quartered (optional)

2 pounds potatoes, cut into big bite-size pieces (optional)

GLAZE

1 (20 ounce) can pineapple chunks in unsweetened juice, 2 tablespoons juice reserved

1 (9 ounce) jar apricot preserves

1 tablespoon Dijon mustard

1 tablespoon soy sauce

2 tablespoons orange juice

1 tablespoon chopped garlic

1 teaspoon white vinegar

1 teaspoon pareve chicken soup mix

½ teaspoon ginger powder

Place beef in a large roasting pan. Cover with water and bring to a rolling boil. Boil for 1 hour, 30 minutes.

Remove half the liquid but reserve to cook cabbage and potatoes in. Add fresh water to cover beef. Cook for an additional 1 hour, 30 minutes or until tender when poked with fork.

Meanwhile, prepare glaze by combining 2 tablespoons pineapple juice and all other glaze ingredients except pineapple chunks. Taste and adjust seasoning as desired.

Spread glaze over cooked beef and scatter pineapple chunks on top. Bake at 350 degrees for 30 to 45 minutes.

While beef bakes, cook cabbage and potatoes in reserved cooking liquid; drain.

Slice beef and serve with cooked cabbage and potatoes.

Mark's Meltdown Chili

Meat

"I started appreciating chili at home (Mom's recipe) and at the JCC day camp in Wilkes Barre, Pa. I started making it in college. I got into hot peppers during the past 6 years."

3 medium onions, diced

Olive oil

1 green bell pepper, diced

6 green jalapeño chiles, seeds and membrane removed, halved

4 red Fresno chiles, seeds and membrane removed, halved

2 habanero chiles, seed and membrane removed, halved

½ pound mushrooms, sliced

1 (14½ ounce) can cooked or stewed tomatoes (tomato sauce is O.K. too)

¼ cup chili powder

1 teaspoon cumin

1 tablespoon cinnamon

1 tablespoon cilantro

Dash of allspice

1 pound lean ground beef or chuck

1 (16 ounce) can dark red kidney beans

12 ounces beer (cheap stuff or non-alcoholic works fine)

Be careful when handling chiles. Use gloves if you have them. Don't touch your eyes. Removing the seeds and webbing reduces the "heat" considerably, particularly from the habaneros which are the hottest of the chiles.

Brown onions in a small amount of olive oil over medium heat. Add all peppers and cover. When onions are clear (do not allow to burn), add mushrooms. Stir for even cooking. Add tomatoes and simmer about 10 minutes.

Add chili powder, cumin, cinnamon, cilantro and allspice. Gradually add the ground meat and cook and stir until meat is done. Add beans and beer. After about 10 minutes, reduce to low heat, cover and allow to simmer several hours, stirring periodically.

Serve with white or brown rice, or unsalted tortilla chips.

Experiment and vary the ingredients. Changing the cooking time can give you different flavor as well. Omit the beer if you want a thicker consistency. Long cooking times, on the order of 5 to 10 hours on lowest setting, gives a blended flavor and smooth consistency. Limit simmer time to about 30 minutes for the ingredients to keep their identity. You can also make a "cooler" version with just enough tang to be interesting by limiting the chiles to 3 jalapeños.

ALL-AMERICAN SLOPPY JOE

Meat

1 tablespoon vegetable oil
1 medium onion, finely diced
2 cloves garlic, minced
2 pounds ground beef
½ cup chili sauce

3 ounces tomato sauce
1 tablespoon Worcestershire sauce
Hot red pepper sauce to taste
Water, beer or red wine to taste

Heat oil in a skillet. Add onions and garlic, stirring frequently until the onion is softened, about 10 minutes. Add ground beef and cook, breaking up lumps with a wooden spoon, until browned, 3 to 4 minutes.

Add chili sauce, tomato paste, Worcestershire sauce and pepper sauce. Add water, beer or red wine, to taste, if too thick.

Serve piping hot on toasted buns.

You can add these optional ingredients:

   Diced tomatoes
   1 small red or yellow pepper, diced
   ½ cup cooked rice
   ½ cup frozen peas
   Cooked rotelle pasta

ARMENIAN BEEF LOAF

Meat

1 (10 ounce) package frozen chopped spinach, thawed and squeezed dry

2 pounds extra lean ground round

1 medium onion, finely chopped

Salt and pepper to taste

½ teaspoon freshly grated nutmeg

½ teaspoon cinnamon

1 cup cooked rice

2 beaten eggs

1½ cups tomato sauce, flavored with ⅛ teaspoon cinnamon

Preheat oven to 350 degrees.

Combine all ingredients, except flavored tomato sauce. Pack beef mixture into a loaf pan.

Bake 45 to 60 minutes or until firm. Serve with the tomato sauce.

Serves 5-6

BBQ MEATLOAF

Meat

"This is a recipe that was included in my wedding cookbook. We like it because it isn't "just some plain ol' meatloaf."

1½ pounds ground beef

1 cup breadcrumbs

1 onion, chopped

1 egg, beaten

1½ teaspoons salt

¼ teaspoon pepper

2 (8 ounce) cans tomato sauce, divided use

½ cup water

1 teaspoon vinegar

3 tablespoons brown sugar

2 tablespoons mustard

2 teaspoons Worcestershire sauce

Preheat oven to 350 degrees.

Mix together beef, breadcrumbs, onions, egg, salt, pepper and ½ can of tomato sauce. Form meat mixture into a loaf in a loaf pan.

Combine remaining tomato sauce, water, vinegar, brown sugar, mustard, and Worcestershire sauce to make the sauce. Pour over meatloaf.

Bake 1 hour, 15 minutes, basting often.

Trudy's Stuffed Meatloaf

Meat

Stuffing

2 tablespoons pareve margarine

½ pound mushrooms, sliced

1 onion, minced

2 cups soft breadcrumbs

½ teaspoon salt

⅛ teaspoon pepper

¼ teaspoon dried thyme

2 tablespoons fresh parsley, minced

Ground Beef Mixture

2 eggs

2 tablespoons water

¼ cup ketchup

1½ teaspoons salt

⅛ teaspoon pepper

¾ teaspoon dry mustard

2 pounds ground beef

Preheat oven to 350 degrees.

To make stuffing, melt margarine in a skillet. Add mushrooms and onion and sauté three minutes. Toss in breadcrumbs, salt, pepper, thyme and parsley. Sauté until lightly browned. Remove from heat.

To make meat mixture, beat together eggs, water and ketchup. Add salt, pepper, mustard and ground beef and mix well.

Pack half of beef mixture into a 2-quart loaf pan. Pack stuffing on top and cover with remaining ground beef mixture.

Bake 1 hour.

Serves 6

STUFFED CABBAGE

Meat

"My Grandpa and my Uncle used to really "chow down" on this one. I remember Grandma would make this dish at holiday time, usually Sukkot. It had a marvelous aroma. The rice in the meat makes it very light and more tender than stuffed cabbage of old. Freshly ground turkey breast can be substituted or mixed with the meat to lower the cholesterol count of this yummy dish. I divide it into groups of 4 and freeze in plastic containers. It seems to be too rich for anyone to finish the entire portion. When serving it to my family, only certain people eat it so I don't need a tremendous amount. Refrigerate after cooking for about 1 to 2 days and then reheat and serve."

Cabbage is so rich in vitamins and minerals that it has been called, "Man's Best Friend," in the vegetable kingdom.

1 firm head green cabbage

1 onion, finely chopped

2 tablespoons margarine

¼ cup long grain rice

½ cup chicken stock (I use a bouillon cube and boiling water)

1 pound ground beef or turkey breast, or both

Salt and pepper

Raisins (optional)

8-10 gingersnaps, crushed (optional)

SAUCE

1 (5 ounce) can tomato purée

3 (5 ounce tomato purée) cans water

¼ cup dark brown sugar

Juice of large lemon

Preheat oven to 300 degrees.

Blanch whole head of cabbage in boiling water for 5 minutes, then plunge into cold water. (I fill the kitchen sink for this part.) Strip off at least 12 outer leaves, removing the tough stalk end; set aside.

Cook onion in margarine until tender. Add rice and cook 3 minutes longer or until opaque. Add stock and cook until it is absorbed.

Mix rice mixture into raw meat and season with salt and pepper. Blend in raisins and gingersnap crumbs, if using.

To make sauce, combine all ingredients.

Place a tablespoon of the filling in the center of each cabbage leaf. Fold over like parcels then squeeze gently between palms to seal. Place in a casserole dish and cover with the sauce.

Bake, covered, for 2 hours. Remove lid and turn oven to 350 degrees. Cook for another 30 minutes to brown meat and thicken sauce.

Makes 12 stuffed cabbage leaves

UNSTUFFED CABBAGE AND MEATBALLS

Meat

"This recipe has become a tradition for the High Holidays for our family. Prepare an extra pan, freeze, and then use during Sukkot. My kids use the leftover meatballs to make meatball subs."

The word, "cabbage," comes from the Latin word, "caput," meaning "head".

According to the Talmud, cabbage is a nourishing food.

2 pounds cabbage, shredded
3 pounds ground beef
2 eggs
1 cup breadcrumbs
1 medium onion, shredded
½ green bell pepper, finely chopped
2 teaspoons mustard
½ teaspoon garlic powder
¼ teaspoon black pepper
1 (10 ounce) bottle chili sauce
⅔ cup water
1 (16 ounce) can whole cranberry sauce
1 (8 ounce) can tomato sauce

Preheat oven to 350 degrees.

Spread shredded cabbage in a large roasting pan.

Combine ground beef, eggs, breadcrumbs, onions, green peppers, mustard, garlic powder and black pepper and shape into about 36 meatballs. Place meatballs over cabbage.

Pour chili sauce evenly over meatballs and cabbage. Pour water over the cabbage. Spread cranberry sauce evenly over the meatballs. Pour tomato sauce over all.

Cover pan with lid or aluminum foil. Bake 1 hour, 30 minutes to 2 hours or until cabbage is softened.

Serve with broad noodles or rice. May be cooked ahead and refrigerated or frozen.

KONCLETON

Meat

"This is either a Russian or Polish dish. My grandmother used to make it. It was considered the poor man's food – you could get a lot of hamburger out of a small amount of meat."

1-2 onions sliced

2-3 tablespoons olive oil

2 pounds ground beef

2 eggs

2 tablespoons crushed garlic or
  to taste

1 teaspoon kosher salt or to taste

Pepper to taste

½ onion, chopped

1-2 squirts ketchup

4-5 tablespoons honey

¾ cup flavored breadcrumbs or
  matzah meal

In a large saucepan, sauté sliced onions in oil.

In a large bowl, combine sautéed onions with beef, eggs, garlic, salt, pepper, chopped onions, ketchup, honey and breadcrumbs.

Form mixture into 2-inch balls. Brown on all sides for 20 to 30 minutes or until cooked and the desired tenderness.

Can be served over mashed potatoes.

STANDING PRIME RIB ROAST

Meat

1 standing rib roast
Garlic cloves, cut into chunks if large

Ground pepper
Kosher salt
Flour

Take whatever size roast you are using and put cloves of garlic in the flesh, using your finger or a small knife to make the holes. Use as few or as many as YOU like.

Sprinkle ground pepper and salt all around the roast (top, bottom and sides) and rub in well. Flour the roast in the same way, making sure it is well distributed (this helps seal the roast).

Take out of refrigerator 1 to 2 hours before cooking to bring to room temperature.

When ready to cook, preheat oven to 550 degrees.

Place roast in oven. Immediately reduce heat to 350 degrees. Cook 15 to 20 minutes per pound; 15 minutes for rare, 18 minutes for medium-rare and 20 minutes for done. Insert a meat thermometer into the thickest center part of the meat but not into the bone. The meat thermometer should register 140 degrees for rare and 170 degrees for well done.

Let roast stand 10 minutes before cutting. Slice and enjoy!

HERB-CRUSTED RACK OF LAMB

Meat

"This recipe is wonderful and easy, and tastes "restaurant good." I found it on-line while looking up how to make a rack of lamb. My butcher told me how to "French" it; to cut away all the meat between the ribs, leaving the bones clean. Ask the butcher to give you these pieces back (you paid for them), and prepare them like the rest of the roast."

1 (8 bone) lamb rack (ask butcher to "French" it)
Salt and pepper
1 clove garlic, minced
1 shallot or small onion, minced
2 teaspoons Dijon mustard
½ teaspoon dried thyme
½ teaspoon dried savory
½ teaspoon dried rosemary
½ teaspoon dried oregano
½ teaspoon dried basil
1 cup breadcrumbs mixed
2 tablespoons margarine, melted

Preheat oven to 400 degrees. Prepare a roasting pan by spraying with nonstick cooking spray or line with foil. Place a rack in pan.

Season lamb with salt and pepper. Rub with garlic and shallots.

Roast 25 minutes. Remove from oven and spread with mustard. Sprinkle with thyme, savory, rosemary, oregano and basil.

Combine breadcrumbs and margarine and sprinkle over roast.

Roast about 20 or 25 minutes longer or until the crumbs are golden; the meat should be rare to medium-rare.

Serves 2-3

Baron Herzog Zin Gris a light-bodied, refreshing summer wine that displays strawberry, citrus and berry flavors is delicious with your Herb-Crusted Rack of Lamb.

MUSTARD-ROASTED RACK OF LAMB

Meat

Ask butcher to "French" the rack of lamb – trim fat from between bones and scrape the protruding bones clean.

2 cloves garlic, chopped
¼ cup Dijon mustard
1 tablespoon red wine
1 teaspoon dried thyme

½ teaspoon fresh ground pepper
Salt to taste
2 (7 to 8 rib) racks of lamb,
   French prepared

Preheat oven and roasting pan to 450 degrees.

Mix garlic, mustard, wine, thyme, pepper and salt in a bowl. Coat lamb with seasoning mixture.

Place lamb in preheated pan and roast 10 minutes. Reduce heat to 350 degrees. Cook until meat thermometer reaches 130 degrees for rare, 15 minutes more for medium-rare. If coating or bones are browning too quickly, cover loosely with foil. Let rest for 15 minutes before serving.

Slice between the bones to divide into portions.

Serves 4

COOK'S NOTES

Lamb Shanks à la Martin

Meat

4 large onions, thinly sliced

4 lamb shanks, cracked
(about 3½ pounds total)

¾ cup dry vermouth

¼ cup soy sauce

¼ cup lemon juice

4 large cloves garlic, minced or
pressed

½ teaspoon pepper

Hot cooked rice

COOK'S NOTES

Preheat oven to 350 degrees.

Arrange onion slices in a 5- to 6-quart baking pan. Top with lamb shanks. Pour vermouth over meat and onions.

In a small bowl, stir together soy sauce, lemon juice, garlic and pepper. Spoon mixture over shanks. Bake, covered, for 3 hours, 30 minutes to 4 hours or until shanks are very tender when pierced and meat pulls from bone.

Serve lamb and onions on a platter with hot cooked rice; keep warm.

Skim and discard fat from pan juices; boil pan juices on high heat until reduced to about ½ cup. Spoon the juices over individual servings of lamb shanks and rice.

Serves 4

Herzog Special Reserve Alexander Valley Cabernet Sauvignon has wonderful complexity, finesse and depth of flavor, with layers of earthy currant, plum, wild berry, spice and cedar. Long elegant aftertaste. We recommend it with your Lamb Shanks à la Martin.

HONEY DELIGHT LAMB SHANKS

Meat /

4 lamb shanks (about 4 pounds total), bones cracked

1 tablespoon olive or salad oil

3 cloves garlic, minced or pressed

1 large onion, chopped

¼ cup honey

1 cup rosé wine or white blush zinfandel

1 (15 ounce) can tomato sauce

¼ teaspoon basil

¼ teaspoon oregano

¼ teaspoon pepper

In a large pan over medium-high heat, brown lamb in oil on all sides. (I brown under broiler, turning until brown.)

Place lamb in a pot with garlic and onion. Stir often until onion is limp, about 10 minutes. Add honey, wine, tomato sauce, basil, oregano and pepper.

Bring to boil. Cover and simmer about 1 hour, 30 minutes or until meat is very tender when pierced.

Transfer lamb to serving dish. Skim and discard fat from pan juices. Boil pan juices over high heat until reduced to about 2 cups. Spoon over lamb.

COOK'S NOTES

DUDU'S FAVORITE LAMB SHANK TZIMMES

Meat /

2 onions, diced

3 cloves garlic, chopped

½ cup oil

2-3 lamb shanks (ask butcher to crack shanks)

1 (8 ounce) can tomato sauce with mushrooms

1 cup chicken broth

1 cup red wine

½ cup honey

2 pounds carrots, cut into chunks

3 sweet potatoes, peeled and cut into chunks

2 parsnips, peeled and cut into chunks

Dash of Herbes de Provence (a dried herb)

Salt and pepper to taste

COOK'S NOTES

Preheat oven to 375 degrees.

Sauté onions and garlic in oil in a pot. Add meat, tomato sauce, broth, wine and honey. Bring to a boil. Add carrots, potatoes, parsnips, herbs and salt and pepper. Return to a boil and cook for a while.

Bake, covered, until the liquid is almost gone. Uncover and bake about 30 minutes longer, basting occasionally. If you want more liquid, add a little extra wine.

Dudu's Favorite Lamb Shank Tzimmes will SING with a Herzog Late Harvest Chenin Blanc. It is full-bodied, luscious and sweet, with fruity and floral aromas.

VEAL AND SHIITAKE MUSHROOM STEW

Meat /

COOK'S NOTES

If you have never used shiitake mushrooms, try them. They add a terrific flavor!

1 tablespoon extra-virgin olive oil

1 pound veal, cut into 1-inch cubes

6 ounces fresh shiitake mushrooms, stems discarded, cut into ½-inch pieces

1 large onion, coarsely chopped

2 teaspoons orange zest

2 large garlic cloves, minced

1 teaspoon rosemary

1 (14½ ounce) can diced tomatoes in juice

1 cup red wine (Cabernet or Chianti)

Salt and pepper

Heat oil in heavy large pot over high heat. Season veal with salt and pepper and add to pot. Sauté until light brown, about 5 minutes. Add mushrooms, onions, orange zest, garlic, and rosemary. Sauté until onion is golden, about 5 minutes.

Add tomatoes with juices and wine; bring to a boil. Reduce heat to medium-low, cover and simmer about 1 hour, 15 minutes or until veal is tender, stirring occasionally. Season with salt and pepper. Serve with rice or orzo.

This can be made a day ahead, if desired.

VEAL PICCATA

Meat

1 pound veal scallops, pounded
    thin

Salt and pepper

Flour

2 tablespoons olive oil

3 tablespoons margarine,
    divided use

¾ cup chicken stock

2 tablespoons lemon juice

2 tablespoons finely chopped
    parsley

Lemon slices, cut paper thin

Pat veal scallops dry and season on both sides with salt and pepper. Dredge lightly in flour and shake off excess.

In a heavy skillet, heat oil and 2 tablespoons margarine. Quickly sauté veal on both sides and arrange in a serving dish. Keep warm while you prepare the sauce.

Pour off any excess fat in the skillet. Return skillet to the heat and deglaze with stock and lemon juice. Stir in the parsley and swirl in the remaining tablespoon of margarine. Pour sauce over veal and garnish with the lemon slices. Serve immediately.

Serves 4

COOK'S NOTES

Herzog Special Reserve Edna Valley Syrah boasting its aromas of violet, raspberry and spice, well structured, with soft mouth-feel is a nice complement to your Veal Piccata.

VEAL SHANKS OSSO BUCO

Meat

4 veal shanks cut into 2 (2 inch) pieces with bone

Salt and freshly ground pepper

Flour

¼ cup olive oil or more, as needed

1 large sweet onion, diced (about 1 cup)

1 cup diced carrots

1 cup diced celery

4 cloves garlic, finely chopped

1 cup dry red wine (Merlot is good)

2 tablespoons orange zest

1 tablespoon lemon zest

½ cup orange juice

¼ cup lemon juice

1 cup crushed plum tomatoes

2 cups hot beef stock

¾ tablespoon Herbes De Provence, or 2 tablespoons fresh thyme, 2 bay leaves and ½ cup chopped fresh Italian parsley

Preheat oven to 350 degrees.

Season veal with salt and pepper. Dust lightly with flour. Heat oil in large skillet and sear veal pieces on all sides until lightly brown, about 10 minutes. This can be done in small batches if there is too much meat. Remove browned meat to an ovenproof casserole dish.

In the same skillet, add onions, carrots, celery and garlic and sauté for 3 to 4 minutes. When vegetables begin to soften and wilt, add wine and deglaze the pan. Add both zests and juices and cook for several minutes to reduce. Add tomatoes and bring to a boil. Pour over the veal.

Add hot stock and herbs and braise, covered, for 1 hour, 45 minutes. The veal should be fork tender, with the meat just beginning to separate from the bone. Adjust salt and pepper. Remove bay leaves before serving, if using.

Serve veal with some of the sauce spooned over the top.

Serves 4

COOK'S NOTES

For Veal Shanks Osso Buco, we recommend Baron Herzog Cabernet Sauvignon, a rich, full-bodied, California wine that boasts layers of berry, currant, and anise flavors with aromas of blackberry and mild oak.

TULKOFF ROOTS

What is now our nation's largest manufacturer of horseradish products is deeply rooted in the history of Baltimore's renowned Jewry. In the early 1920's, Harry and Lena Tulkoff added their own recipe for a pungent product to their family produce business located on the city's famed "Corned Beef Row". Tulkoff's Horseradish became so popular among caterers and consumers that the family began to focus solely on the production, bottling, and distribution of the aromatic accompaniment for everything from gefilte fish to brisket. Now headquartered in a large modern facility just east of Baltimore's Inner Harbor, with a second facility in California—Tulkoff has blanketed the country with its signature brand and private labeling of award winning products.

This page courtesy of
Martin and Sylvia Tulkoff,
Beth Tfiloh Congregation

GRANDMA'S SWEET & MILD GEFILTE FISH

Pareve /

"The amount of seasoning (sweet or savory) depends on that particular fish. Therefore, when seasoning, the best way to determine how the fish is going to taste is to taste it raw. DO SO AT YOUR OWN RISK. Also, you may want to season it a bit more since the broth will dilute it slightly. I only use white fish and yellow pike in equal proportions. Carp is permissible but only if it is FRESH ROE carp."

BROTH

Fish bones and heads from the whitefish and pike ONLY. Try to use bones and head from more fish than was ground

2 white parsnips, cut into a few pieces

3 celery stalks, cut into a few pieces

2-3 whole onions

4-5 carrots, cut into a few pieces

Parsley

Dill

Salt and pepper to taste

Sugar to taste

Put the bones and heads in a big pot with all the vegetables and seasonings. Add enough water to just cover. Cook 45 minutes.

Taste and adjust seasoning. Strain broth, keeping the carrots (unless you prefer fresh carrots to be cooked later) and onions (Use the onions to keep the gefilte fish moist). Return to a boil.

GEFILTE FISH

8 pounds ground white fish and yellow pike

8 eggs, beaten until fluffy (1egg per pound of fish)

2½- 3 tablespoons salt

10 tablespoons sugar

1-1½ teaspoons pepper

2 pounds Vidalia, Bermuda or any sweet onion, ground (Use the food processor to grind. It is fine to make it mushy)

Mix all ingredients together well. If mixture is too sticky, add water, a small amount at a time. You shouldn't need matzah meal if the fish is fresh, but if you do, use only a scant amount. Taste and adjust seasoning.

(Continued on next page)

Wet hands (keep bowl of water near to wet hands when needed), and form mixture into balls. Keep in mind when forming balls that they WILL puff up. DO NOT overhandle, the less the balls are handled, the fluffier they will be. Put them GENTLY into the strained boiling broth. Cook for 1 hour, 30 minutes.

At about the 1 hour mark, if you wanted fresh sliced carrots, now is the time to add them. Keep the lid on the pot so the balls do not get dry. Cook in pot while still covered. Take fish out of pot very carefully so not to damage the balls, lay in a heat resistant container and cover with fish broth, and onions and carrot, if you wish. Chill.

COOK'S NOTES

HELEN'S TRADITIONAL GEFILTE FISH

Pareve /

"My aunt helped me make Gefilte fish for Passover in 1968. I have been making it for Rosh Hashanah and Passover ever since that first time. I always made it early in the day. When I started to work full time I began making it at 5 am. This astounded my family and everyone asked why not make it at night. For me coming home from work and cooking is too hard. The fish is always expensive and I was always so afraid that it would not be tasty. Many a time I would wake up at 3 or 4 a.m. and decide to make it then. I was afraid that I would fall asleep and not get up in time to make it. We have a saying in our family, "Where is it written in the Torah that Gefilte fish should be made very early in the morning?"

Bones and heads and make sure that fish man takes the eyes out

6-8 onions, peeled

4 medium carrots

Salt to taste

White (not black) pepper to taste

8 eggs

10 pounds ground rock, whitefish or pike (no carp)

8 onions, ground

In 2 large pots put heads and bones. Add enough water to cover. Bring to a boil. Remove foam that may accumulate. Divide whole onions and carrots to each pot. Add salt and a lot of white pepper to the water. Cover and bring to a boil and then let simmer.

Beat eggs. Add eggs to ground fish. Stir in ground onions. Mix well. Season fish mixture with salt and pepper.

After stock has simmered for about 15 to 20 minutes add a "taster ball" to each pot. Cover pot and cook 15 to 20 minutes. Cool and taste. Season as needed.

Remove the bones, heads and onions and strain the stock. Return stock to a simmer.

Wet hands and take a handful of the fish and make into a ball. Drop the ball onto an oval mixing spoon, then shape ball into an oval and drop into the water. The spoon helps keep the balls uniform in size and keeps you from burning your hands in the hot water.

Simmer fish balls for 1½ hours. When gefilte fish balls are completely cooked, place cooked balls in a heat resistant glass dish to cool. After cooling, place them into plastic container. Pour some of the stock over the fish. Refrigerate until ready to serve. Serve cold or at room temperature.

Garnish with 1 coin shaped slice of cooked carrot on top of each fish ball. Serve with horseradish.

Chef Tio Pepe Filet of Sole Topped with Bananas

Pareve /

1 ounce margarine, melted	Dash of white pepper
1 shallot, chopped	4 ounces white wine
2 pounds filet of sole	4 bananas, sliced diagonally
1 teaspoon of salt	

Place margarine and shallots in a fish poacher or large pan. Roll each filet of sole and place in the pan. Add salt, pepper and white wine to the fish. Cover and poach for 5 minutes.

Remove fish rolls from pan and place in a broiler approved dish or platter. Cover each fish roll completely with sliced bananas, neatly arranged.

Place fish under the broiler for 2 minutes. Remove from broiler and spoon Hollandaise Sauce (see below) on top of bananas. Return dish to the broiler for 1 minute.

Hollandaise Sauce

1 cup (2 sticks) pareve margarine, melted	1 lemon, squeezed
4 egg yolks, beaten	Dash of salt and pepper

Over a double boiler, whisk margarine into egg yolks. Add lemon juice, salt and pepper gradually.

"Chiquita Banana," in her famous song of the 1940's, told housewives never to put bananas in the refrigerator as they will turn brown under 40 degrees. Maintain bananas at room temperature.

Herzog's Late Harvest White Riesling is a pleasantly sweet wine with rich, ripe concentrated fruit flavors. This easy drinking wine would be delicious with this marvelous fish dish.

CRISPY BAKED FILETS

Pareve

1 pound flounder filets	¼ teaspoon salt
Pepper	2 tablespoons oil
Paprika	⅓ cup corn flake crumbs

Preheat oven to 400 degrees.

Wash and dry filets and cut into serving pieces. Season with pepper, paprika and salt and brush with oil. Coat fish with crumbs and arrange in a single layer in a greased shallow baking dish.

Bake 10 minutes without turning or basting. Flake fish with a fork to check for doneness.

Serves 2-3

FLAVORFUL VENETIAN SOLE OR SARDINES

Pareve

This recipe has been translated from the Italian to English from "La Cucina Nella Tradizione Ebraica", Cooking in the Hebrew Tradition. It is a staple of Jewish Venetian Cooking, but its roots are in the Judeo/Arab community of Sicily due to its use of raisins, zest, and pine nuts. The recipe came to Venice with Jews expelled from Sicily by the Spanish in the 1490's. It is wonderful. Enjoy!

2 pounds filet of Sole or large fresh sardines	1½ cups cider or wine vinegar
3 heaping tablespoons flour	1 teaspoon of either lemon, lime, or citron zest
3 tablespoons olive, canola, or peanut oil	¼ cup of pine nuts
1 large onion, sliced	¼ cup of raisins

Rinse and dry the fish. (If using whole fish, gut and clean first.) Dredge the fish in the flour. In a large sauté pan, heat oil until almost smoking and fry fish for 1½ to 2 minutes until cooked through. Transfer fish to plate and lower heat under oil. When temperature is lowered, add sliced onions and cook for 25 minutes, making sure the onions do not brown. In the last 5 minutes, add the vinegar. Remove from heat, add zest, pine nuts and raisins. In a baking dish to fit, layer the fish, onions, condiments and vinegar mixture. Refrigerate. The flavor improves with 2 or 3 days of marinating. Serve at room temperature.

Serves 6

Elliott's Tuna Over Pasta

Pareve

½ cup soy sauce

¼ cup seasoned rice wine vinegar

2 tablespoons sesame oil

1 pound fresh tuna steak, cubed

3 large scallions, sliced

½ pound snow peas

1 large Portabello mushroom, cubed

12 ounces firm tofu*, cubed

2 teaspoons dried basil, or 2 tablespoons fresh, minced

1 teaspoon garlic powder

Salt and pepper to taste

1 tablespoon sesame seeds

2-4 tablespoons olive oil, divided use

1 tablespoon cornstarch

10 ounces Chinese noodles or linguini, prepared per package directions

COOK'S NOTES

Mix soy sauce, vinegar and sesame oil in a glass dish. Add tuna and marinate 30 to 60 minutes.

Toss together scallions, snow peas, mushrooms, tofu, basil, garlic powder, salt and pepper and sesame seeds. Heat half the olive oil in a large skillet. Add vegetable mixture and sauté until crisp-tender, about 5 minutes. Transfer to a bowl.

Add remaining oil to skillet. Using a slotted spoon, remove tuna pieces from marinade, reserving marinade, and sauté tuna in oil until tuna is just done, still pink (do not overdo, or tuna will become overly dry). Put cornstarch in a bowl with a little bit of marinade and combine until smooth. Pour remaining marinade into skillet and then add marinade with cornstarch mixture. Mix around for about 1 minute. Add vegetables to heat. Serve over noodles.

Serves 4

*See page 215 for how to prepare tofu for cooking.

ROCKFISH CAKES

Pareve

1 pound rockfish (or other meaty white fish)

Salt and pepper, to taste

1 egg

2 heaping tablespoons mayonnaise

1 tablespoon yellow mustard

1 teaspoon dry mustard

1 teaspoon Old Bay seasoning

Dash hot sauce (optional)

3½ tablespoons ground cracker crumbs

3 tablespoons Worcestershire sauce

2 tablespoons fresh parsley

Paprika, to taste

Cocktail sauce

Season fish with salt and pepper. Preheat oven to 350 degrees. Bake fish until cooked thoroughly, about 10 minutes; cool. Flake fish off the skin and put in bowl. Add egg, mayonnaise, mustards, Old Bay seasoning, hot sauce, cracker crumbs, Worcestershire sauce, and parsley. Form into patties; sprinkle with paprika. Bake at 400 degrees for 8 to 12 minutes. Check for doneness. Broil for 2 minutes to finish. Serve with cocktail sauce.

When you purchase the rockfish buy a little extra to allow for the skin you take off. And try to avoid the tails. Purchase the meaty part of the fish.

Optional: Add chopped red pepper and/or celery. You can substitute frozen pollack. Quick and easy.

Enjoy Alfasi Chardonnay with your delicious homemade Rockfish Cakes. Dry, crisp, and well balanced, this Chilean wine displays fresh apple and pear flavors.

FLORENTINE FISH ROLL-UPS

Dairy

1 (10 ounce) box frozen chopped
   spinach, cooked and drained

2 eggs, beaten

8 tablespoons matzah meal,
   seasoned with salt and pepper

4 flounder filets

2 tablespoons butter

2 medium onions, chopped

2 tablespoons flour

1 teaspoon salt

⅛ teaspoon pepper

1½ cups milk

Ketchup for color (optional)

Preheat oven to 350 degrees.

Mix cooked spinach with eggs and matzah meal. Divide mixture
among filets. Roll up each filet and place in a shallow greased pan.

In a saucepan, melt butter. Add onions and cook until translucent.
Add flour and salt and pepper and mix well. Pour in milk. Cook and
stir over moderate heat until thickened. Add ketchup, if desired. Pour
sauce over fish.

Bake 30 minutes.

4 servings

GRILLED HALIBUT WITH
TOMATO AND CAPER SAUCE

Dairy / Pareve

The sauce can be made up to 2 days in advance, and the fish grilled at the last minute. This recipe is also delicious served at room temperature.

⅓ cup extra-virgin olive oil, plus more for brushing

2 cups finely chopped onions

2 cups chopped fennel

2 garlic cloves, minced

2 (28 ounce) cans Italian plum tomatoes, drained

Kosher salt and freshly ground pepper

¼ cup dry white wine

¼ cup pareve chicken broth or vegetable broth

¼ cup capers, drained and coarsely chopped

1 cup coarsely chopped basil, plus small leaves for garnish

2 tablespoons unsalted butter or unsalted pareve margarine

8 (6 to 7 ounce, 1-inch thick) skinless halibut filets

In a large deep skillet, heat ⅓ cup olive oil. Add the onions and fennel and cook over medium-low heat, stirring occasionally, for about 10 minutes or until softened. Add garlic and cook about 1 minute or until fragrant.

Add tomatoes to the skillet and break them up with a fork. Season with salt and pepper. Simmer 15 to 20 minutes. Add wine, broth and capers and cook over low heat for 10 minutes. Stir basil and butter into the sauce.

Preheat a grill. Brush the halibut filets with olive oil and season generously with salt and pepper. Grill over high heat until just cooked through, about 4 minutes per side. Spoon the sauce onto a large deep platter. Set the filets on the sauce and garnish with basil leaves. Serve hot or at room temperature.

The sauce can be refrigerated for up to 2 days. Reheat gently before serving.

Serves 8

You can cut this recipe in half - and it's still great.

MACADAMIA NUT CRUSTED SEA BASS

Pareve

½ cup all-purpose flour

2 eggs

3 cups macadamia nuts

Flaked coconut (optional)

6 (6 ounce) sea bass, mahi-mahi
or snapper filets

¼ cup olive oil

Preheat oven to 350 degrees.

Place flour in small bowl. Whisk eggs in a separate small bowl. Finely grind nuts in food processor and place in another bowl with coconut, if using.

Coat each fish filet with flour, then dip into eggs and coat with nuts.

Heat at least 2 tablespoons of oil in a skillet over medium heat. Place 2 or 3 filets in skillet to brown the nut topping - watch carefully so nuts do not burn. Repeat with additional filets, adding more olive oil if necessary.

Transfer to a baking sheet and put in oven. Bake until fish are opaque and cooked through in the center. Cooking time can vary by type of fish.

Serve with coconut rice, if desired.

Serves 6

For coconut rice, use coconut milk instead of water when making rice.

Sea Bass may be called:

Sea bass

Rock bass

Bluefish

Blackwill

Hannahill

Humpback

Giant Sea Bass

Black Sea Bass

Grouper Bass

Teal Lake Shiraz is wonderful with this special Sea Bass. Light and distinctive for its spicy cherry and anise flavors, this Australian wine's fruity flavors echo nicely on a soft finish.

BONNIE'S FRESH FISH SALAD
Dairy

Very light and really delicious. Great summertime hors d'oeuvre.

1 large head radicchio lettuce
⅓ cup plain yogurt
⅓ cup mayonnaise
2 teaspoons Dijon mustard
2 teaspoons capers
2 tablespoons minced red onion
1 tablespoon lemon juice

¼ cup minced red bell pepper
2 teaspoons raspberry vinegar
Salt and white pepper to taste
1 pound cooked and flaked
   halibut or pollack
2-3 tablespoons chopped parsley
   for garnish

Pull off 6 of the outer leaves from head of radicchio to use for serving; reserve remaining radicchio for a later use in a salad.

Whisk together yogurt, mayonnaise and mustard until smooth. Stir in capers, red onions, lemon juice, bell peppers and raspberry vinegar. Season mixture with salt and white pepper. Gently fold in fish.

Place one-half cup servings in radicchio leaves. Serve individually or from one serving platter. Garnish with parsley as desired.

Serves 6

MALAYSIAN LIME COCONUT MAHI MAHI
Pareve

"My family has a taste for hot spices. In fact, we grow a variety of hot peppers each summer. This will make your tongue and head tingle."

⅓ cup light coconut milk
¼ cup chopped fresh cilantro
2 tablespoons thinly sliced
   peeled lemon grass, or
   1 tablespoon lime zest
2 tablespoons soy sauce
1 tablespoon brown sugar

1 teaspoon lime juice
½ teaspoon chili paste with garlic
2 shallots, peeled
1 clove garlic, peeled
1½ pounds Mahi Mahi
Cilantro sprigs and lemon
   wedges for garnish (optional)

Preheat broiler. Combine all ingredients except fish and garnish and coarsely chop in a food processor. Place fish on a greased broiler pan and spread half of mixture on top. Broil 15 minutes.

Serve with remaining sauce. Garnish with cilantro sprigs and lemon wedges.

Serves 4

A fish's eye is always open, so it is a good luck protector against the "evil eye."

We suggest Verbau Gewürztraminer to accompany your Mahi Mahi. This semi dry white wine is imported from Alsace, France and features spicy aromas and flavors.

RED CURRANT CHILEAN SEA BASS WITH MUSHROOMS

Pareve

6 (8 ounce) Chilean sea bass filets
Salt and pepper

¼ cup canola or vegetable oil
½ cup red currant jam
1-3 tablespoons water (optional)

COOK'S NOTES

Preheat oven to 400 degrees.

Pat sea bass filets dry and season with salt and pepper. In a nonstick skillet, heat 2 tablespoons oil until hot but not smoking. Place 3 filets into pan, flesh side down, and cook until golden, about 3 minutes. Turn fish over and sauté 2 minutes more. Remove from pan, add rest of oil and repeat with remaining 3 filets. (This can be done earlier in the day and the fish then refrigerated.)

Melt jam in a small saucepan over low heat until consistency is of a thick glaze. Add water if jam is still too thick to brush. Brush tops of filets with red currant glaze and finish in oven, about 2 to 4 minutes depending on doneness when removed from sauté pan.

Top each filet with mushrooms (recipe below).

MUSHROOMS

1 pound mixed fresh wild mushrooms (shiitake, cremini, porcini, and chanterelle)
2 shallots, minced

¼ cup olive oil
⅓ cup chopped fresh tarragon or parsley
Salt and pepper

Sauté mushrooms and shallots with oil in large skillet over medium-high heat, stirring occasionally. Cook until mushrooms begin to brown, 8-10 minutes. Toss with chopped herb, and salt and pepper to taste. (This may be prepared a day in advance and reheated.)

Serve this dish with Backsberg Chardonnay. Hailing from South Africa, this wine is off dry and medium bodied with lively apple, pear and melon flavors.

ENTRÉES—FISH

SALMON CUPS

Dairy

1 (14¾ ounce) can salmon, drained (or 2 cans tuna)

3 eggs

½ cup mayonnaise

2 tablespoons all-purpose flour

12 (½ inch) cheese cubes

Preheat oven to 350 degrees.

In a medium bowl with a fork, mash together salmon, eggs, mayonnaise and flour. Divide salmon mixture evenly among 12 greased muffin cups. Place a piece of cheese in the center of each and press down slightly.

Bake 15 minutes or until puffed and golden. Cool in pan on a wire rack for 5 minutes before removing. To remove, run a knife along the rim of each muffin cup. Use a fork to help get out the salmon cakes.

This dish can be baked in mini-muffin cups and served as appetizers.

SALMON EN CROÛTE

Dairy

⅔ pound Brie cheese, white rind removed

1 pound frozen puff pastry, thawed

1⅔ pounds salmon filets

2 tablespoons butter, melted

Salt and pepper to taste

1 cup sliced sautéed shiitake mushrooms

1 egg, beaten

Place Brie in the freezer for 30 minutes; then thinly slice with a cheese slicer.

Roll out the puff pastry on a pastry board to form a rectangle 12x20 inches. Place it on a large baking sheet and chill for 30 minutes.

Preheat the oven to 350 degrees.

Lay salmon filet down the middle of the puff pastry. (It may be necessary to tuck the tip end under to fit.) Drizzle butter over fish and season with salt and pepper. Lay cheese slices over the filet and sprinkle with sliced mushrooms.

Fold the dough over like a turnover, overlapping the sides. Crimp the ends together firmly to seal.

Brush the pastry with the beaten egg. Bake for 30 minutes. Cut into 6 equal pieces and serve at once.

6 portions

Salmon with Maple Balsamic Glaze

Pareve

¼ cup maple syrup

2 tablespoons balsamic vinegar

¼ cup orange juice

1 teaspoon minced garlic

2 tablespoons olive oil

¼ teaspoon pepper or to taste

½ teaspoon salt

1 pound salmon filets or steaks

In a small saucepan, mix maple syrup, balsamic vinegar, orange juice and garlic together. Bring to a boil, reduce heat and simmer for 5 minutes or until mixture is reduced. Remove from heat and stir in oil. Chill. Divide marinade in half.

Marinate salmon for 10 minutes in half of the marinade. Remove from marinade and discard marinade. Sprinkle salmon with salt and pepper. Liberally brush with remaining half of marinade.

Broil or grill 4 to 5 inches from heat on an uncovered grill directly over medium coals for 12 minutes per inch of thickness.

For filets, baste again halfway through cooking time. For steaks, turn halfway through cooking time and baste with marinade.

Serves 2-4

COOK'S NOTES

We recommend a Herzog Special Reserve Russian River Chardonnay—rich and complex, drawing on pear, citrus, hazelnut and mineral flavors, all framed in a creamy-smooth texture with plenty of toasty oak to enjoy with your salmon.

ENTRÉES—FISH

LABYRINTH ROAD SALMON CAKES

Pareve

"When I was small, my mother would make salmon cakes for dinner on Wednesday nights. At six years of age, it was the worst dinner anyone could hope for. To make matters worse she served them with baby peas and spaghetti which would run all over into everything. It was my least favorite meal ever! My mother and father loved this meal. I simply did not get it.

Time passes and behold – I have a 17 year old daughter and a 14 year old daughter who one day eat these same exact salmon cakes at my sister's house which our Mother made especially for that evening. They love them. 'Mom', they exclaim, 'Why don't you make these for us? We love them!' They tell me they will even take them for lunch each day for school if I make a batch and freeze them. I am shocked. I cannot believe my ears. Enjoy them with your family if you dare!"

1 jumbo egg, beaten
1-2 tablespoons mayonnaise
1 teaspoon baking powder
1 tablespoon chopped parsley

½ teaspoon Worcestershire sauce
1 (14½ ounce) can Red Sockeye Salmon
⅛ cup cracker crumbs or cornflake crumbs

Whisk together egg, mayonnaise, baking powder, parsley, and Worcestershire sauce.

Debone and drain salmon. Mix it with egg mixture. Form into patties and roll into crumbs on both sides.

Sprinkle paprika on top of each patty for color. Broil 10 minutes until brown on a greased cookie sheet or pan. Or bake in oven at 350 degrees for 7 minutes or until solid but moist inside.

May be serve hot, cold or warm. Serve with spicy mustard.

Fresh cooked salmon as an alternative is also delicious in this recipe.

Simple Salmon Sampler

Salmon Teriyaki

Pareve

1 pound salmon filet

**Thick teriyaki baste
(Make sure thick baste)**

Spread teriyaki baste on top of salmon. Bake at 375 degrees for about 12 to 15 minutes. You can also place on the grill 12 to 15 minutes. Do not turn over – this only needs to be cooked on one side.

Serve with steamed spinach or string beans and baked potato.

Salmon Italian Style

Pareve

1 pound salmon filet

Italian salad dressing

Pour salad dressing on top of salmon. Broil or grill about 10 to 15 minutes until done. Do not turn over.

Serve with spaghetti, salad or garlic bread.

Mustard Salmon

Pareve

1 pound salmon filet
**1½ tablespoons mayonnaise
    (regular or light)**

3 tablespoons Dijon mustard

Mix together mustard and mayonnaise until blended. Spread on top of salmon. Bake at 375 degrees for 12 minutes. Then broil for an additional 2 to 3 minutes until it browns around edges. You can also grill this.

Serve with broccoli and whipped or baked potatoes.

Cook's Notes

ARTICHOKE-MUSTARD SAUCE

Pareve

¼ cup Dijon mustard
6 tablespoons boiling water
¾ cup olive oil
Pepper to taste

2 teaspoons lemon juice
14 ounce can artichoke hearts,
    drained and coarsely
    chopped

This sauce can be used as a condiment over cooked meats, chicken or vegetables; just as you would use dill sauce.

Place mustard in a bowl. Gradually add boiling water, beating constantly until all the water is mixed in.

In a slow, steady stream, add olive oil, whisking constantly until all oil has been added and the sauce is creamy. Stir in the pepper and lemon juice, mixing well. Add the chopped artichoke hearts and stir to blend.

May prepare sauce ahead and refrigerate. Bring to room temperature to serve.

HONEY MUSTARD MARINADE

Pareve

A delicious glaze for salmon or tuna.

2 tablespoons honey
1 tablespoon sugar

3 tablespoons regular or light
    soy sauce
1 tablespoon Dijon mustard

Combine all ingredients and pour ½ marinade over salmon or tuna. After approximately half of cooking time, pour remaining marinade over fish. Tent aluminum foil over fish and continue to grill until cooked through.

MEL'S TERIYAKI MARINADE FROM KAUAI

Pareve

3 cups low sodium soy sauce
1 tablespoon garlic powder
½ teaspoon ground ginger

1 pound light brown sugar
1 tablespoon onion flakes

Mix in batches in a blender. Marinate fish in mixture for 30 minutes before baking, grilling, or broiling.

Joe's Mustard Sauce

Dairy

1 tablespoon plus ½ teaspoon dry mustard or more, divided use

1 cup mayonnaise

2 teaspoons Worcestershire sauce

1 teaspoon steak sauce

1 tablespoon heavy cream

1 tablespoon milk

Pinch of salt

Use this as you would any dill sauce. Drizzle over any cold or cooked fish.

Place 1 tablespoon mustard in a mixing bowl or the bowl of an electric mixer. Add mayonnaise and beat for 1 minute. Add Worcestershire sauce, steak sauce, cream, milk and salt. Beat until the mixture is blended and creamy.

If you'd like a little more mustard flavor, whisk in about ½ teaspoon more dry mustard until well-blended.

Chill the sauce, covered, until ready to serve.

Makes about 1 cup

Mediterranean Fish Sauce

Dairy / Pareve /

3 cloves chopped fresh garlic

2-3 chopped shallots

2 tablespoons olive oil

1 (28 ounce) can diced tomatoes

1 tablespoon fresh lemon juice

1 teaspoon sugar

Fresh pepper

1 tablespoon chopped fresh basil

¼ cup half-and-half (optional)

Sauté garlic and shallots in olive oil until translucent. Add tomatoes, lemon juice, sugar and pepper. Simmer for 20 minutes.

Add basil and half-and-half and simmer for a few minutes. Serve over grilled or fried fish.

Serves 4

How to Make Sushi 101

What you need before you start:

Rolling bamboo mat

Plastic wrap

Sushi rice

Rice wine vinegar (seasoned)

Salt

Sugar

Nori (toasted seaweed sheets)

Wasabi (powdered or ready made)

Pickled ginger (prepared or see recipe on page 175)

Any vegetables, in matchstick cut (carrots must be parboiled)

Fish (also sliced thinly)

To make sushi rice:

3 cups water

2 cups raw rice

4 tablespoons sugar

3 tablespoons rice wine vinegar

1 tablespoon salt

Bring water to boil, turn off heat. Add rice (some like to rinse their rice first to lessen the starch factor), bring back to boil and simmer on lowest setting for about 15-20 minutes. Start checking after 10 minutes to see if rice is cooked. If rice is still hard keep cooking, adding water if needed.

While rice is cooking, prepare the flavoring of sugar, salt, and rice wine vinegar. Make sure to stir well until it is thoroughly mixed.

Mix rice with vinegar mixture while fanning (to help cool off and be sure water evaporates). Once the rice is well coated, sushi can be prepared. (Make sure rice is cool enough to handle.)

* Adjust seasoning to your liking.

* Makes about 9 rolls of sushi.

To assemble Sushi:

Cover mat with plastic wrap (it makes clean up SO easy as the rice doesn't get stuck between the bamboo).

Lay the sheet of nori on the mat, shiny side down.

Put rice on about a ⅓ of the sheet. Put veggies or whatever on top of the rice.

Start rolling from bottom to top, VERY TIGHTLY. After each rotation, pull back to pack it well.

Once mat is rolled around nori, squeeze a bit to tighten. You may need some water on edge to seal, but try without first. If you let the roll lay for a few minutes on the seam, it will usually self seal.

Using a serrated knife or very sharp knife, slice roll. First, slice in half. Then slice each half in half, and then again to produce eight even pieces of sushi. Serve with wasabi and pickled ginger.

ENJOY!!!

To make pickled ginger:

2 large gingerroots   **5-7 tablespoons sugar**
1 cup rice vinegar   **1 teaspoon salt**

Peel the gingerroot. Cut the ginger into medium-sized pieces and salt it. Leave the ginger in a bowl for 30 minutes, then put into a jar.

Mix rice vinegar and sugar in a pan and bring to a boil. Pour the hot mixture of vinegar and sugar on the ginger. Cool, then cover with a lid and place in the refrigerator.

In a week, the ginger changes its color to light pink. Slice thinly to serve. The pickled ginger lasts about a month in the fridge.

Pickled ginger is served with sushi. Try to eat pieces of pickled ginger between different kinds of sushi. It helps to clean your mouth and enhance the flavors.

COOK'S NOTES

TOFU LASAGNA

Dairy

1 pound lasagna noodles

2 tablespoons vinegar

1 tablespoon oil

1 pound soft tofu, not silken

¼ cup Parmesan cheese

1 teaspoon onion powder

1 teaspoon garlic powder

1 tablespoon parsley

1 tablespoon basil

½ teaspoon salt

1 quart Italian-style tomato sauce

8 ounces mozzarella cheese, grated

Preheat oven to 350 degrees.

Boil lasagna noodles for 5 minutes. Add vinegar and oil to boiling water to prevent noodles from sticking - vinegar will not affect the taste. Drain and rinse thoroughly with cold water.

Drain and mash tofu. Combine tofu with Parmesan cheese, onion powder, garlic powder, parsley, basil and salt in a mixing bowl. Blend well.

In a greased 9x13-inch pan, arrange a layer of lasagna noodles. Spread a layer of tofu mixture over noodles, then cover with a layer of tomato sauce. Repeat layering until all ingredients are used. Top with grated mozzarella cheese. Bake 30 minutes.

TOFU MANICOTTI

Dairy

1 pound soft tofu

1 tablespoon olive oil

¼ cup Parmesan cheese

8 ounces mozzarella cheese, grated, divided use

2 teaspoons parsley

1 teaspoon salt

1 teaspoon basil

½ teaspoon oregano

⅛ teaspoon black pepper

¼ teaspoon garlic powder

12 manicotti shells

1 quart Italian-style tomato sauce

Preheat oven to 350 degrees.

Drain and mash tofu. Combine tofu with oil, Parmesan cheese, half the mozzarella cheese, parsley, salt, basil, oregano, pepper and garlic powder. Mix well.

Pour 1 cup tomato sauce into a 13x9x2-inch baking pan. Fill uncooked manicotti shells with tofu mixture. Place filled shells in sauce, allowing room for shells to expand while cooking. Pour remaining sauce over shells. Sprinkle remainder of mozzarella on top. Cover with foil and bake 40 minutes.

For a cheesier dish, sprinkle extra mozzarella and Parmesan on top.

Tofu Parmigiana

Dairy

3 tablespoons oil

½ cup soy sauce

1 teaspoon garlic powder

¾ cup dry white wine

1 pound Soydairy firm tofu

1 egg beaten with 2 tablespoons milk

¾ cup seasoned breadcrumbs

2 cups Italian style tomato sauce

1 tablespoon oregano

4 tablespoons Parmesan cheese, grated

4 ounces mozzarella cheese, grated

Preheat oven to 350 degrees. Spread 3 tablespoons oil over a baking sheet.

Combine soy sauce, garlic powder and wine for a marinade. Drain tofu and slice into about ten (¼-inch) pieces. Place sliced tofu in marinade and let sit for 1 hour, turning once to marinate both sides evenly.

Remove tofu slices from marinade. Dip in egg mixture and then into breadcrumbs. Place on prepared baking sheet. Bake about 10 minutes or until brown on each side.

Pour ⅔ cup tomato sauce into a 1-quart baking dish. Layer half of the breaded tofu slices on sauce. Sprinkle with half the oregano, Parmesan cheese and mozzarella cheese. Pour another ⅔ cup sauce over slices. Layer with remaining tofu slices and sprinkle with remaining oregano. Cover with remaining sauce again. Top with remaining mozzarella and Parmesan cheeses.

Cover and bake 30 minutes or until sauce bubbles and cheese melts. Serve with spaghetti, garden salad and garlic bread.

TOFU TACO STUFFING

Dairy

1 pound soy firm tofu
Oil for sautéing
½ cup onions, chopped
1 clove garlic, crushed
1 teaspoon cumin
1 teaspoon coriander
¼ teaspoon cayenne pepper
1 teaspoon chili powder

1 (28 ounce) can kidney beans
½ cup tomato purée
1 tablespoon Worcestershire sauce
1 package taco shells
Grated cheese, shredded lettuce, chopped onions, sliced fresh tomatoes, hot sauce and sour cream for topping

COOK'S NOTES

Drain and crumble tofu. Add to heated oil in a skillet. Add onions and garlic and sauté. Add cumin, coriander, cayenne pepper and chili powder and stir continuously until tofu stops steaming.

Mash kidney beans with tomato purée and Worcestershire sauce and mix into tofu mixture.

Serve in taco shells and add toppings as desired.

This filling is also great in burritos and enchiladas.

Makes 12 tacos

SPICY TOFU HOT POT

Pareve

This is good for those with a weakness for spicy cuisine!

2 teaspoons peanut oil

2 tablespoons grated ginger

6 cloves garlic, minced

2 teaspoons chili paste with garlic

4 cups pareve chicken stock

1 tablespoon dark brown sugar

¼ cup low-sodium soy sauce

2 pounds extra firm tofu, drained and cut in cubes

4 cups thinly sliced bok choy

4 ounces fresh shiitake mushrooms or more to taste, stems discarded, sliced

½ pound fresh lo mein noodles or fresh linguine

½ cup chopped fresh cilantro

Heat oil in large Dutch oven over medium heat. Add ginger, garlic, chili paste, broth, sugar and soy sauce and bring to a boil. Add tofu, bok choy, mushrooms.

Cover and simmer 2 minutes. Increase heat to high. Add noodles, cooking uncovered for 2 minutes. Remove from heat and stir in cilantro.

Serves 4 generously

KUGELS, QUICHES
AND
PASTAS, TOO!

KUGELS, QUICHES AND PASTAS, TOO!

FINE NOODLE KUGEL SOUFFLÉ

Dairy

1 (12 ounce) bag fine egg
    noodles

4 eggs

1 cup sugar

1 cup sour cream

1 (8 ounce) container whipped
    cream cheese

2 teaspoons vanilla

1 cup (2 sticks) butter, softened

Cinnamon for topping

Preheat oven to 325 degrees.

Cook noodles and drain. Blend eggs, sugar, sour cream, cream cheese, vanilla and butter. Put cooked noodles at the bottom of a greased 13x9x2-inch baking dish. Pour egg mixture over noodles. Sprinkle with cinnamon.

Bake, uncovered, for 40 to 45 minutes or until golden. Cool 15 minutes, then cut into squares.

Serves 12

The word, "kugel," is generally translated as "pudding." It is pronounced "koo-gel" or "ki-gel," depending on where your grandmother comes from.

ZIPPY'S EXCEPTIONAL JERUSALEM KUGEL

Pareve

10 ounces fine noodles or
    spaghetti

¾ cup sugar

¾ cup oil

3 eggs

Salt and pepper to taste

Preheat oven to 350 degrees.

Cook noodles according to package directions; drain and return to pot.

In a skillet, heat sugar in oil, stirring constantly, until caramelized and golden brown. Do not overcook or it will be bitter.

Add caramelized sugar slowly into pot with noodles, stirring until completely mixed. Add eggs and salt and pepper. Transfer to a greased and heated round aluminum disposable pan.

Bake 45 minutes or until golden brown.

Makes 1 pie

EVIE'S DAIRY KUGEL

Dairy

Our friend, Evie, came to dinner. After eating my kugel, she said "Your kugel was good, but I'll give you a recipe that is the best." She was right.

1 (8 ounce) package cream
   cheese, softened

½ cup (1 stick) butter, softened

4 eggs, beaten

2 cups milk

½ cup sugar

1 teaspoon vanilla

8 ounces noodles, cooked and
   drained

TOPPING

Crushed corn flakes

Cinnamon

Sugar

   Mix cream cheese, butter, eggs, milk, sugar and vanilla until smooth. Add mixture to drained noodles and mix well. Transfer to a greased 2-quart oblong casserole dish. Cover with plastic wrap and refrigerate overnight.

   The next day, preheat oven to 350 degrees. Mix all topping ingredients together and sprinkle over kugel. Bake 1 hour, 15 minutes or until golden brown on top.

Serves 8-10

INA'S CHEESE KUGEL

Dairy

This is outstanding! You can use low-fat ingredients, but the fattening ones are best.

8 ounce package egg noodles, ½-inch size

6 eggs

1 cup sugar

8 ounces farmer's cheese

4 ounces cream cheese

16 ounces creamed cottage cheese

1 cup sour cream

2 cups regular milk

6 tablespoons melted butter

1 teaspoon salt

TOPPING

1 teaspoon sugar

1 teaspoon cinnamon

2 packages slivered almonds

Preheat oven to 350 degrees.

Cook noodles in boiling water for 5 minutes; drain.

Beat eggs and add sugar, farmer's cheese, cream cheese, cottage cheese, sour cream, milk, butter and salt. Beat until smooth. Add noodles and mix.

Transfer mixture to a 13x9x2-inch glass baking dish sprayed with vegetable spray.

For topping, combine cinnamon and sugar and sprinkle over kugel. Top with almonds.

Bake, uncovered, for 1 hour.

Sprinkle cinnamon and sugar on top for a new taste.

Add 1-2 teaspoons of allspice to add some "zip" to your kugel.

Raisins are fun, too. Any kind of dried or canned fruit will work well.

AUNT GOLDYE'S KUGEL

Dairy

Aunt Goldye was the greatest lady. She made this kugel for brunches at her house and we all adored it! Aunt Goldye is gone but her kugel lives on. It's delicious-enjoy our legacy.

1 pound medium noodles

1 pint regular, low-fat or fat-free sour cream

6 eggs, slightly beaten

1½ (8 ounce) packages regular or low-fat cream cheese, softened

1½ teaspoons vanilla

2 teaspoons lemon juice

1 (16 ounce) can crushed pineapple

2 cups sugar, divided use

1 cup (2 sticks) butter, melted, divided use

2 cups crushed corn flakes

Parboil noodles; drain. Add sour cream, eggs, cream cheese, vanilla, lemon juice, pineapple, 1½ cups sugar and ¾ cup butter.

Pour mixture into a greased 13x9x2-inch pan. Sprinkle cereal crumbs and remaining ½ cup sugar over kugel. Drizzle remaining 4 tablespoons melted butter on top. Refrigerate overnight.

When ready to bake, preheat oven to 325 degrees.

Bake 1 hour, 30 minutes.

JOANIE'S APPLESAUCE KUGEL

Pareve

This freezes well.

1 pound noodles, cooked and drained

1 cup raisins

5 eggs

2 teaspoons cinnamon

1 cup sugar

1 cup applesauce

1 can apple pie filling

½ cup (1 stick) margarine

Preheat oven to 375 degrees.

Combine all ingredients and place in a disposable aluminum deep-dish pan. Bake, uncovered, for 1 hour.

Applesauce Noodle Kugel

Dairy

1 (8 ounce) package noodles

8 ounces cottage cheese

1 cup sour cream

1 cup applesauce

4 tablespoons (½ stick) butter

3 eggs, well beaten

1 teaspoon salt

Cinnamon sugar (optional)

Raisins (optional)

Preheat oven to 350 degrees.

Cook the noodles according to package directions; drain and rinse in cold water. Combine noodles with remaining ingredients except butter. Transfer to a greased casserole dish. Top with butter pieces.

Bake 1 hour. Raise the heat to 400 degrees during the last 15 minutes so that the pudding is crisp and brown.

Kugel can be either a side dish or a dessert. As a side dish, it is a casserole of potatoes, eggs and onions. As a dessert, it is usually made with noodles and various fruits and nuts in an egg-based pudding. Kugel made with noodles is called, "lokshen kugel."

Apricot Kugel

Dairy

1 (12 ounce) bag noodles

6 ounces cream cheese, softened

6 tablespoons (¾ stick) butter, softened

3 eggs

½ cup sugar

¾ cup milk

1 (16 ounce) can apricots with juice, chopped

12 dried apricots, chopped

1 tablespoon vanilla

Preheat oven to 350 degrees.

Cook noodles according to package directions; drain. Place cream cheese and butter in a mixing bowl. Top with hot, drained noodles and mix until blended. Mix in eggs, sugar, milk, all apricots and vanilla. Place mixture in a greased baking dish.

Bake 40 to 60 minutes or until done.

"Sometimes I double the recipe, but still only use one can of apricots with the juice."

STICKY BUN KUGEL

Pareve

"This can be made days in advance and frozen. I usually invert onto a plate lined with foil so when it cools, I can lift it off the plate and wrap for the refrigerator or freezer. If you are serving it immediately, this is not necessary. This tastes good hot, cold or room temperature, but we like it best warmed up."

½ cup (1 stick) margarine

1 cup brown sugar

4 eggs, beaten

6 tablespoons (¾ stick) margarine, melted

1 teaspoon cinnamon

½ cup sugar

1 pound medium noodles, cooked and drained

Raisins (optional)

1 cup pecan halves, or more to taste

Preheat oven to 350 degrees.

Melt ½ cup of margarine and add 1 cup of brown sugar; stir until mixed. Put mixture in the bottom of a Bundt pan and refrigerate 30 minutes.

Mix eggs, ¾ stick melted margarine, cinnamon and sugar, and add to cooked, drained noodles along with raisins, if using.

Remove pan from refrigerator and spread refrigerated mixture up sides of Bundt pan. Put pecan halves around side of pan. Spoon noodle mixture carefully over pecans.

Bake 1 hour. It will turn dark brown and look like it is burning towards the end of the hour. When you remove it from the oven, it will be sizzling.

Let sit about 3 minutes or until the sizzling calms down. You may want to stick a knife around the edges of the pan to be sure it won't stick.

Invert onto a plate to serve. Delicious!!

CARDIAC KUGEL

Dairy

"Not for the faint of heart! Made once a year in our house to break Yom Kippur Fast."

8 ounces medium noodles

½ cup (1 stick) butter, softened

8 eggs

½ cup sugar

½ tablespoon cinnamon

½ tablespoon allspice

4 ounces cream cheese
(not whipped)

¼ pound ricotta cheese

8 ounces sour cream or yogurt

¾ cup milk

1½ teaspoons vanilla

½ cup raisins (optional)

Ricotta, farmer's or cottage cheeses may be used interchangeably. (You may need some milk to soften the farmer's cheese.)

Preheat oven to 375 degrees.

Boil noodles, drain and mix with butter until melted.

Beat eggs in a bowl. Mix in sugar, cinnamon, and allspice. Add cream cheese, ricotta cheese and sour cream. Mix well. Pour this mixture over the noodles. Add milk, vanilla and raisins.

Transfer to a greased 9x13-inch pan.

Bake 45 to 60 minutes.

TZIVIAH'S CARROT KUGEL

Pareve

2 cups grated carrots

1 cup (2 sticks) margarine, softened

½ cup brown sugar

1 egg

3 tablespoons orange juice

1½ cups flour

1 teaspoon baking powder

½ teaspoon baking soda

1 teaspoon salt

½ teaspoon cinnamon

Preheat oven to 350 degrees.

Grate carrots with grating blade of a food processor and put aside.

Using "s-shaped" steel blade of processor, blend margarine, brown sugar and egg until creamy. Add orange juice, flour, baking powder, baking soda, salt and cinnamon one at a time, blending well before each next addition. Add carrots and blend about 20 seconds more. Pour mixture into an ungreased pan. Bake 30 minutes or until firm.

KUGELS, QUICHES AND PASTAS, TOO!

VEGETABLE KUGEL

Pareve /

"Can be used for Pesach, Rosh Hashanah or any holidays. My family looks forward to the kugel and it's always a 'HIT'!"

¼ cup chopped green pepper	3 eggs, beaten
1 cup chopped onion	1½ teaspoons salt
½ cup chopped celery	⅛ teaspoon pepper
1½ cups grated raw carrots	¾ cup matzah meal
6 tablespoons margarine	Oil
1 (10 ounce) package frozen chopped spinach	

Preheat oven to 350 degrees.

Sauté green pepper, onion, celery and carrots in margarine for about 10 minutes, stirring occasionally.

Cook spinach, drain. Add spinach to sautéed vegetables. Add eggs, salt, pepper and matzah meal. Spoon into 12 well greased large muffin tins or a casserole dish.

Bake 45 minutes or until firm. Allow to cool 10 minutes before removing from pan or cut up in portions if using casserole dish.

CHEESE BLINTZES
Dairy

BATTER

2 eggs
½ cup all-purpose flour
¾ cup liquid (half milk, half water)

1 tablespoon butter, melted, plus extra for cooking

FILLING

¾ pound farmer's or hoop cheese
2½ tablespoons sugar
1 tablespoon sour cream
2 teaspoons grated lemon zest

1 teaspoon vanilla
½ teaspoon cinnamon
Sour cream and strawberry preserves

In a bowl, beat eggs. Add flour alternately with liquid, beating until smooth. Add 1 tablespoon melted butter and stir until well blended. Cover and chill 1 to 2 hours.

Heat a 7-inch skillet and butter well. Reduce heat, pour about 2 tablespoons batter into pan, tip and swirl to cover bottom evenly. Cook until underside is set. Turn and cook other side. Turn out on a towel.

Repeat, stirring batter before making each blintz and adding butter to pan as needed. Cool blintzes, stacking with waxed paper between each.

For filling, in a food processor, blend cheese, sugar, sour cream, lemon zest, vanilla and cinnamon.

Lay a blintz flat, brown side up. Place a few tablespoons filling on one end. Fold edges to center and roll up envelope fashion. (May be made in advance and chilled.)

Fry in hot butter until golden brown on both sides and center is heated. Serve with sour cream and preserves.

Makes 12 blintzes

Blintzes are of Hungarian origin, related to the Ukranian blinchiki and the Russian blini.

Two cheese blintzes are traditionally served side by side on the holiday of Shavout to represent the two tablets of The Ten Commandments.

CHEESE AND MUSHROOM BRUNCH EGGS

Dairy

SAUCE

2 tablespoons margarine or
butter

2 tablespoons all-purpose flour

1 cup milk

⅓ cup shredded Swiss cheese

3 tablespoons grated Parmesan
cheese

2 tablespoons dry white wine or
milk

EGGS

1½ cups sliced fresh mushrooms

¼ cup thinly sliced green onions

1 tablespoon margarine or butter

12 eggs, beaten

1 medium tomato, chopped

For sauce, in a medium saucepan melt margarine. Stir in flour and cook 1 minute. Add milk all at once. Cook and stir over medium heat until thickened and bubbly. Stir in cheeses. Cook and stir over medium heat until cheeses melt. Remove from heat and stir in wine. Set aside.

For eggs, spray an unheated large skillet with nonstick coating. Preheat skillet over medium heat. Add mushrooms and green onions to the hot skillet; cook 2 to 3 minutes or until tender. Transfer vegetables to a small bowl; set aside.

In the same skillet melt margarine. Add eggs. Cook over medium heat without stirring until eggs begin to set around the edge. Using a large spatula, lift and fold the partially cooked egg mixture so the uncooked portion flows underneath. Continue cooking until eggs are set, but still glossy and moist. Transfer half of the scrambled eggs to a 2-quart square baking dish or an au gratin dish.

Spread half of the mushroom mixture over the eggs in the baking dish. Drizzle with about half the sauce. Top with the remaining scrambled eggs, remaining mushroom mixture, and remaining sauce. Cover and chill overnight.

When ready to bake, preheat oven to 350 degrees.

Bake, uncovered, for about 30 minutes or until heated through. Top with tomato. Let stand 10 minutes.

Serves 6

For a lower-fat version: Use skim milk and reduced-fat Swiss cheese and use 2½ cups refrigerated or frozen egg product (thawed) instead of the whole eggs.

SPINACH QUICHE

Dairy

¼ cup Parmesan cheese

9 inch pie shell, baked

3 eggs

8 ounces creamed cottage cheese

1 cup heavy whipping cream

1 small onion, chopped

Salt (optional)

¼ teaspoon nutmeg

¼ teaspoon pepper

1 (10 ounce) package frozen chopped spinach, thawed and well drained

1 teaspoon margarine, melted

Preheat oven to 375 degrees.

Sprinkle Parmesan cheese in cooled pie shell.

Beat eggs until frothy. Cream cottage cheese and add to eggs. Mix cream, onion, salt, nutmeg and pepper and add to egg mixture.

Add spinach to egg mixture and pour into pie shell. Drizzle margarine on top.

Bake 25 to 30 minutes.

This freezes well.

"SCHORRLY" DELICIOUS ONION QUICHE

Dairy

Courtesy of Mrs. Zipora Schorr, Beth Tfiloh Dahan Community Day School's Director of Education.

16 ounces mushrooms, sliced

3 large onions, chopped

2 tablespoons oil

1 cup milk

3 tablespoons flour

2 eggs

1 cup marinara sauce

2 prepared pie shells

¼ cup grated Parmesan or mozzarella cheese

Preheat oven to 350 degrees.

Sauté mushrooms and onions in the oil. Add milk, flour, eggs and marinara sauce.

Pour mixture into pie shell. Sprinkle with cheese.

Bake 45 minutes.

Makes 2 pies

SPINACH MUSHROOM ONION QUICHE

Dairy

1 large onion, sliced

4-5 large mushrooms, sliced

2 tablespoons butter or olive oil

1 (10 ounce) package frozen chopped spinach

2 (10 ounce) packages frozen leaf spinach

1 (8 ounce) package cream cheese

2 eggs

Kosher salt to taste

Ground pepper to taste

½ cup Parmesan cheese

2 tablespoons crushed garlic

Flavored breadcrumbs

2-3 deep dish pie shells

4 ounces mozzarella cheese, shredded

4 ounces Cheddar cheese, shredded

Preheat oven to 350 degrees.

Sauté onions and mushrooms in butter until slightly translucent.

In a separate pot, cook all spinach until almost done; drain well. Add cream cheese, eggs, salt, pepper, Parmesan cheese, garlic and breadcrumbs. Mix well and set aside.

Bake empty pie shells for about 10 to 15 minutes. Remove from oven. Sprinkle mozzarella cheese in crust. Add sautéed vegetables and sprinkle with Cheddar cheese. Top with spinach mixture.

Return to oven and bake 25 minutes.

Enjoy this tasty Baron Herzog Sauvignon Blanc, a fresh, herbal, crisp, lemony and pear character wine; velvety-smooth and medium-bodied with your delicious Spinach and Mushroom Onion Quiche!

Cousin Gail's Three Cheese Macaroni

Dairy

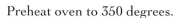

- 1½ pounds (about 6 cups) small elbow macaroni
- 2 cups grated Cheddar cheese, divided use
- 2 cups grated fontina cheese, divided use
- 8 tablespoons (1 stick) butter
- ¼ cup flour
- 2 cups milk
- 1 teaspoon salt
- 1 egg
- ½ teaspoon paprika
- ½ cup breadcrumbs (1 slice, toasted and crumbled)
- 3 tablespoons grated Parmesan cheese
- 2 tablespoons extra-virgin olive oil

Cook's Notes

Preheat oven to 350 degrees.

Cook pasta as directed on package; drain and transfer to a greased 3-quart casserole dish. Sprinkle Cheddar and fontina cheeses on top, reserving ½ cup of each. Stir lightly with a fork.

To make the sauce, melt butter in a saucepan over medium heat. Stir in flour until smooth. Slowly add milk and salt, whisking to prevent lumps. Add sauce to macaroni, reserving 1 cup. Mix egg into reserved sauce and pour over macaroni.

Sprinkle macaroni with remaining Cheddar and fontina cheeses and paprika.

Combine breadcrumbs, Parmesan cheese and olive oil in a small bowl and spread on top. Place casserole dish on a foil-lined baking sheet. Bake on middle rack of oven for 25 minutes or until bubbly and golden brown.

Serves 8

Easy Spinach Lasagna

Dairy

24 ounces fat-free ricotta cheese

1 egg

1 (10 ounce) package frozen chopped spinach, thawed and drained

1 teaspoon salt

Pepper to taste

2 cups shredded-light mozzarella cheese, divided use

1 (12 ounce) package regular lasagna noodles, do not cook these

1 (32 ounce) jar spaghetti sauce

½-1 cup water

Preheat oven to 350 degrees.

In a bowl, mix ricotta cheese, egg, spinach, salt, pepper and 1½ cups mozzarella cheese.

In a greased 13x9x2-inch baking dish, layer one-third spaghetti sauce, one-third uncooked noodles, and one-half cheese mixture. Repeat layers until ingredients are used up, ending with noodles.

Sprinkle remaining ½ cup mozzarella cheese on top. Pour water along the sides.

Cover tightly with foil and bake 1 hour, 15 minutes to 1 hour, 30 minutes. Let cool, uncovered, for about 10 minutes before serving.

COOK'S NOTES

Mexican Lasagna

Dairy

Quick, easy and healthy vegetarian meal. Serve with your favorite bread and salad!

1 (15 ounce) can black beans, rinsed and drained

1 (14 ounce) can diced tomatoes (can use Italian or garlic seasoned)

1 (4 ounce) can chopped chili peppers (optional)

2 cups frozen corn kernels, thawed, or more to taste

2 green onions, minced

½ teaspoon oregano

6-8 tortillas (depending on size)

1½ cups shredded Cheddar cheese

Sour cream and salsa

Preheat oven to 400 degrees.

In a large mixing bowl, combine beans, tomatoes, chili peppers, corn, green onions and oregano. Mix thoroughly.

Line a greased 2-quart casserole or baking dish with 3 to 4 tortillas, overlapping if necessary.

Spread half of the bean mixture in a layer over the tortillas. Sprinkle with half the cheese. Repeat layers.

Bake 15 to 20 minutes or until cheese is bubbly. Let stand 1 to 2 minutes, then slice. Top with sour cream and salsa! Yummy!

Serves 6

COOK'S NOTES

HOMEMADE TOMATO SAUCE FOR PASTA

Pareve

¾ cup olive oil

2 large onions, finely chopped

6 large cloves garlic, chopped

5 (28 ounce) cans Italian plum tomatoes, diced

1 (6 ounce) can tomato purée or tomato paste

2 cups dry white wine

2 tablespoons lemon juice

2 tablespoons sugar

1 bunch Italian flat leaf parsley, chopped

1 bunch fresh basil, chopped

2 sprigs fresh oregano

Salt and pepper

Heat a large pot, add olive oil. Immediately add finely chopped onion and chopped garlic. Sauté and cover with lid. Turn down heat. Do not allow onions and garlic to brown.

Add tomatoes and bring to boil. Reduce heat. Add tomato purée, wine, lemon juice, sugar, parsley, basil and oregano. Season with salt and pepper to taste.

Cover and simmer on low heat about 1½ to 2 hours, stirring often.

Remove oregano stems. Adjust seasonings.

This tomato sauce freezes very well.

Did you know that the average American eats 92 pounds of tomatoes a year? Eighty percent of that, however, comes in a processed form, such as ketchup or sauces.

THREE PEPPER PIZZA

Dairy

1 cup ricotta cheese

1 (1 ounce) package ranch salad dressing mix

1 (12 inch) pre-baked pizza crust

1 small green pepper, thinly sliced

1 small red bell pepper, thinly sliced

1 small yellow bell pepper, thinly sliced

1 small onion, thinly sliced

2 cups fresh mushrooms, thinly sliced

2 medium Roma tomatoes, thinly sliced

2 teaspoons olive oil

½ teaspoon dry oregano

½-1 cup grated Parmesan cheese

Preheat oven to 450 degrees.

Combine ricotta cheese and salad dressing mix, blending well. Spread cheese mixture over pizza to cover within ½-inch of edge.

Arrange peppers, onions, mushrooms and tomatoes on top. Add oregano and drizzle olive oil over pizza before adding cheese. Sprinkle with Parmesan cheese.

Bake 15 to 20 minutes or until bubbly and cheese has melted.

Serves 4

The American version of pizza has changed from the Italian version by adding cheeses and tomato sauce to the flattened dough.

• Pizza may be traced back as far as the Israelites and other ancient peoples, who created flat bread topped with olive oil and native spices.

• By the beginning of the 1900's, pizza made its way to the inner cities of America, most notably New York and Chicago. These cities had a high population of Italian immigrants.

• Pizza became especially popular after our soldiers returned from WWII.

• Today, pizza has become just as American as baseball and apple pie.

Feta Pasta

This entrée is good with garlic bread and salad. The recipe multiplies easily and satisfies your vegetarian friends!

Dairy

4 ounces spaghetti

1 garlic clove

2 tablespoons extra-virgin olive oil

8 cherry tomatoes, halved

Nutmeg

Salt and pepper (optional)

3 ounces feta cheese, crumbled

1 tablespoon chopped fresh basil, plus extra for garnish

Small quantity black olives, halved or chopped

Prepare pasta per package instructions in lightly salted water; drain thoroughly.

In a large frying pan, gently heat garlic clove in olive oil for 1 to 2 minutes. Add cherry tomatoes. Increase heat to lightly fry tomatoes for 1 minute. Remove garlic and discard.

Add drained spaghetti to pan and stir. Add just a touch of nutmeg to taste. If desired, season with salt and pepper.

Add feta cheese and basil and stir very lightly. Top with black olives.

Serve hot. Garnish with additional basil if desired.

Serves 2

Cook's Notes

Broccoli Pasta with Pine Nuts

Dairy/Pareve

"I invented this recipe one day in the kitchen when I was hungry for pasta, but wanted something different. I hope you enjoy it as much as my family and I do."

1 large bunch broccoli, chopped
Olive oil as needed
1 onion, chopped
1 garlic clove, minced
Salt and pepper to taste
Lemon pepper to taste

Onion powder to taste
Oregano to taste
½ cup pine nuts, toasted
½ pound angel hair pasta,
   cooked and drained
Parmesan cheese (optional)

Sauté broccoli in olive oil; remove from pan. Add onions to pan and sauté in olive oil; remove from pan. Add garlic to pan and sauté in oil, adding more oil if necessary.

Mix broccoli, onions, garlic and a little olive oil. Season with salt and pepper, lemon pepper, onion powder and oregano. Pour mixture over pasta. Sprinkle pine nuts on top.

Add Parmesan cheese (optional).

Italian Broccoli and Pasta

Pareve/Dairy

3 tablespoons scallions
2 cups broccoli florets
½ teaspoon thyme
½ teaspoon oregano
½ teaspoon pepper

1 (14½ ounce) can stewed
   tomatoes, not drained
2 cups spaghetti or thicker
   noodles (#17), cooked and
   drained
Parmesan cheese (optional)

Spray skillet with non-stick spray and stir-fry scallions and broccoli for about 3 minutes.

Add thyme, oregano, pepper and tomatoes and simmer.

Spoon mixture over noodles. Add Parmesan cheese on top (optional).

Serves 4

PASTA WITH "CREAM" AND VEGETABLE SAUCE

Pareve

1 onion, sliced

1 green bell pepper, sliced in strips

1 red bell pepper, sliced in strips

1 zucchini, coarsely chopped

2 tablespoons oil

¼ cup Tofutti cream cheese

Salt and pepper to taste

8 ounces pasta, cooked and drained

Sauté onion, bell peppers and zucchini in oil until softened. Add Tofutti cream cheese. Continue to sauté and mix until well blended.

Season with salt and pepper to taste.

Pour mixture over drained pasta.

PASTA RAPHAEL

Dairy

2 (6 ounce) jars marinated artichoke hearts

¼ cup olive oil

2 cups chopped onion

2 tablespoons minced garlic

½ teaspoon dried oregano

¼ cup fresh basil, or 1-2 teaspoons dried

½ teaspoon salt

1 tablespoon ground black pepper

¼ cup fresh parsley

1 (28 ounce) can plum tomatoes, peeled

1 pound cooked and drained pasta

¼ cup fresh Parmesan cheese, grated

Drain artichoke hearts; reserving marinade.

Heat olive oil in a large sauce pan. Add reserved marinade, onion, garlic, oregano, basil, salt and pepper. Stir in artichokes, parsley and tomatoes. Serve with pasta, sprinkled with Parmesan cheese.

Serves about 10

The artichoke is considered an aphrodisiac!

Penne with Arugula and Walnut Pesto

Dairy

2 cloves garlic, cracked

½ cup extra-virgin olive oil, divided use

12 ounces arugula, stems removed

½ cup walnut pieces or ⅔ cup walnut halves, toasted

¼ teaspoon ground or grated nutmeg

Salt and pepper

½ cup grated Parmigiano-Reggiano cheese

1 pound penne rigate (with lines) pasta

⅓ pound fresh green beans, cut into thirds

Cook's Notes

In a small saucepan cook garlic over medium heat in ¼ cup oil for 5 minutes, then remove pan from heat.

Fill a food processor with arugula, loosely packed. Add walnuts, oil and garlic to the arugula in the processor. Add nutmeg and salt and pepper to the processor bowl, set lid in place and pulse grind the mixture into a thick paste.

Add any remaining arugula to the processor and grind into the paste by pulsing the processor again. Transfer arugula paste to a large pasta bowl. Stir in the remaining oil and the cheese. Taste pesto sauce and adjust seasonings.

While cooking penne according to package directions for al dente, watch the time. After about 6 minutes, add green beans to the pasta pot. The beans will cook along with pasta the last 2 or 3 minutes. Drain pasta and beans together in a colander, then transfer hot pasta and beans to the pasta bowl with the pesto in the bottom.

Toss pasta and beans with pesto for 2 to 3 minutes to combine and evenly coat the pasta and beans with the pesto sauce. Serve immediately.

Serves 4-6

Kasha Varnishkes

Pareve

1 cup medium or whole kasha
  (buckwheat groats)

1 egg

2 cups water

3 onions, diced

Oil

Garlic powder

Salt (optional)

Pepper

Paprika

2 cups dry bowtie noodles
  (varnishkes)

Mix the kasha with the egg in a medium saucepan over low heat, stirring constantly until each grain is separate and dry.

Boil 2 cups water in a kettle. Add the boiling water to the saucepan containing the dry separated grain. Cover tightly and simmer 15 minutes, stirring the mixture a few times while cooking.

In another pot, sauté onions in oil with garlic powder, salt, pepper and paprika. Add the sautéed onions to the kasha mixture and stir. Simmer for another 5 minutes. Kasha is now ready. In another pot, cook noodles according to package directions; rinse and drain. Combine cooked kasha with cooked noodles and serve.

Serves 4-6

Asian Sesame Noodles

Pareve/Meat

This is a great dish to take to a picnic or buffet dinner.

¼ cup sesame oil

½ cup teriyaki sauce

1 pound of linguine, cooked and
  drained

1-2 green bell peppers, sliced

1-2 red or yellow bell peppers,
  sliced

1-2 carrots, sliced thin or curled
  with a vegetable peeler

1 bunch of scallions, sliced

Chopped cooked chicken or beef
  (optional)

Mix sesame oil and teriyaki sauce in the bottom of a large bowl. Add drained noodles and mix well until noodles are coated.

Add bell peppers, carrots and scallions and mix well again. Add meat, if desired.

VEGETABLES
AND
SIDE DISHES

VEGETABLES AND SIDE DISHES

Roasted Asparagus with Bell Pepper Sauce

Pareve /

Fresh asparagus spears　　　**Black pepper**
Coarse salt　　　　　　　　　　**Olive oil**

Preheat oven to 425 to 450 degrees.

Wash fresh asparagus, cut off bottom of stalks.

Sprinkle with salt and pepper. Drizzle olive oil on asparagus and toss well. Place on a baking sheet.

Bake 15 minutes. Take out when bright green color.

BELL PEPPER SAUCE

2 large bell peppers (yellow,　　**¼ cup olive oil**
　　orange or red)　　　　　　　**1 tablespoon fresh lemon juice**

Char peppers all around on an open flame or under the broiler. Place in paper bag until cool enough to handle. Peel and seed. Put in food processor or blender with oil. Purée until smooth. Add lemon juice and blend again until smooth. Salt and pepper to taste.

To keep asparagus fresh longer, store upright in a dish of cold water in the refrigerator.

SAUTÉED SUGAR SNAP PEAS AND ASPARAGUS

Pareve

2 pounds asparagus

¼ pound sugar snap peas

2 tablespoons olive oil

Kosher salt

Freshly ground black pepper

Red pepper flakes

Sea salt (optional)

Cut off the tough ends of the asparagus and slice the stalks diagonally into 2-inch pieces. Snap off the stem ends of the snap peas and pull the string down the length of the vegetable.

Warm the olive oil in a large sauté pan over medium heat and add the asparagus and snap peas. Add kosher salt, pepper, and red pepper flakes, if desired to taste. Cook approximately 10 minutes or until crisp-tender, tossing occasionally. Sprinkle with sea salt, if desired, and serve hot.

Serves 6-8

ROASTED BROCCOLI

Pareve /

"Delicious! I have shared this recipe so many times."

¼ cup olive oil

1 tablespoon lemon juice

2 large garlic cloves, crushed

Salt and pepper to taste

5 cups broccoli florets, cut into serving-size pieces

Preheat oven to 425 degrees.

Combine olive oil, lemon juice, garlic, salt and pepper. Add the broccoli and toss until evenly coated.

Put in large roasting pan in a single layer. Roast 25 minutes, stirring after 15 minutes. Serve hot.

WALNUT BROCCOLI

Dairy

4 packages frozen chopped
    broccoli

¼ cup water

¼ cup butter or margarine,
    melted

⅓ cup flour

2 cups milk

½ teaspoon salt

1 tablespoon heaping granular
    pareve chicken bouillon

⅓ cup chopped walnuts, or more
    to taste

Kosher stuffing mix or seasoned
    breadcrumbs

Preheat oven to 350 degrees.

Cook broccoli slightly in water, drain. Place in a greased casserole dish.

Whisk butter, flour, milk, salt and bouillon to make sauce and pour over broccoli.

Add chopped walnuts to stuffing mix or breadcrumbs and sprinkle over broccoli. Bake 30 minutes.

For a simple and attractive way to present this recipe, place the cooked broccoli in a decorative and colorful oven-to-table casserole dish. Makes a wonderful accompaniment to any dairy meal.

Broccoli comes from the Latin, "Bracchium," meaning "branch" or "arm."

Introduced to America around the 1960's, broccoli is an Italian vegetable and was originally called, "calabrese."

Sliced carrots look coin shaped and are golden in color, symbolizing prosperity. They are traditionally eaten on Rosh Hashanah for a successful New Year.

CARROTS VICHY

Pareve /

This recipe is classically cooked with bottled Vichy water or with plain bottled water to which a pinch of soda has been added.

1½ pounds baby carrots or large carrots, cut into very thin rounds or cut into 2-inch diagonal lengths

Water or pareve chicken stock to cover

Salt and pepper

Nutmeg

2 tablespoons sugar

4 tablespoons margarine

Finely chopped parsley

Place carrots in a heavy saucepan, adding enough water or chicken stock to just cover. Add the salt, pepper, and nutmeg. Bring to a boil and cook for about 10 to 12 minutes or until almost tender.

Pour off all but about ¼ cup of water. Add the sugar and margarine. Boil carrots and liquid, watching and shaking the pan occasionally so that they do not stick, until the liquid has reduced to a syrupy glaze.

Turn into a hot vegetable dish and sprinkle with minced parsley.

Serves 6

SPICED-UP CAULIFLOWER

Pareve

1 large head cauliflower

Salt and pepper to taste

½ cup mayonnaise

Pinch cayenne pepper or to taste

1 tablespoon Dijon mustard

½ cup dry breadcrumbs

4 tablespoons (½ stick) margarine, melted

Preheat oven to 350 degrees.

Separate cauliflower into florets; steam 8 minutes. Drain well and place in a baking dish. Season with salt and pepper.

Combine the mayonnaise, cayenne and mustard and pour over the steamed florets, mixing well. Sprinkle with breadcrumbs and drizzle with the melted margarine.

Bake 10 to 15 minutes or until golden. Serve piping hot.

PORTOBELLOS PICCATA

Dairy

3 large portabello mushrooms

½ cup non-fat egg substitute, or
   2 eggs

½ cup breadcrumbs

¼ cup Parmesan cheese, grated

Dash black pepper

3½ teaspoons olive oil

1 (28 ounce) jar spaghetti sauce

Rinse mushrooms and pat dry. Cut into slices about ⅛-inch thick. Pat dry again.

Beat eggs in a deep plate. Combine crumbs, cheese and pepper on another plate. Dip mushroom slices in egg, then crumb mixture.

In a skillet, heat oil. Add mushrooms a few slices at a time. Pan fry until golden brown.

Serve with sauce.

GREEN BEANS AND
MUSHROOM GREMOLATA

Pareve

1 pound green beans, trimmed

½ pound mushrooms, sliced
   (preferably shiitake)

2 tablespoons pareve margarine

4 tablespoons pareve margarine,
   melted

¼ cup fresh parsley

1 teaspoon grated lemon peel

2 large garlic cloves, crushed

Salt and pepper to taste

Poach green beans for 5 minutes until they are crisp-tender.

Sauté the mushrooms in 2 tablespoons margarine until cooked through, about 2 to 3 minutes.

To prepare sauce, combine melted margarine, parsley, lemon peel, garlic and salt and pepper.

Drain the beans. Combine beans, mushrooms and sauce. Toss to blend and serve.

Green Beans with Gingered Walnuts

Pareve

Gingered Walnuts

1 tablespoon vegetable oil	¼ teaspoon garlic powder
1 teaspoon low sodium soy sauce	¾ cup walnut halves
¼ teaspoon ground ginger	

Preheat oven to 250 degrees.

Spread oil in small baking dish and put in oven. When pan is hot, remove from oven and stir in soy sauce, ginger and garlic powder. Add walnuts and stir until well coated.

Bake 25 minutes or until nuts are brown. Cool and drain.

Green Beans

1 pound fresh green beans, rinsed, ends trimmed	2 teaspoons lemon juice
	1 tablespoon olive oil

Steam beans for 5 minutes until crisp-tender. Toss beans with lemon juice and olive oil. Add gingered nuts and toss again.

Serves 4

GREEN BEANS WITH ROASTED ONIONS

Meat / Pareve

6 medium onions (about 2½ pounds), each cut vertically through root end into 12 to 14 wedges

6 tablespoons (¾ stick) pareve margarine, divided use

Salt and pepper

2 cups canned low-salt chicken broth or pareve powder

3 tablespoons sugar

2 tablespoons red wine vinegar

3 pounds slender green beans, ends trimmed

Preheat oven to 450 degrees.

Spray 2 large heavy baking sheets with vegetable oil spray. Arrange onions in single layer on prepared sheets.

Dot onions evenly with 4 tablespoons margarine. Season with salt and pepper. Bake until onions are dark brown on bottom, about 35 minutes.

Meanwhile, boil broth in a heavy large skillet over high heat until reduced to ½ cup, about 6 minutes. Add sugar and vinegar and whisk until sugar dissolves and mixture comes to boil.

Add onions to sauce; reduce heat to medium-low. Simmer until liquid is slightly reduced, about 5 minutes. Season with salt and pepper. (Can be prepared 1 day ahead. Cover and refrigerate. Rewarm over low heat before continuing.)

Cook green beans in a large pot of boiling salted water until crisp-tender, about 5 minutes. Drain well. Return beans to same pot. Add remaining 2 tablespoons margarine and toss to coat. Mound beans in a large shallow bowl. Top with onion mixture and serve.

Serves 12

Zucchini is a summer squash of the variety that is green-skinned and shaped like a cucumber. Yellow squash is a vegetable of the gourd family.

Ratatouille means to "stir about" a medley of vegetables with a variety of herbs.

RATATOUILLE

Pareve /

1 large onion, sliced

1 tablespoon olive oil

2-3 zucchini or yellow summer squash, sliced

1 (8 ounce) can diced tomatoes

1 red bell pepper, diced

2-3 garlic cloves, chopped

Basil, rosemary, oregano and thyme (or any other combination, to taste)

Sauté onion in olive oil in a saucepan, cooking 5 to 7 minutes on medium-high heat.

Add squash and sauté 5 to 10 minutes, stirring often. Add tomatoes, bell pepper, garlic and seasonings. Mix well.

Cover and cook over low heat for about 20 minutes or until squash is tender.

Option #1: After mixture is sautéed, add 1 to 2 teaspoons powdered pareve chicken soup mix.

Option #2: Add 2 tablespoons yellow mustard.

WILTED SPINACH

Pareve /

2 tablespoons olive oil

1 small garlic clove, thinly sliced

3 (10 ounce) bags spinach, tough stems removed

½ teaspoon salt

¼ teaspoon ground black pepper

In a 12-quart saucepan, heat the oil over medium-high heat until hot. Add garlic and cook about 1 minute or until golden brown.

Add the spinach and stir until the leaves are coated with oil.

Cover and let cook until the spinach wilts, about 2 minutes. Season with salt and pepper.

Serves 8

Spinach Mushroom Gratin

Dairy

2 (10 ounce) packages chopped frozen spinach, thawed

2 bunches green onions, chopped

2 tablespoons olive oil

8 ounces mushrooms, sliced

2 cloves garlic, crushed

1 teaspoon salt

Pinch of cayenne pepper, or more to taste

¼ teaspoon nutmeg

½ teaspoon dried oregano

1 (8 ounce) carton ricotta cheese, divided use

3 eggs, divided use

4 ounces light or regular cream cheese, softened

6 ounces Monterey Jack cheese grated, divided use

1 (14 ounce) can Italian tomatoes

1 cup crushed croutons or dried breadcrumbs

¼ cup melted butter or margarine (optional)

COOK'S NOTES

Preheat oven to 350 degrees.

Squeeze the spinach to remove as much moisture as possible. Sauté green onions in oil until soft. Add mushrooms and garlic and sauté until soft. Stir in spinach and cook for 3 minutes while stirring constantly.

Season mixture with salt, cayenne pepper, nutmeg and oregano and remove from heat. Add 4 ounces of ricotta, 2 eggs, cream cheese and one-third of grated cheese.

Grease a 9x9-inch casserole dish and cover the bottom with the tomatoes (you may have to slice them if they are whole), then layer the spinach mixture on top. Combine the remaining egg with the remaining ricotta and grated cheeses and spoon over the spinach. Sprinkle the croutons over the top and drizzle with butter.

Bake 30 minutes or until casserole is browned and bubbly.

HERB BAKED TOMATO TARTS

Pareve /

"After making these, the house smells so good. No matter how many I make, there are never any left. Enjoy."

1 dozen plum tomatoes	**½ scant teaspoon salt**
1½-2 tablespoons chopped fresh thyme	**¼ teaspoon sugar**
2 large cloves garlic, chopped	**¼ scant teaspoon pepper**

Preheat oven to 250 degrees. Line a baking sheet with heavy duty foil.

Cut tomatoes horizontally in half. Remove stems and flatten bottom of tomatoes so they will stand. Set on baking sheet, cut side upward.

Mix together thyme and garlic. Add salt, sugar and pepper. Sprinkle on top of tomatoes.

Bake 3 hours. Reduce heat to 200 to 225 degrees and bake 1 hour more. The tomatoes shrink a lot.

To make this a dairy dish, sprinkle Parmesan cheese on top of the tomatoes.

"Absolutely To Die For" Tomato Pie

Dairy

"I have had to freeze these and send them out of town because friends adore them! The crust is heavenly."

Filling

3 pounds whole tomatoes – strained and squeeze all juice out. Keep only the meat of the tomatoes. You can use canned or fresh tomatoes.

2 cups grated sharp Cheddar

½ cup mayonnaise

2 tablespoons grated or chopped onion

2-4 teaspoons Parmesan cheese

Crust

½ cup flour

2 teaspoons baking powder

¼ cup wheat germ

½ teaspoon salt

½ cup butter

½ cup sour cream

Preheat oven to 350 degrees.

Mix all filling ingredients in a food processor.

Mix all crust ingredients together by hand. Pat into 2 pie plates. Add the filling.

Bake at least 1 hour or until the center is firm.

Thomas Jefferson, America's third President, was one of the first Americans to eat tomatoes.

The tomato has been known as a "love apple" since the 1500's.

The first tomatoes were yellow and were known as the "golden apple."

BARLEY CORN PILAF

Meat / Pareve

2 tablespoons olive oil

1 medium-size yellow onion, chopped

1 medium-size red bell pepper, chopped

1 cup pearl barley

1 teaspoon dried thyme

1½ cups chicken broth or vegetable broth

⅔ cup chopped scallions

1½ cups corn kernels, fresh or frozen

Salt and pepper to taste

Heat olive oil in a 3-quart saucepan. Add onion and bell pepper and sauté over medium heat until tender, about 5 minutes. Add barley and stir constantly until all the barley kernels are coated with oil.

Stir in thyme and broth and mix well. Bring to a boil. Reduce heat, cover and simmer 40 minutes or until the barley is tender and all the liquid is absorbed. Add scallions, corn and salt and pepper, stirring until evenly mixed. Heat through and serve.

Serves 6

Sautéed Asian Greens & Grilled Tofu

Pareve

1 (14 ounce) block firm tofu, drained

¼ cup low-sodium soy sauce

1 teaspoon Asian sesame oil

1½ teaspoons dark brown sugar

1½ teaspoons finely grated fresh ginger

1 small garlic clove, minced

¼ teaspoon hot sauce or dried hot red pepper flakes

1 tablespoon plus 1 teaspoon vegetable oil, divided use

2 (5 ounce) bags Asian greens or baby spinach

Pressing excess moisture out of your tofu will increase its firmness and its ability to absorb the flavors of the marinade.

Cut tofu crosswise into 6 slices. Arrange in 1 layer on a triple layer of paper towels and top with another triple layer of towels. Weight with a shallow baking pan or baking sheet and let stand 2 minutes. Repeat process 2 more times.

Stir together soy sauce, sesame oil, brown sugar, ginger, garlic, hot sauce, and 1 tablespoon vegetable oil in a glass pie plate. Add tofu slices in 1 layer and marinate, turning over every couple of minutes, 8 minutes total.

Heat a lightly oiled well-seasoned ridged grill pan over moderately high heat until hot but not smoking. Lift tofu from marinade with a slotted spatula (reserve marinade) and grill, turning over once carefully with a spatula, until grill marks appear and tofu is heated through, 4 to 6 minutes total.

While tofu grills, heat remaining teaspoon of vegetable oil in a 12-inch skillet over moderately high heat until hot but not smoking. Add greens and sauté, tossing with tongs, until greens start to wilt. Add reserved marinade and sauté, tossing, until greens are just wilted, about 1 minute. Lift greens from skillet with tongs, letting excess marinade drip off, and divide between 2 plates.

Serve greens with tofu slices.

Serves 2

There are 160 varieties of potatoes grown in the United States. California is the largest potato producer.

The best baking potatoes are the Russet Burbanks potato and the White Rose potato from Idaho, the Green Mountain potato from New York, the Irish Cobbler potato from Wisconsin and the Sebagos potato from Washington state.

CRISPY ONION BAKED POTATOES

Pareve /

"Our family went to Israel during the summer of 2002. We discovered this delicious recipe at a "Sheva Brachos" and decided to bring it home to America."

4-6 large baking potatoes
⅓ cup olive oil
¼ cup onion soup mix
1 teaspoon potato starch
2 tablespoons mayonnaise

1 teaspoon sugar
2 cloves garlic crushed
½ teaspoon salt
¼ teaspoon black pepper
½ teaspoon paprika

Preheat oven to 350 degrees.

Wash potatoes and cut into bite-sized pieces. Set aside.

Mix all remaining ingredients in a small bowl.

Place potato sections in a large bowl and coat with mixture. Spread coated potato sections onto a greased baking sheet. Bake, uncovered, for 1 hour.

For extra crispiness, bake an additional 10 minutes at 400 degrees.

Serves 6

AMY'S FAVORITE DOUBLE BAKED POTATOES

Dairy /

4 medium potatoes
8 tablespoons (1 stick) butter
½ cup light cream
1 teaspoon salt

4 teaspoons grated onion
1 cup grated sharp yellow cheese
½ teaspoon paprika

Bake potatoes. Cut potatoes lengthwise and scoop out pulp into a mixing bowl, reserving shells.

Whip potatoes with butter, cream, salt, onion and cheese.

Refill shells with potato mixture. Sprinkle with paprika and reheat in a very hot oven for 15 minutes.

Freezes well.

Mom's Sweet Potato Casserole

Dairy / Pareve /

12 sweet potatoes or 8 large yams

8 tablespoons (1 stick) butter or margarine

¼ cup skim or regular milk (or pareve non-dairy creamer)

2 tablespoons dark brown sugar

1 (10 ounce) package marshmallows (mini or regular)

1 (8 ounce) can crushed pineapple (optional)

Preheat oven to 350 degrees.

Bake sweet potatoes 1 hour or until soft enough for a knife to go through a potato.

Slice down the center of each potato. Scoop out the pulp and put directly into mixer. Add butter, milk and brown sugar. Beat until smooth and put into a greased casserole dish. At this point, dish can be frozen or refrigerated until needed.

Bake for 30 to 45 minutes or until hot. Cover top with marshmallows and bake 5 to 10 minutes longer or until marshmallows are golden brown. Serve immediately.

You can adjust the size of the casserole by using the formula of 1 sweet potato for 2 people.

GRANDMA ROSE'S CANDIED SWEET POTATOES

Dairy / Pareve /

"Grandma's candied sweet potatoes were a real Friday night dinner staple. Everyone loved them. Everyone ate them. Everyone took as much sugary sauce as they could to heap on their potatoes. Talk about comfort food. My sister has picked up this recipe now and treats us all to these yummy potatoes whenever she gets the chance. Thank heavens for sisters!"

5 medium sweet potatoes
½ stick butter or margarine
1 cup dark brown sugar
1 cup granulated sugar

¼ cup maple syrup
1 teaspoon vanilla extract
1 teaspoon cinnamon

Preheat oven to 350 degrees.

Boil sweet potatoes until tender. Cool, peel and slice lengthwise. Place in a greased baking dish.

Combine butter, both sugars and syrup in a saucepan and cook on a low heat until thick. Remove sauce from heat and add vanilla and cinnamon. Pour sauce over sweet potatoes. Bake 1 hour.

SIMPLE HOLIDAY TZIMMES

Pareve /

Save time by using a food processor to slice vegetables and apples.

¼ cup honey

¼ cup unsweetened orange juice

2 tablespoons brown sugar

2 teaspoons grated orange rind

6 cups peeled and thinly sliced sweet potatoes (about 2 pounds)

6 cups peeled and thinly sliced Rome apples (about 1½ pounds)

1⅓ cups thinly sliced carrots

1 cup small pitted prunes, halved

Combine honey, orange juice, brown sugar and orange rind in a saucepan. Cook until mixture forms a syrup. Add potatoes, apples, carrots and prunes and simmer 45 minutes or until tender.

To prepare in oven, combine all ingredients in a baking dish. Cover and bake at 350 degrees for 1 hour and 30 minutes or until fruits and vegetables are tender.

Tzimmes is any kind of sweet stew. It is usually orange in color and includes carrots, sweet potatoes and/or prunes. A wide variety of dishes fall under the heading, "tzimmes." Some people commonly make a tzimmes of carrots and pineapple chunks boiled in pineapple juice. On Thanksgiving, some people serve a tzimmes of sweet potatoes, white potatoes, carrots and stewing beef.

Tzimmes is commonly eaten on Rosh Hashanah, the Jewish New Year, because it is sweet and symbolizes our hopes for a sweet New Year.

The word, "tzimmes," is often used in Yiddish to mean making a big fuss about something.

Acorn Squash Soufflé

Pareve

This has become a popular family side dish and easy to adjust for "carbohydrate watchers." Great for Thanksgiving and year round.

1 medium acorn squash	2 teaspoons baking powder
1 cup (2 sticks) margarine	2 teaspoons vanilla
6 eggs	2 teaspoons cinnamon or
¾ cup sugar	pumpkin pie spice (optional)
6 tablespoons flour	Handful of dried cranberries (optional)

Preheat oven to 350 degrees.

Cut squash in half with a sharp knife. Place both halves face down on a baking sheet. Bake 1 hour or until soft. Peel when cooled.

Meanwhile, combine margarine, eggs and sugar in a food processor and mix with the dough blade. Add squash and mix until smooth. Transfer contents to a large bowl. Add flour, baking powder, vanilla and cinnamon. Mix well. Stir in cranberries, if desired.

Pour into a 1¾-quart greased casserole dish. Sprinkle with extra cinnamon.

Bake, uncovered, for 1 hour, 30 minutes or until set.

To soften acorn squash, pierce the squash with a knife and microwave for about 4 to 5 minutes on high.

CARROT SOUFFLÉ

Pareve

Great for Thanksgiving!

1 pound carrots, sliced or
    2 (1-pound) cans sliced carrots
3 eggs
½ cup sugar
3 tablespoons flour

1 teaspoon baking powder
1 teaspoon vanilla
1 stick margarine, melted
Nutmeg and cinnamon to taste

TOPPING

¼ cup corn flake crumbs
2 tablespoons margarine
Dash of cinnamon

2 tablespoons brown sugar
¼ cup nuts (optional)

Preheat oven to 350 degrees.

Boil carrots until tender, drain. Place carrots in a food processor with eggs and blend.

In a mixing bowl, mix sugar, flour, baking powder, vanilla and margarine. Add spices to taste.

Blend sugar mixture with carrot mixture and pour into a greased 1½-quart casserole dish.

Combine all topping ingredients and spread over carrot mixture. Bake 1 hour, 30 minutes.

COOK'S NOTES

PILGRIM CORN PUDDING

Dairy

2 eggs
1 tablespoon sugar
1 tablespoon flour
4 tablespoons (½ stick) butter, melted

1 cup milk
1 (11 ounce) can whole kernel corn, drained
Salt and pepper

Preheat oven to 325 degrees.

Beat eggs with a whisk. Add sugar, flour, butter and milk. Fold in corn.

Pour mixture into a 1-quart casserole. Bake 45 minutes.

Recipe can be doubled.

Serves 4-6

PINEAPPLE CHEESE COMPOTE

Dairy

It's very light, and a wonderful addition to a heavy meal.

1 (20 ounce) can pineapple chunks, drained well, reserving 6 tablespoons liquid
6 tablespoons flour
½ cup sugar
1 (20 ounce) can crushed pineapple

2 cups Cheddar cheese, shredded
½ cup corn flake crumbs or graham cracker crumbs
8 tablespoons (1 stick) butter or margarine, melted

Preheat oven to 350 degrees.

Mix reserved 6 tablespoons pineapple juice, flour and sugar. Add pineapple chunks, crushed pineapple and cheese.

Pour into an 8-inch square baking pan. Sprinkle with crumbs. Drizzle butter over top. Bake 45 minutes.

Tip-Top Corn Pudding

Dairy / Pareve

2 (16 ounce) cans whole kernel
    corn, drained well

6 eggs, beaten

Pinch of salt

¼ cup sugar

1 teaspoon vanilla

1 cup milk (or pareve milk – rice
    or soy – for pareve pudding)

8 tablespoons (1 stick) butter or
    margarine, melted

1 teaspoon flour

2 cups corn flakes or frosted
    corn flakes

Preheat oven to 350 degrees.

Mix all ingredients except corn flakes. Pour mixture into a greased 13x9x2-inch casserole dish. Sprinkle cereal on top.

Bake 40 to 45 minutes.

Corn was the most important source of food for the English who came to North America in the early 1600's.

Apricot Stuffing

Meat

1 celery stalk, sliced

1 onion, chopped

1½ cups turkey broth or
    reduced-sodium chicken
    bouillon

16 slices reduced-calorie bread,
    cubed and dried

2 tablespoons dried parsley

1½ teaspoons poultry seasoning

¼ teaspoon salt

2 egg whites

¼ cup dried apricots

Preheat oven to 350 degrees.

Combine celery, onion and broth in a small saucepan. Bring to a boil. Reduce to low heat, cover and simmer 5 minutes or until vegetables are tender.

In a large bowl, combine celery mixture, bread, parsley, poultry seasoning, salt, egg whites and apricots.

Spoon mixture into a lightly greased 2-quart casserole dish. Cover and bake 30 minutes.

Serves 8

Raisin Bread Stuffing

Pareve

"When I first needed a stuffing recipe, I was unable to duplicate my mother's recipe. (I had the directions, but I couldn't match the taste to my memories.) I decided to find a recipe that would become a special favorite for my family. With a husband who has an insatiable sweet tooth, this raisin bread stuffing recipe became the perfect choice. I've kept it even more special by only making it on special occasions."

1 cup (2 sticks) margarine
3 celery stalks, diced
1 medium onion, diced
16 cups raisin bread cubes
   (approximately 2 raisin breads)

2 eggs
¾ cup water
¼ teaspoon marjoram

Melt margarine in a 5- to 8-quart Dutch oven over medium heat. Add celery and onions and cook until tender, stirring frequently. (I prefer the vegetables on the firm side of tender.) Remove Dutch oven from heat.

Add bread cubes, eggs, water and marjoram to vegetables and mix. Stuff into a 12- to 14-pound turkey.

Bake according to the time required for the turkey.

"If raisin bread is left over, I form balls, which I then add to the turkey pan along the sides or in the back during the last half-hour of baking time.

Double the recipe for turkeys over 14 pounds in weight.

If you want to bake the stuffing separately spoon into a greased ovenproof 9x13-inch dish and bake at 350 degrees covered for 45 minutes to 1 hour uncovering the last 15 minutes."

POTATO LATKES

Pareve

6 medium to large russet
   potatoes, cut into chunks

2 large yellow onions, cut into
   chunks

3 eggs

4-6 tablespoons flour

Salt and pepper to taste

1 teaspoon baking powder

Vegetable oil

Place potatoes and onions in a food processor and process using the grater blade. Remove grated vegetables and squeeze out as much liquid as possible.

Place squeezed vegetables into a large bowl. Add eggs, flour, salt and pepper and baking powder. Mix until well blended.

Heat 1-inch of oil in a skillet over medium heat. For each pancake, place a heaping tablespoon of batter into skillet, spreading batter to flatten; pancakes should be thin.

Cook until brown and crisp on both sides. Drain on paper towels. Keep warm in a 200 to 250 degree oven while preparing remaining latkes.

Serve with applesauce, or at dairy meals, serve with sour cream.

"Latke" is the Yiddish word for pancake. They have become a versatile delicacy and can be eaten for breakfast, lunch or dinner!

To make latkes ahead of time and freeze, place cooked latkes in a single layer on a baking sheet and place in freezer. After frozen, remove from baking sheet and place in a plastic bag. Return to freezer until needed. To serve, place frozen latkes on a baking sheet and heat at 450 degrees for 7 to 10 minutes. Voila!

Asian Potato Pancakes

Pareve

"My husband spent a number of years in Japan and we always enjoy putting an Asian touch on a lot of dishes."

3 pounds russet potatoes, peeled, grated and drained well
½ cup chopped peanuts
¼ cup flour

2 tablespoons fresh minced ginger
3 eggs
1 cup chopped scallions
½ cup vegetable oil

Place all ingredients except oil in a large bowl and stir well.

Heat half the oil in large nonstick skillet over medium-high heat until hot. Drop a heaping tablespoon of potato batter per latke into hot oil and spread with a spoon to about 3 inches round. Repeat to fill skillet without crowding.

Cook until browned on both sides. Drain on paper towels. Repeat until all batter is used, using remaining oil as needed. Serve with plum sauce or sweet and sour sauce.

Makes 1-2 dozen latkes

Potatoes change their chemical content when stored – the starch will diminish and the sugar will increase.

Potatoes are graded by quality: No. 1 means second grade; US Fancy means 1st grade.

CARROT PANCAKES

Pareve /

Good for Passover, too.

2 green bell peppers, diced

¼ cup vegetable oil plus oil for
    frying, divided use

6 medium carrots, quartered

4 eggs

Salt and pepper to taste

2 tablespoons sugar

¼ cup water

½-1 cup matzah meal

Sauté bell peppers in ¼ cup oil. Drain and set aside.

Grate carrots in a food processor or on a hand grater until medium fine. Mix in sautéed peppers, eggs, salt and pepper, sugar, water and matzah meal until mixture is the consistency of potato pancake batter.

Fry in oil in a heated skillet until pancakes are golden on both sides. Drain well.

Serves 4-6

In Yiddish, carrot is "mern," meaning, "increase." It is thought to be good luck to eat this food.

SWEET POTATO LATKES

Pareve

2 cups sweet potato, peeled and grated

2 cups (washed and unpeeled) zucchini, grated

½ cup chopped parsley

½ cup chopped onion

3 eggs, lightly beaten

4 tablespoons flour

1 tablespoon corn flakes, crusted to crumbs

½ tablespoon salt

Ground black pepper, to taste

4 tablespoons vegetable oil

In a large bowl, mix together the sweet potato, zucchini, parsley, onion, eggs, flour, corn flake crumbs, salt and pepper.

Heat a large nonstick pan, adding oil when pan is ready. Carefully drop tablespoons of batter into the pan and fry the latkes, turning carefully when crisp on the bottom.

Using a spatula in combination with a spoon helps to turn without breaking up the latkes. Oil may be added to the pan in small amounts when needed. When browned, remove latkes from pan. Lay on paper towels to absorb any excess oil.

A food processor is perfect for grating and chopping of vegetables, using appropriate blades.

Botanically, sweet potatoes and yams are not related. Yams are sweeter and juicier than sweet potatoes, yet much less nutritious. The sweet potato is one of the richest sources of carotene and has three times as much vitamin C as yams.

WILD RICE PANCAKES WITH MUSHROOMS

Dairy

Really, really, yummy!!

COOK'S NOTES

1 tablespoon olive oil

12 medium mushrooms

1 teaspoon salt, divided use

1 teaspoon minced garlic

2 teaspoons fresh lemon juice

4 eggs

¼ cup flour

4 scallions, minced

1 cup cooked wild rice

5-6 ounces goat cheese

⅛ teaspoon pepper

Heat a skillet over medium heat. Add olive oil and mushrooms and cook 5 minutes. Stir in ½ teaspoon salt and cook 5 minutes more. Stir in garlic and lemon juice and remove pan from heat.

Beat eggs in a bowl. Whisk in flour and remaining ½ teaspoon salt. Stir in cooked mushrooms, including all juices.

Add scallions, wild rice, goat cheese and pepper and stir well.

Place skillet over medium-high heat and spray with non-stick spray.

Pour ½ cup of batter into skillet. Cook 2 to 3 minutes on each side or until pancakes are golden.

Makes about 8 large pancakes, serves 4-6

Zucchini Latkes

Pareve

This recipe is courtesy of the Jewish Museum of Maryland—15 Lloyd Street, Baltimore, MD 21202.

4 medium zucchini, unpeeled and grated	2 tablespoons seasoned breadcrumbs
1 medium white potato, grated	Ground black pepper to taste
1 medium onion, chopped	½ teaspoon garlic powder
3 eggs, beaten	3 tablespoons vegetable oil
3 tablespoons flour	

In a large bowl, mix together zucchini, potato and onion. Add eggs and mix well.

In a separate bowl, combine flour, breadcrumbs, pepper and garlic powder. Add to vegetables and mix.

Heat a large nonstick pan, adding oil when pan is hot. Drop batter by tablespoonfuls into hot oil and fry until crisp, turn to fry on the other side. When nicely browned, remove from pan and drain on prepared paper towels. Serve quickly, best while hot.

These latkes can be frozen and reheated in the oven when needed. Do not defrost before heating.

This is a modern-day latke, yet they are fried in oil – appropriate for Chanukah because oil is symbolic of the miracle of the holiday.

DESSERTS
CAKES, PIES, COOKIES AND SAUCES

DESSERTS

BUBBY ATTMAN'S
CHOCOLATE CHIP HONEY CAKE
Pareve

"This is my all time favorite cake. My Bubby, Ida, used to bake this cake every Jewish New Year. My mother and Aunt Mildred sat with her when she baked it so they could measure out the ingredients before she "threw them" into the cake. From that day on we had a family recipe. It's a very special cake that holds special meaning for me. It's a family cake - enjoy it with yours."

COOK'S NOTES

3 eggs

2 cups sugar

¾ cup oil

2 heaping tablespoons honey

1 cup applesauce

2 heaping tablespoons chocolate syrup

3 cups flour

1 teaspoon dry instant coffee

2 teaspoons baking soda

½ cup boiling water

6 ounce package semi-sweet chocolate chips

Preheat oven to 350 degrees.

Beat eggs in a mixing bowl. Mix in sugar, oil, honey, applesauce, syrup and flour in order listed.

In a separate bowl, combine coffee, baking soda and boiling water. Add coffee mixture to batter and mix well.

Pour batter into a greased 13x9x2-inch pan like Bubby used to do. Sprinkle chocolate chips on top. Bake 55 to 65 minutes.

I find this cake bakes best when using a tube pan or 2 loaf pans. Shorten baking time for tube pan to 45 to 55 minutes.

The cake will be moist and very delicious. It freezes beautifully.

DESSERTS—CAKES

GRANDMA SALLY'S
PUMPKIN CHOCOLATE CHIP CAKE
Dairy / Pareve

This is an easy, great last minute dessert. Great for Sukkot!

2 cups sifted flour

2 cups sugar

1 teaspoon baking powder

1 teaspoon baking soda

½ teaspoon salt

1½ teaspoons cinnamon

¼ teaspoon ginger

¼ teaspoon allspice

4 eggs

1 (16 ounce) can pumpkin

1 cup oil

1 cup All-bran cereal

12 ounce bag chocolate chips

Preheat oven to 350 degrees.

Sift flour, sugar, baking powder, baking soda, salt, cinnamon, ginger and allspice together. Set aside.

Beat eggs in a separate bowl. Add pumpkin, oil and cereal. Add dry ingredients and beat with a mixer. Fold in chocolate chips.

Pour batter into greased and floured Bundt pan. Bake 50 to 55 minutes.

Bubby Kaplan's Raisin Cake

Pareve

"A family favorite usually served at Rosh Hashanah lunch after shul in our household. This is Bubby Kaplan's recipe from the old country."

2 eggs

1 cup sugar

¼ cup shortening or margarine, melted

1 teaspoon vanilla

2 tablespoons applesauce

½ teaspoon cinnamon

¼ teaspoon nutmeg

1 cup raisins

¼ cup water

¼ cup orange juice

2 cups flour

1 teaspoon baking powder

1 teaspoon baking soda

Dash of salt

Preheat oven to 350 degrees.

Combine eggs and sugar. Blend in shortening. Mix in vanilla, applesauce, cinnamon, nutmeg and raisins. In a separate bowl, sift together flour, baking powder, baking soda and salt and add to the liquid ingredients.

Mix well and pour into a greased and floured 9-inch square pan. Bake 30 to 40 minutes.

APPLE NUT COFFEE CAKE

Dairy

2 cups flour

1 teaspoon baking powder

1 teaspoon baking soda

¼ teaspoon salt

½ cup shortening

1 cup sugar

2 eggs

1 teaspoon vanilla

1 cup sour cream

2 cups finely chopped apples

TOPPING

½ cup chopped nuts

½ cup brown sugar

1 teaspoon cinnamon

2 tablespoons butter, melted

Preheat oven to 350 degrees.

In a mixing bowl, sift together flour, baking powder, baking soda and salt.

In a separate mixing bowl, cream together shortening and sugar. Add eggs and vanilla and beat well. Add dry ingredients to creamed mixture alternately with sour cream. Fold in chopped apples. Spread batter in greased 13x9x2-inch pan.

Combine all topping ingredients and sprinkle over batter. Bake about 40 minutes.

QUICK APPLE CAKE

Pareve

12 cooking apples
Cinnamon sugar (see sidebar)
1 cup sugar
1 cup oil
2 eggs, beaten

1 cup flour
1 teaspoon baking powder
Pinch of salt
2 teaspoons vanilla

*Cinnamon sugar:
¼ cup sugar plus
½ teaspoon
cinnamon*

Preheat oven to 350 degrees.

Peel and slice apples. Layer slices in a 13x9x2-inch baking dish, filling about two-thirds full.

Sprinkle with cinnamon sugar. Combine sugar, oil, eggs, flour, baking powder, salt and vanilla and pour over apple slices.

Bake about 45 minutes or until brown. Serve warm.

DEBBYE'S JEWISH APPLE CAKE

Pareve

"My friend, Debbye, gave me this recipe when I got married. She got it from her mother and now I am passing it on to the next generation of bakers and their families. Enjoy!"

3 cups flour
2 cups sugar
3 teaspoons of baking powder
1 cup oil
4 eggs

½ cup orange juice
½ teaspoon of salt
3 medium apples, peeled and
    cubed (I use slices for the
    top)
Cinnamon sugar

Preheat oven to 350 degrees.

Mix together all ingredients in order listed, except apples and cinnamon sugar.

Put some dough on the bottom of a greased and floured tube pan. Sprinkle with cubed apples and cinnamon sugar. Repeat dough and apple layers, ending with sliced apples and cinnamon sugar on top.

Bake 1 hour, 30 minutes.

FROMA'S LIGHT AND AIRY
CARROT PUDDING CAKE

Pareve

This cake is delicious with a cup of hot coffee or tea, at breakfast or anytime!

COOK'S NOTES

6 eggs, separated
1 teaspoon salt
1 cup oil
1 cup brown sugar
2¼ cups flour
4 tablespoons water

1 teaspoon baking powder
2 teaspoons baking soda
2 teaspoons vanilla extract
2 cups grated carrots
Powdered sugar (optional)

Preheat oven to 350 degrees.

Beat 3 egg whites with salt until stiff; discard remaining 3 egg whites.

In a separate bowl, mix together 6 egg yolks, oil, brown sugar, flour, water, baking powder, baking soda, vanilla. Fold mixture into egg whites along with grated carrots.

Pour batter into a greased Bundt pan. Bake 30 minutes.

When cake is cool, take out of pan. Sprinkled lightly with powdered sugar, if desired.

5¢ YEAST COFFEE CAKE

Dairy

"This is one of my grandmother's recipes that evokes many fond childhood memories. I just loved to help Bubby make this coffee cake in her kitchen. It made an ordinary day so special for me. Bubby did all of her cooking and baking without written recipes. My mother took it upon herself to jot down these recipes many, many years ago. Note the use of a ½ of a 5 cent piece of yeast in this recipe!"

½ of a 5-cent piece of yeast (about 1 cake of yeast)

1 cup plus 1 teaspoon sugar, divided use

½ cup lukewarm water

6 cups sifted flour, plus extra for working with dough

2 eggs beaten with a little warm water

½ cup vegetable shortening

1½ teaspoons salt

2 cups milk, water or sour cream (or combination)

Melted butter

Sugar

Cinnamon

Raisins

1 cake of yeast is the equivalent of 1 packet of yeast or 2¼ teaspoons.

Put yeast and 1 teaspoon sugar into ½ cup lukewarm water. Cover and let sit 5 minutes.

In a separate bowl, sift flour and make a well. Add beaten eggs, yeast mixture, remaining 1 cup sugar, shortening, salt, and milk. Knead until mixed and place in a lightly greased bowl. Cover and let stand in draft-free, warm place for 2 hours.

Separate dough into 3 pieces. Place about 6 tablespoons of flour on a board. Roll each piece of dough to about ¼-inch thickness. Cover and let stand 10 minutes. Spread melted butter, sugar, cinnamon and raisins over dough.

Roll up each piece of dough and place each in a loaf or round pan. Let stand 30 minutes. Drizzle with melted butter and sprinkle sugar and cinnamon on top. Bake at 350 degrees for 40 minutes.

Makes 3 loaves

ANNE'S COFFEE CAKE

Dairy

"My mother-in-law, Anne Fox, gave me this recipe almost forty years ago when my husband Bill and I were first married. It is still a family favorite."

1 cup (2 sticks) butter, softened	Pinch of salt
1½ cups granulated sugar	½ pint sour cream
3 eggs	1 teaspoon vanilla
2½ cups flour	½ cup chopped nuts
2 teaspoons baking powder	½ cup brown sugar
1 heaping teaspoon baking soda	Cinnamon to taste

Preheat oven to 350 degrees.

Cream together butter and sugar. Add eggs one at a time.

Mix together flour, baking powder, baking soda, and salt. Alternate adding dry ingredients and sour cream to batter. Add vanilla and mix well.

Pour half the batter into a greased 10-inch tube pan. Combine nuts, brown sugar and cinnamon and sprinkle over batter, leaving a little for top of cake. Add rest of batter. Sprinkle remaining nut mixture on top. Bake 45 to 60 minutes.

This page is sponsored by
Myra and Bill Fox in loving memory of
Bill's mother, Anne Fox.

Neysa's Banana Pudding Cake

Dairy / Pareve

"My children still ask my mother to make this cake. It is so easy and tastes like it's truly from scratch. What a great way to use overly ripened bananas!"

1-2 small ripe bananas

1 (18¼ ounce) package yellow cake mix

1 (4 serving) package banana cream or pareve vanilla instant pudding mix

4 eggs

1 cup water

¼ cup oil

½ cup finely chopped nuts (optional)

Powdered sugar

Lemon juice

COOK'S NOTES

Preheat oven to 350 degrees.

Mash bananas in a large bowl. Beat with an electric mixer until well mashed. Add cake mix, pudding mix, eggs, water, oil and nuts. Blend on low speed until dry ingredients are moistened. Increase to medium speed and beat for 2 minutes. Pour into a well-greased and floured 10-inch tube pan. Bake 60 to 70 minutes. Cool before removing from pan. Combine powdered sugar and lemon juice to make an icing. Drizzle icing over cooled cake.

Can also bake cake in a 13x9x2-inch pan for 50 to 55 minutes at 350 degrees.

This page is sponsored by Myra and Bill Fox in honor of Myra's mother, Neysa Lafferman.

DESSERTS—CAKES

COOK'S NOTES

CARIBBEAN RUM CAKE

Dairy

"In honor of my husband's 50th birthday, my husband and I went sailing around the British Virgin Islands with a captain and a gourmet cook. It sounds exotic and actually it was. Our Captain's bikini-clad girlfriend, first mate and cook was kind enough to share all her secret recipes with us. She even supplied the index cards. This rum cake was one of our favorite desserts."

1 cup chopped pecans

1 (18 ounce) package yellow cake mix

1 (3 ounce) package instant vanilla pudding mix

½ cup water

½ cup vegetable oil

½ cup dark rum

4 eggs

GLAZE

8 tablespoons (1 stick) butter

¼ cup water

¼ cup sugar

¼ cup dark rum

Preheat oven to 325 degrees.

Sprinkle pecans over the bottom of a greased and floured 10-inch tube pan. Mix cake mix, pudding mix, water, oil, rum and eggs together and pour into pan. Bake 1 hour.

Meanwhile, prepare glaze. Melt the butter in a pan. Stir in water and sugar and boil 5 minutes. Remove from heat and stir in rum.

Invert baked cake onto a serving plate. Prick the cake with a long fork or any thin pointy object. Brush and spoon glaze all over the cake.

HARRIET'S FIRST PRIZE SOUR CREAM CAKE

Dairy

"This cake is our favorite and won first prize at the Maryland State Fair in 1980."

3 cups flour
¼ teaspoon baking soda
¼ teaspoon salt
1 cup butter, softened
3 cups sugar

6 eggs
¼ teaspoon lemon juice
2 teaspoons vanilla
1 cup sour cream

COOK'S NOTES

Preheat oven to 350 degrees.

Combine flour, baking soda and salt in a bowl. In the bowl of a mixer, cream butter and sugar until mixed well. Add eggs, one at a time. Add lemon juice and vanilla. Blend in dry ingredients, alternating with sour cream and beat until smooth.

Bake in a greased Bundt pan for 1 hour, 15 minutes.

Sprinkle cinnamon and sugar on the top before baking and even add some mini chocolate chips to the batter, if you like.

SOUR CREAM POUND CAKE

Dairy

"I've made many pound cakes, all good, but not as good as this one. It is moist, buttery, and foolproof if directions are followed. It is delicious and loved by all who have tried it."

2½ cups all-purpose unbleached flour

2 teaspoons baking powder

½ plus ⅛ teaspoon salt

1 cup (2 sticks) unsalted butter, slightly softened

2½ cups sugar

5 eggs, room temperature

1 teaspoon pure vanilla extract

1 cup sour cream

Powdered sugar

Preheat oven to 300 degrees.

Whisk together the flour, baking powder and salt until well blended; set aside.

In a separate bowl, beat butter until very pale. Sprinkle in sugar and beat until slightly fluffy, then scrape bowl. Add eggs, one at a time, beating until blended before adding the next egg. Add vanilla and sour cream and mix well. With mixer on low add dry ingredients until almost incorporated, but not quite. Stop mixer and fold batter with a spatula until well blended and smooth.

Scrape batter into a greased and floured 10- to 12-cup Bundt pan. Bake 1 hour to 1 hour, 15 minutes or until golden brown and a toothpick inserted in the center comes out with a few moist crumbs. Start checking for doneness after 50 minutes due to differences in oven temperatures.

Cool in pan for 15 minutes. Invert onto a rack and cool completely.

Sprinkle with powdered sugar. Serve plain or with whipped cream.

TOLL HOUSE MINI MORSEL POUND CAKE

Dairy

3 cups flour
1 teaspoon baking powder
½ teaspoon salt
2 cups sugar
1 cup (2 sticks) butter, softened
3 teaspoons vanilla extract

4 eggs
¾ cup milk
1 (12 ounce) package semi-sweet
  chocolate mini morsels (2 cups)
Powdered sugar or melted
  chocolate (optional)

Preheat oven to 325 degrees.

In a small bowl, combine flour, baking powder and salt; set aside.

In a large mixer bowl, beat sugar, butter and vanilla extract until creamy. Beat in eggs, one at a time, beating well after each addition. Gradually beat in dry ingredients alternately with milk. Stir in chocolate morsels.

Pour into a greased and floured 10-inch Bundt pan. Bake 70 to 80 minutes (check after 60 minutes) or until a skewer inserted in center of cake comes out clean.

Cool in pan 15 minutes. Invert and remove from pan to cool completely.

Sprinkle with powdered sugar or drizzle with melted chocolate, if desired.

Serves 16

FAMILY FAVORITE BLUEBERRY CAKE

Dairy

"My aunts were caterers – this was one of their favorites."

2 cups flour
¼ teaspoon salt
1 teaspoon baking powder
1 teaspoon baking soda
8 tablespoons (1 stick)
　margarine or butter, softened
1 cup sugar

2 eggs
1 cup sour cream
1 teaspoon vanilla
1 pint fresh blueberries
　separated with some flour
Cinnamon sugar, to taste

Preheat oven to 350 degrees.

Sift together flour, salt, baking powder and baking soda; set aside.

In a large bowl with a mixer, beat margarine. Add sugar and beat until smooth. Add eggs, one at a time. Add dry ingredients alternately with sour cream mixed with vanilla.

Spoon half of the batter into a greased Bundt pan. Add half the blueberries and sprinkle with cinnamon sugar. Add remainder of batter. Add remaining blueberries and sprinkle with cinnamon sugar. Bake 50 minutes.

IDA'S CHOCOLATE CHIP CHOCOLATE CAKE

Pareve

This decadent cake is a great dessert for a Shabbat crowd!

3 cups flour	2 cups water
2 cups sugar	¾ cup canola oil
½ cup cocoa	2 tablespoons vinegar
2 teaspoons baking soda	2 teaspoons vanilla extract
1 teaspoon salt	1 (12 ounce) bag chocolate chips

Preheat oven to 350 degrees. Mix together all ingredients except chocolate chips. Mix in half of the chips into batter with spoon. Pour into greased 9x13-inch pan. Sprinkle rest of chips on top. Bake 40 minutes or until toothpick comes out clean.

COOK'S NOTES

CHOCOLATE AND WHITE INTRIGUE CAKE

Dairy / Pareve

2 cups sugar	½ teaspoon salt
1 cup (2 sticks) butter or margarine, softened	1 cup milk or non-dairy creamer
3 eggs	1½ teaspoons vanilla
3 cups flour	1 cup chocolate syrup
2 teaspoons baking powder	¼ teaspoon baking soda

Preheat oven to 350 degrees.

Cream together sugar and butter. Add eggs and beat well.

Mix flour, baking powder, and salt together. Mix vanilla with milk. Beginning and ending with dry ingredients, alternate adding dry and wet ingredients to the creamed mixture.

Pour two-thirds of the batter into a well-greased and lightly floured 10-inch tube pan.

To remaining batter, add chocolate syrup mixed with baking soda. Spoon chocolate batter over white batter. Do not mix.

Bake 1 hour, 10 minutes. Cool completely before removing from pan.

Chocolate Chinchilla

Pareve

7 egg whites
Pinch of cream of tartar
⅔ cup sugar
2 ounces unsweetened cocoa

Flavoring of choice: 2 teaspoons cinnamon or 2 tablespoons instant coffee or ¼ cup finely ground almonds

Preheat oven to 325 degrees. Grease the inside of a 1½ quart soufflé dish and dust out with sugar. (You may also use any baking dish or tin of about the same capacity, with high sides.)

Beat egg whites with cream of tartar until stiff. Very gradually beat in the sugar.

In a separate bowl, mix together cocoa and the flavoring of choice. Sprinkle over the meringue mixture and fold in gently but thoroughly.

Turn into prepared baking dish. Mixture should be nearly full to the top. Place in a pan filled with 1-inch warm water. Bake in the center of the oven for about 45 minutes. It will be puffed, like a soufflé.

Serve immediately, with rum- or brandy-flavored whipped cream.

If you have any left over, it will be delicious eaten cold the next day!

Zippy's Famous Chocolate Mousse

Dairy / Pareve

"When our school was a little smaller, teachers would all come over for a Succah party or Chanukah party. I always served this and it was always a favorite."

4 eggs, separated
2 tablespoons sugar
2 tablespoons Sabra liqueur
6 ounces chocolate chips, melted

1 (8 ounce) container pareve whipping cream, whipped (optional)
Chocolate curls for garnish

Beat egg whites with sugar until peaks form. Beat egg yolks separately with Sabra. Add melted chocolate to the yolks and beat well.

Fold whites and yolks mixtures together. Pour into a decorative crystal bowl or individual glasses. Decorate with whipped cream and chocolate curls. Refrigerate or freeze.

Well-balanced and refreshing, Gamla Muscat is an Israeli boutique wine that exhibits sweet lingering flavors and is the perfect match for this exceptional dessert.

Linwood's Famous Chocolate Bread Pudding

Dairy

14 ounces bittersweet chocolate

1¼ cups (2½ sticks) sweet butter

¾ pound white bread, crusts removed

1¼ cups heavy cream

1¼ cups ground almonds

1½ cups sugar

10 eggs, separated

4 ounces bittersweet chocolate chunks

COOK'S NOTES

Preheat oven to 350 degrees.

Melt 14 ounces bittersweet chocolate and butter in a double boiler.

Soak bread in cream for 45 minutes. Put bread in a mixer and beat with a paddle on low speed for 15 minutes. Add almonds, scrape bowl very well. Mix in sugar and egg yolks.

When chocolate and butter are melted, cool slightly and add to bread mixture. Add 4 ounces chocolate chunks and mix well.

In a separate mixing bowl, whip egg whites. Fold whites into bread mixture. Transfer to a well-greased 13x9x2-inch pan. Bake 45 minutes or until firm.

Remove from oven and allow to cool. Place in refrigerator.

When chilled, cut into pieces and heat in microwave.

Serve warm with crème anglaise custard sauce and raspberry sauce.

LIZ'S PUMPKIN CHEESECAKE
WITH BOURBON SOUR CREAM TOPPING

Dairy

CRUST

¼ cup graham cracker crumbs

½ cup butter, melted

¼ cup granulated sugar

½ cup finely chopped pecans

FILLING

1½ cups solid pack pumpkin

1½ teaspoons cinnamon

½ teaspoon ground ginger

½ cup light brown sugar

3 (8 ounce) packages cream
    cheese

1 tablespoon cornstarch

3 eggs

½ teaspoon nutmeg

½ teaspoon salt

½ cup granulated sugar

2 tablespoons heavy cream

1 tablespoon bourbon

TOPPING

2 cups sour cream

1 tablespoon bourbon

2 tablespoons granulated sugar

16 pecan halves for garnish

Combine the crust ingredients and press into the bottom of a springform pan. Chill 1 hour.

Preheat oven to 350 degrees.

To make filling, combine all ingredients in a food processor and process. Pour over chilled crust. Bake 50 to 55 minutes.

For topping, combine sour cream, bourbon and sugar. After cheesecake bakes 50 to 55 minutes, spread topping over cheesecake and bake 5 more minutes.

Allow cake to cool in pan. Chill and garnish with pecans before serving.

CHOCOLATE ROYALE CHEESECAKE

Dairy

1½ cups crushed chocolate sandwich cookies (about 18 cookies)

2 tablespoons butter or margarine, melted

4 (8 ounce) packages cream cheese, softened

1 cup sugar

2 tablespoons flour

1 teaspoon vanilla

1 package (8 squares) semi-sweet baking chocolate, melted and slightly cooled

¼ cup hazelnut liqueur (optional)

4 eggs

COOK'S NOTES

Preheat oven to 325 degrees.

Mix crumbs and butter; press into the bottom of a 9-inch springform pan. Bake 10 minutes, if using a silver springform pan. (Bake at 300 degrees for 10 minutes if using a dark, nonstick springform pan.)

Beat cream cheese, sugar, flour and vanilla with an electric mixer on medium speed until well blended. Blend in melted chocolate and liqueur. Add eggs, one at a time, mixing on low speed after each addition until blended. Pour over crust.

Bake 55 to 60 minutes or until center is almost set, if using a silver springform pan. (Bake at 300 degrees for 60 to 65 minutes or until center is almost set if using a dark, nonstick springform pan.) Run a knife or metal spatula around the rim of pan to loosen cake; cool before removing rim of pan. Refrigerate 4 hours or overnight.

Serves 12

BLACK BOTTOM CHEESECAKE

Dairy

2½ cups sugar, divided use

1 (8 ounce) package cream cheese, softened

2 teaspoons vanilla, divided use

3 eggs, divided use

6 ounce package chocolate chips

1 cup oil

3 cups flour

¾ cup cocoa

2 teaspoons baking soda

2 teaspoons baking powder

1 cup hot water

1 tablespoon lemon juice

1½ teaspoons salt

1 cup milk

This recipe can also be used to bake Black Bottom Cupcakes. Use mini muffin tins and mini cupcake holders. Bake 35 to 40 minutes at 350 degrees.

Preheat oven to 350 degrees.

In a small bowl, cream ½ cup sugar and cream cheese. Add 1 teaspoon vanilla and 1 egg. Beat until creamy. Stir in chocolate chips; set aside.

In a large bowl, beat remaining 2 cups sugar, remaining 2 eggs and oil for 1 minute at high speed. Blend in flour, cocoa, baking soda, baking powder, hot water, lemon juice, salt, milk and remaining 1 teaspoon vanilla. Beat 3 minutes or until completely smooth.

Pour chocolate batter into a well greased tube pan. Spoon cream cheese batter on top. Bake 1 hour, 15 minutes.

Cool in pan 30 minutes and remove.

Cake is very heavy so be careful when removing it from the pan. This cake is very rich and moist and does not need frosting.

VANILLA CHEESECAKE WITH BERRIES

Dairy

CRUST

3 tablespoons Grape-Nuts cereal or finely crumbled shredded wheat

1 tablespoon sugar

FILLING

¼ cup plus 2 tablespoons unsifted flour

¼ teaspoon salt

1½ (8 ounce) packages low-fat cream cheese, softened

1¼ cups sugar, divided use

2 eggs, separated

1 tablespoon vanilla

2 cups low-fat vanilla yogurt

Berries, of choice (strawberries, raspberries, blueberries, etc)

COOK'S NOTES

Preheat oven to 300 degrees.

Coat a 9-inch springform pan with cooking spray. Combine cereal and sugar and add to the pan. Tilt and rotate the pan until crumbs are evenly distributed over bottom of pan.

For filling, sift together the flour and salt; set aside. In a large bowl, beat cream cheese with an electric mixer until smooth. Beat in 1 cup sugar, egg yolks and vanilla until well blended. Reduce speed to low and add flour mixture and yogurt, alternately. Beat until smooth.

In a clean bowl, whip egg whites until foamy. Gradually beat remaining ¼ cup sugar into whites and whip until whites are stiff but not dry. Fold whites into the batter in several additions. Pour batter over crust in pan and set on a heavy baking sheet.

Bake 1 hour or until the edges are slightly puffed up and the center is dry to the touch but slightly wobbly. Turn off the heat and leave the cake in the oven with the door closed for 1 hour. Set the cake on a wire rack until thoroughly cool. Cover and refrigerate 4 hours or overnight.

To unmold, run top of a paring knife between the cake and the pan. Loosen the spring and lift off the pan sides, leaving the pan bottom intact.

Remove cake from refrigerator 30 minutes before serving. Decorate top with berries.

ALMOND AND BLOOD ORANGE TART
Dairy / Pareve

ALMOND CRUST

1 cup all-purpose flour

2 cups cake flour

¼ teaspoon salt

8 tablespoons (1 stick) unsalted
    butter or margarine, softened

¼ cup sugar

¾ cup ground blanched almonds

1 egg yolk

2 teaspoons almond extract

ALMOND FILLING

1 cup (4 ounces) blanched
    almonds

¾ cup sugar

¼ teaspoon salt

1 teaspoon vanilla extract

2 teaspoons almond extract

2 eggs

4 tablespoons (½ stick) unsalted
    butter or margarine, softened

7 blood oranges

Butter the bottom of a 9-inch metal tart pan with a removable bottom.

For the crust, sift both flours and salt into a medium bowl. Set aside. In the large bowl of an electric mixer, beat butter and sugar on medium speed until smooth and creamy. Mix in ground almonds. Mix in the egg yolk and almond extract until blended. On low speed add dry ingredients, beating just until incorporated and until the dough holds together. Gather the dough into a ball and flatten into a disk. Wrap the dough in plastic wrap and refrigerate about 40 minutes or until firm.

Press the dough between 2 large pieces of wax paper. Remove one side of wax paper and place, dough side down, in the prepared pan. Press dough into the pan, folding in any overhanging dough to form a slightly thickened sides, ¼-inch thick. Use dough scraps to patch any cracks in the dough. Cover and refrigerate while you make the filling.

Preheat oven to 350 degrees.

For the filling, in a food processor, process the almonds, sugar, salt, vanilla, almond extract and eggs until a thick mixture forms, about 1 minute. Add butter and process until it is incorporated. Use a rubber spatula to scrape the filling over the chilled crust, spreading evenly.

(Continued on next page)

Place the filled tart pan on a baking sheet, so it is easy to move around. Bake about 20 minutes or until the filling is light brown and firm. Check to see if the tart is set by giving it a gentle shake; the center should remain firm. Cool thoroughly, about 1 hour. The tart can be prepared 1 day ahead up to this point. Cover and store at room temperature.

Use a sharp knife to cut off ends of oranges and then cut them crosswise into ⅜-inch thick slices. Trim the peel, including the white pith, from the slices. Spread orange slices on paper towels and pat gently to remove excess liquid.

Arrange overlapping slices of oranges to cover almond filling. Loosen the edges of the crust from the tart pan side with a small sharp knife and remove the sides. Use a sharp knife to cut the tart into slices and serve.

Hiding underneath the red orange slices covering the top of this tart is a soft almond filling baked in a crisp almond crust. Slicing blood oranges before cutting their rind away from the flesh is a good way to help peeled orange slices hold their shape for a decorative topping.

You can substitute apricot preserves for blood oranges.

PECAN PIE

Pareve

"I've been making this recipe for 24 years. People love the addition of the chocolate."

4 tablespoons (½ stick) margarine, softened

1 cup sugar

3 eggs, well beaten

¾ cup light corn syrup

1 teaspoon vanilla

½ cup semi-sweet chocolate chips

1 deep dish pie crust, unbaked

½ cup pecan halves

Preheat oven to 350 degrees.

Cream margarine and sugar. Add beaten eggs. Mix in corn syrup, vanilla and chocolate chips. Pour into crust.

Arrange pecans on top of pie in a circular pattern. Bake 45 minutes.

As American As Apple Pie

Pareve

"My 13 year old son makes this to rave reviews every time."

CRUST

3 cups all-purpose flour

2 teaspoons lemon zest (from 1 medium lemon)

1 cup margarine, chilled

6-8 tablespoons ice water

FILLING

1 cup plus 1 tablespoon granulated sugar, divided use

1 teaspoon ground cinnamon

¼ cups cornstarch

6 large Granny Smith apples, peeled and thinly sliced (about 4 cups)

¼ cup salted margarine, chilled and cut into small pieces

1 egg, beaten

To prepare crust, mix flour and lemon zest together with a wire whisk in a medium bowl. With a pastry cutter or knives, cut margarine into flour until dough resembles coarse meal. Add ice water and blend until dough can be gathered into a ball. Divide dough in half, flatten into disks and wrap tightly in plastic wrap or a plastic bag. Refrigerate 1 hour until firm.

For filling, combine 1 cup sugar, cinnamon and cornstarch with a wire whisk in a large bowl. Add apples to sugar mixture and toss with a wooden spoon until dry ingredients coat the apples completely.

Preheat oven to 400 degrees.

On a floured surface using a floured rolling pin, roll out a piece of dough into a 11-inch diameter circle. Fold the crust in half, then in quarters. Place point of folded crust in center of a 9-inch pie plate and carefully unfold. Trim excess dough, leaving about ¾-inch hanging over edge of plate. Spoon in apple filling and scatter butter pieces on top.

Roll out second piece of dough into a 10-inches diameter circle. Again, fold in half, then quarters, and place over filling. Fold extra crust of the top layer over the bottom layer. Crimp layers together decoratively.

Cut several steam slits in pie top. Brush crust with beaten egg and sprinkle with 1 tablespoon sugar.

Place pie on center rack of oven. Bake 20 minutes, then reduce heat to 350 degrees. Bake an additional 30 minutes or until crust is deep golden brown and filling is bubbling through steam slits. Remove from oven and cool to room temperature on rack.

French Quarter Ice Cream Torte

Dairy

Fudge Sauce

8 ounces semi-sweet chocolate baking squares

1 cup heavy cream, not whipped

1 teaspoon dry instant coffee

1 tablespoon rum

Torte

35-40 chocolate wafer cookies, crushed

1 quart chocolate chocolate chip ice cream, softened

1 quart coffee ice cream, softened

½ Almond Roca candy, coarsely chopped

Melt chocolate with cream and coffee, stirring until smooth. Remove from the heat and add rum; set aside.

Spread half the crushed cookies on the bottom of a 9-inch springform pan.

Spread softened chocolate ice cream over cookie crust. Drizzle half of fudge sauce over the ice cream. Spread the rest of the cookies on top, then cover with coffee ice cream. Drizzle the rest of the fudge sauce over top. Distribute the crushed candy evenly over the surface. Freeze.

Creamy Smooth Hot Fudge Sauce

Dairy

The big chocolate flavor of this heavenly sauce over ice cream and a brownie is sure to satisfy the craving of any sweet tooth.

1 (14 ounce) can sweetened condensed milk

4 (1 ounce) squares semi-sweet chocolate

2 tablespoons butter (no substitutes)

1 teaspoon vanilla extract

In a heavy saucepan, combine milk, chocolate and butter. Cook and stir over medium-low heat until chocolate is melted. Remove from heat and stir in vanilla.

Makes about 1½ cups

Serve over pound cake, ice cream and strawberries.

EVERYONE'S FAVORITE ICE CREAM CAKE

Dairy

"My grandchildren like to decorate this cake with sprinkles or jimmies. I have been making this for years, and it is always a hit."

8 tablespoons (1 stick) butter, softened	1 cup flour
1 cup sugar	1½ teaspoons baking powder
4 eggs	½ gallon vanilla ice cream, or favorite flavor, softened
1 (16 ounce) can chocolate syrup	6 ounces chocolate chips
2 teaspoons vanilla	¼ cup milk

Preheat oven to 350 degrees.

Cream butter and sugar. Beat in eggs, chocolate syrup, vanilla, flour and baking powder.

Pour batter into a greased 13x9x2-inch baking pan. Bake 30 minutes. Freeze when cool.

Cover frozen cake with ice cream. Melt chocolate chips with milk and drizzle over ice cream.

VERY RICH HOT FUDGE SAUCE

Pareve

"This is my favorite chocolate sauce to pour over ice cream for company. It's really amazing over a piece of homemade pound cake with vanilla anything (frozen yogurt or ice cream). Once you make a batch, you can keep it forever in your freezer and use as desired. Always serve it piping hot from stove or microwave."

½ cup water	2 ounces unsweetened chocolate
½ cup sugar	1 teaspoon vanilla

Combine water and sugar and stir until dissolved. Cook, without stirring, to the syrup stage, about 5 minutes.

Add chocolate and cook over medium-low heat for about 10 minutes or until chocolate melts. Cool. Stir in vanilla.

If the syrup is too thick, thin to desired consistency with dry sherry, brandy or boiling water.

Fresh Fruit Platter with Fruit Sauce

Pareve

½ small cantaloupe

12 strawberries

3 kiwis

1 medium bunch seedless grapes

2 apples

2 large bananas

Sauce

1½ cups frozen blackberries, thawed on paper towels to absorb liquids

2 ripe pears

2 teaspoons sugar, or 1 teaspoon honey

1 teaspoon fruit brandy or liqueur (optional)

Vary this recipe according to your own tastes and according to what is available in the market at any season.

Cut cantaloupe into thin wedges or half wedges. Hull the strawberries. Peel and cut the kiwi into wedges or slices. Divide the grapes into tiny bunches or 3 or 4. Core and slice the apples. Peel the bananas and cut into short stick-like pieces. If the fruits are being prepared several hours ahead of time, the apple slices and banana pieces can be put into a small bowl of orange juice, then drained when ready to use.

To make sauce, combine blackberries, pears, sugar and brandy in a food processor bowl. Process until puréed. Push through a sieve.

Arrange the fruits artfully on a platter, perhaps garnishing with tiny mint sprigs or edible flowers. Pour sauce into a small bowl to serve.

BANANA CHOCOLATE WRAPPERS

Dairy

1 quart peanut oil, for frying

1 banana, quartered

4 wonton wrappers

4 teaspoons semi-sweet
   chocolate, chopped into small
   pieces

2 tablespoons cane or granulated
   sugar

4 ounces caramel ice cream

Preheat oil to 350 degrees in a large, deep (at least 2-quart) pot.

Place 1 piece of the quartered banana and 1 teaspoon chocolate pieces at the bottom of a wonton wrapper. Sprinkle with sugar and wet the edges with water. Wrap like a burrito. Repeat with remaining banana pieces, chocolate pieces, and wrappers.

Drop rolls into hot oil and fry until golden brown. Place on a plate with paper towels to soak up excess oil.

Sprinkle again with sugar. Place 2 each on an individual serving plate with a scoop of ice cream.

Serves 2

MANDEL BREAD

Pareve

1 cup canola oil
1 cup sugar
3 eggs, beaten
3 cups flour

1 teaspoon baking powder
1 cup chopped pecans
2½ teaspoons vanilla
Cinnamon sugar

For variations, add or substitute: Shredded coconut, dried cranberries, raisins and ¼ teaspoon orange or almond extract for ½ teaspoon vanilla.

Blend oil and sugar. Add beaten eggs; mix well.

Combine flour, baking powder and pecans. Stir into egg mixture until thoroughly mixed. Add vanilla. Refrigerate at least 4 hours.

Preheat oven to 375 degrees.

Shape dough into 4 equal parts, about 12x4-inches, and place on 1 to 2 parchment paper-lined baking sheets. Sprinkle with cinnamon sugar.

Bake 20 minutes. Remove from oven and cut into slices. Lay pieces on their sides and sprinkle with cinnamon and sugar mixture. Repeat for other side.

Bake another 10 minutes to brown.

Substitute ½-1 cup chocolate chips for the nuts.

AUNT SYLVIA'S FAMOUS MANDEL BREAD

Dairy

2 cups flour
½ teaspoon baking powder
½ teaspoon salt (optional)
1 cup sugar

8 tablespoons (1 stick) butter, softened
3 eggs
1 teaspoon vanilla
Cinnamon sugar

Preheat oven to 350 degrees

Combine flour, baking powder and salt; set aside.

Cream sugar and butter together on medium speed of a mixer. Add eggs and vanilla and mix well. Reduce speed and add dry ingredients. Mix well.

Add 2 cups of any of the following to the batter:

chocolate chips, butterscotch chips, maraschino cherries, chopped walnuts, raisins, craisins.

Spray a large baking sheet with nonstick cooking spray. Make four ¾-inch thick rolls from batter and place them lengthwise on baking sheet. Sprinkle with cinnamon sugar.

Bake 20 minutes. Check and take out of oven when light brown. Slice the rolls into ½-inch wide pieces and lay pieces on side. Return to oven for 5 minutes to brown; watch carefully so they don't burn.

PISTACHIO-ORANGE BISCOTTI

Pareve

This dessert migrated to Baltimore from a gourmet cook in Riverside, New York.

1¾ cups all-purpose flour
½ teaspoon baking soda
½ teaspoon baking powder
⅛ teaspoon salt
½ cup unsalted margarine,
    softened

1 cup granulated sugar
2 tablespoons orange zest
1½ teaspoons vanilla extract
2 eggs
1½ cups unsalted shelled
    pistachio nuts

Sift together flour, baking soda, baking powder and salt in a bowl; set aside.

Combine margarine, sugar, orange zest and vanilla in a large bowl. Using an electric mixer set on high speed, beat until light and fluffy. Mix in the eggs, one at a time, beating well after each addition. Reduce the speed to low and mix in the pistachio nuts. Add dry ingredients and mix just until incorporated. Cover and refrigerate until well-chilled, about 1 hour.

Preheat an oven to 350 degrees.

Divide the dough in half. Using lightly floured hands, roll each half on a lightly floured surface into a log 1½ inches in diameter. Arrange logs on a greased and floured baking sheet, spacing them 5 inches apart.

Bake until light brown and firm to the touch, about 30 minutes. Logs will spread during baking. Remove from the oven and cool slightly on the baking sheet.

Using a spatula carefully transfer the logs to a work surface. Using a serrated knife, cut on the diagonal into ¾-inch thick slices. Arrange the slices, cut-side down, on the baking sheet. Bake at 350 degrees for 10 to 15 minutes or until golden brown. Transfer cookies to a wire racks to cool. Store in an airtight container at room temperature for up to 2 weeks.

Makes about 3 dozen

Would be delicious dipped in white chocolate with crushed nuts.

This dessert is:

Nice to give as a gift.

*Good to serve when
entertaining.*

*Gorgeous in a pretty
container.*

AMIE'S BISCOTTI

Dairy

1¾ cups flour

1 cup sugar, plus extra for topping

1 teaspoon baking powder

¼ teaspoon salt

4 tablespoons (½ stick) butter, cold and cut into chunks

1 cup chocolate toffee candy bars, approximately 3 bars, chopped

1 cup pecan pieces, chopped

2 eggs

1 teaspoon vanilla

Preheat oven to 350 degrees.

In a food processor, mix flour, sugar, baking powder and salt. Add butter and process. Add chocolate toffee candy bars and pecan pieces and process.

In a separate bowl, mix eggs and vanilla. Add to mixture in processor and blend.

Pour all into another bowl and work with hands to knead dough into 2 logs. Place logs on a greased baking sheet. Sprinkle with sugar.

Bake 30 minutes. Let stand 10 minutes. Slice and bake 10 minutes more. Remove to wire racks to cool.

COOK'S NOTES

A wonderful dessert wine to enjoy with this Biscotti is Binyamina Portok, the Israeli version of a classic full-bodied Port wine. Sweet, luscious, full flavored and simply delicious, this Israeli wine boasts a long lingering finish.

ROYAL PEANUT BUTTER CROWN CUPCAKE COOKIES

Dairy

8 tablespoons (1 stick) butter or margarine, softened

½ cup granulated sugar

½ cup light brown sugar

½ cup creamy or chunky peanut butter (not natural variety)

1 egg

½ teaspoon vanilla extract

1¼ cups all-purpose flour

½ teaspoon baking soda

¼ teaspoon salt

1 (14 ounce) package miniature peanut butter cups

Can put candy-coated peanut butter pieces on top of melted chocolate peanut butter cups for more color, or add colored sprinkles or powdered sugar when serving.

Preheat oven to 350 degrees.

In a large mixing bowl with an electric mixer on high speed, beat butter, both sugars and peanut butter until smooth and creamy. Mix in egg and vanilla until blended. Add flour, baking soda and salt and mix on low speed until incorporated. Increase to medium speed and mix for 1 minute.

Roll into 1-inch balls. Place each ball into is own compartment of an ungreased mini-muffin tin. Press each ball gently with your thumb so that the dough fills the compartment.

Bake 8-10 minutes or until lightly browned. (Remove wrapping from peanut butter cups while cookies bake.)

Remove from oven and let cookies cool 3 minutes. Press a peanut butter cup into the warm center of each cookie until only the top shows (but do not press down too far).

Cool 5 to 10 minutes more. Remove from tins by inserting the tip of a sharp knife into one edge.

Freezes well.

CHOCO-PEANUT BUTTER BARS

Dairy / Pareve

"This yummy recipe was the favorite of my twin sons when they were growing up and is now the favorite of their children. Looks pretty too!"

8 tablespoons (1 stick) margarine, softened
½ cup peanut butter
½ cup granulated sugar
½ cup brown sugar
1 egg
2 tablespoons water

1¼ cups flour
¾ teaspoon baking soda
½ teaspoon baking powder
¼ teaspoon salt
2 (6 ounce) packages chocolate chips, divided use
½ cup chopped salted peanuts

Preheat oven to 375 degrees.

Mix margarine, peanut butter, both sugars and egg thoroughly. Stir in water, flour, baking soda, baking powder, salt and 1 package chocolate chips. Spread in a greased 13x9x2-inch pan. Bake 20 minutes.

Remove from oven. Immediately sprinkle remaining package of chocolate chips evenly over baked layer. Place baking sheet over pan so contained heat will soften chocolate chips. Spread softened chocolate evenly. Sprinkle with peanuts.

Cut into 1x3-inch bars.

Makes 32 bars

FAIGIE'S HAMANTASHEN

Pareve

"My mother made these with her kindergarten class every Purim for 30 years (she doubled the recipe for school). She'd be happy to know the recipe was passed on to new generations!"

8 tablespoons (1 stick)
   margarine
¾ cup sugar
1 egg

¼ cup orange juice
2½ cups flour or as needed
1½ teaspoons baking powder
Salt to taste

FOR FILLINGS, TRY:

Poppy seed and honey
Prune and orange zest
Cherry pie filling

Nuts
Raisins and cinnamon mixed
   together

Preheat oven to 350 degrees.

Cream margarine and sugar. Add egg and juice and mix well. Add flour, baking powder and salt and mix. More flour may be added until the dough is a rolling consistency.

Roll out dough and cut into 3-inch rounds. Add a dollop of filling and pinch twice to make 3 corners. Press 2 sides together, and then fold third side over and press the ends together. Place on a greased baking sheet. Bake 20 minutes.

Makes 60

There are 3 times in the year that we eat Hamantashen. Purim, Hoshana Rabba (the 7th day of Succot outside of Israel) and Erev Yom Kippur.

These are all days that are holidays (really, semi-holidays) but not with the same obligations as the other Biblical holidays. In Yiddish, they are called "fashtelt"-hidden or covered-holidays. So the sweets we eat in the Hamantashen are covered by the dough!! (But don't worry-the rest of the meal does not have to be all wrapped up!!)

DESSERTS—COOKIES

WENDE'S APPLE-PEAR CRUMBLE

Pareve

5-6 large Granny Smith apples, peeled

2-3 Bartlett pears, peeled

1 cup flour

½ cup sugar

1 teaspoon cinnamon

8 tablespoons (1 stick) margarine

Preheat oven to 350 degrees.

Cut apples and pears into wedges and place in a 9-inch pie pan, filling above top of pan as fruit will cook down.

Combine flour, sugar, cinnamon and margarine in a food processor until well blended but a little chunky. Spoon mixture over apples and pears until completely covered in a thick layer.

Bake 45 to 60 minutes or until topping is well browned.

If serving with a dairy meal, especially great when served warm with ice cream.

CRANBERRY APPLE CRUNCH

Pareve

5-6 apples, peeled and sliced

1 (16 ounce) can whole berry cranberry sauce

1 cup rolled oats

½ cup flour

1 cup brown sugar

8 tablespoons (1 stick) margarine, softened

Preheat oven to 350 degrees.

Cover bottom of greased 13x9x2-inch pan with apple slices. Top with cranberry sauce.

Combine oats, flour, sugar and margarine and sprinkle over fruit. Bake 1 hour.

PEACH CRUNCH

Pareve

4-5 peaches, sliced

1 cup flour

½ cup sugar

½ cup brown sugar

1 teaspoon cinnamon

½ teaspoon baking powder

1 egg, beaten

4 tablespoons (½ stick) margarine, melted

Preheat oven to 350 degrees.

Place sliced peaches in a greased pie pan.

Combine flour, sugar, cinnamon and baking powder. Stir in egg to make a crumb topping. Sprinkle topping over peaches. Drizzle margarine on top.

Bake 30 minutes or until topping is browned and bubbly.

Top with ice cream or whipped cream, if serving with dairy meal.

This works well with apples in the fall when all the good peaches are gone. It also works well with fresh cherries, but you have to pit them first.

OLD-FASHIONED GINGERBREAD

Pareve / Dairy

1 cup light or dark molasses

½ cup boiling water

6 tablespoons (¾ stick) butter or margarine

1 egg

2½ cups flour

½ teaspoon salt

1 teaspoon baking soda

1½ teaspoons ginger

½ teaspoon cinnamon

Few dashes of cayenne pepper

Preheat the oven to 350 degrees.

Place molasses into a mixing bowl. Pour in boiling water and add the butter, mixing well. Beat in egg.

In a separate bowl, sift together flour, salt, baking soda, ginger, cinnamon and cayenne pepper and gradually add to molasses mixture.

Pour batter into a greased and floured 9-inch square baking pan. Bake 25 to 30 minutes or until the cake springs back when touched and is pulling away from the sides of the pan.

Serve warm, with applesauce, ice cream or lightly sweetened whipped cream.

Ginger Crisps

Dairy / Pareve

12 tablespoons (1½ sticks)
  butter or margarine, melted

1 cup sugar, plus extra for
  coating

¼ cup molasses

1 egg

2 cups flour

2 teaspoons baking soda

½ teaspoon salt

1 teaspoon cinnamon

½ teaspoon ground cloves

1 teaspoon ground ginger

Combine butter, sugar and molasses and mix well. Add the egg and beat until smooth and thick. Add flour, baking soda, salt, cinnamon, cloves and ginger and blend thoroughly. Cover and chill the dough for 2 hours or as much as overnight.

When ready to bake, preheat oven to 350 degrees.

Form chilled dough into small balls using about 1 tablespoon of dough for each cookie. Dip each ball in the sugar, coating only one side and place, sugar side up, at least 2 inches apart on foil-lined baking sheets. Dipping the dough in the sugar gives the cookie a crispy topping.

Bake 10 to 12 minutes or until the cookies are dark, golden brown. While baking, the cookies will first puff up and then flatten. They are not done baking until they have flattened. Remove from oven and let cool about 2 minutes on the baking sheets. Remove to a wire rack to cool completely.

Makes about 3 dozen

ARLENE'S GOOD OLD-FASHIONED STRUDEL

Pareve

DOUGH

2 cups flour
½ cup oil

½ cup water from tap, not boiled
Pinch of salt

FILLING

Oil
Cinnamon
Sugar
1 (9 ounce) jar apricot preserves

Chopped nuts
Golden raisins
Coconut

Preheat oven to 350 degrees.

Mix all dough ingredients and divide into 3 parts. Refrigerate until filling ingredients are ready.

On a floured surface, roll out each dough section thin. Brush with oil; sprinkle with cinnamon and sugar. Dab teaspoons of preserves all over, but no too close to the edges. Sprinkle nuts and coconut over dough.

Roll up strudel and seal ends.

Brush top with oil and sprinkle with cinnamon and sugar. With a knife, score top of strudel. Place on a greased baking sheet.

Bake 35 to 45 minutes until lightly browned. Remove from oven and cut where scored.

Makes about 25-30 slices

BAKE SHOP STRUDEL

Dairy

DOUGH

½ cup butter

1 teaspoon salt

½ cup sour cream

2 cups flour

FILLING

1 (12 ounce) jar apricot jam or jelly

1 cup chopped pecans

1 cup shredded coconut

1 cup raisins

½ cup cinnamon and sugar

1 egg

1 tablespoon water

Combine dough ingredients; mix together and refrigerate overnight. Divide dough in half after chilled.

Preheat oven to 350 degrees. Roll on floured board to ⅛-inch thick. Spread lightly with apricot jelly. Sprinkle with nuts, coconut and raisins. Top with cinnamon and sugar. Roll jelly-roll fashion, tucking in ends first. Beat 1 egg with water. Brush roll with egg wash and sprinkle with cinnamon and sugar. Repeat with remaining dough.

Place rolls on ungreased shallow pan. Bake 45 minutes. Remove from pan while still hot. Cut into slices about 1-inch thick when cooled.

LEVINDALE BROWNIES

Dairy

¾ cup butter

6 ounces baking chocolate

6 eggs

3 cups sugar

2 teaspoons vanilla extract

1½ cups flour

1 teaspoon baking power

½ teaspoon salt

1½ teaspoons chopped pecans

Preheat oven to 325 degrees. Melt butter and chocolate together in saucepan; let cool slightly. Beat eggs and sugar together in large bowl until very light and fluffy. Add vanilla. Stir in chocolate mixture, then flour, baking powder, salt and nuts. Bake in greased and floured jellyroll pan for 25 minutes. Cut into squares when cool.

In the late 1960's, about twenty women comprised the Ladies Auxiliary of the Levindale Hebrew Home and Hospital. Each week, this dedicated group met in Levindale's kitchen to make the most delicious brownies, crescents, chocolate candy chews, mondel bread, and so much more. Loyal customers phoned in their orders and picked up their fresh sweets starting at 3PM. All the money raised went directly to enhancing the lives of the patients.

CHOCOLATE CANDY CHEWS

Dairy

1½ cups sugar

½ teaspoon salt

2 cups golden corn syrup

¼ pound butter

8 squares unsweetened chocolate

1 tablespoon vanilla extract

Combine sugar, salt, corn syrup, butter, and chocolate in large saucepan. Cook over medium heat, stirring constantly, until boiling. Using candy thermometer, cook without stirring, to 243 degrees. Remove from heat and add vanilla.

Pour into greased pan and allow to cool slightly. Pull and cut while warm. Roll into 1-inch balls. Then wrap in pre-cut cellophane candy wrappers and twist tightly.

To make Almondettes: Wrap each piece around almond.

To make Pecan Delights: Cook to 244 degrees. Form candy into small balls and press into broken pecans.

LEVINDALE CRESCENTS

Dairy

3 egg yolks beaten

1 teaspoon vanilla extract

1 package dry yeast

1 cup sour cream

1¼ cups butter or margarine

4 cups sifted flour

½ teaspoon salt

Confectioners' sugar

FILLING

3 egg whites, stiffly beaten

1 cup chopped pecans or walnuts

1 cup sugar

1 teaspoon vanilla extract

Preheat oven to 350 degrees. Mix egg yolks, vanilla, sour cream and yeast together. In a separate bowl, cut butter into flour and salt with pastry blender until mixture resembles meal. Mix yeast mixture into flour and salt mixture. Divide into 7 balls. Roll each ball separately in powdered sugar and roll out with rolling pin quite thin into a circle. Cut each circle into 8 pie-shaped wedges. In a separate bowl, mix all ingredients together for filling. Put 1 teaspoon of filling onto each triangle and roll tightly, starting at broad end. Shape as a crescent and place on ungreased cookie sheet. Bake 20 to 25 minutes. Remove from pan immediately. Sprinkle with powdered sugar when cooled.

These crescents freeze well.

Each June, the ladies would bake the full week before the annual Levindale Fair to fill the many orders the event would demand. As time went by and lifestyles changed, it became harder to recruit younger women to help in the Bake Shop. Eventually, it closed. It was like the end of an era. But, the recipes live on in each of their homes and hopefully, now in yours. America Cooks Kosher is proud to bring some of these sweet memories to your kitchen.

Lemon Bars

Dairy

Crust

12 tablespoons (1½ sticks)
   butter, softened

½ cup powdered sugar

1½ cups flour

Filling

3 eggs, beaten

1½ cups granulated sugar

3 tablespoons flour

Juice of 1 lemon or more
   (I use 1½ lemons)

Powdered sugar for topping

Preheat oven to 350 degrees.

Mix together butter, powdered sugar and flour and pat into a greased 13x9x2-inch baking pan. Bake 20 minutes.

Combine all filling ingredients except powdered sugar and pour over crust.

Bake another 20 minutes. Sprinkle with powdered sugar and cut into bars.

Fifkes

Dairy

1 cup (2 sticks) butter, softened

2 cups flour

1 package yeast

¼ cup warm water

2 eggs, unbeaten

Cinnamon

Sugar

Raisins

Nuts

Cut butter into flour. Dissolve yeast in warm water. Mix yeast into eggs and add to flour mixture. Knead and cover. Let sit for 1 hour.

Preheat oven to 350 degrees.

Break dough into small pieces, flatten to round. Sprinkle raisins, cinnamon and nuts in each one and roll up. Then roll each piece in cinnamon and sugar.

Bake 25 to 30 minutes.

Dream Bars

Pareve

Crust

8 tablespoons (1 stick)
    margarine, softened

½ cup brown sugar

1¼ cups flour

Filling

2 eggs, beaten

½ teaspoon baking powder

1 cup brown sugar

½ teaspoon salt

1 cup shredded coconut

1 teaspoon vanilla extract

Preheat oven to 350 degrees.

Combine ingredients for crust and pat into a 9-inch cake pan. Bake 15 minutes.

Mix all filling ingredients and spread over baked crust.

Bake another 20 to 25 minutes. Cut into squares.

Cook's Notes

DELECTABLE DATE-NUT BARS

Pareve

"This cake was first given as Mishloach Manot in 1917. I've been making it for more years than I want to admit."

2 eggs	1 teaspoon baking powder
1 cup sugar	8 ounces pitted soft dates, cut
1 teaspoon vanilla	into thirds
1 cup flour	1½ cups walnut pieces

Preheat oven to 325 degrees.

Mix eggs with sugar and vanilla. Mix in flour, which has been combined with baking powder. Add dates and mix well to distribute. Add nuts and stir to evenly mix in nuts and dates; very little mixing is needed.

Press into a greased metal 9x5-inch loaf pan. (I put parchment paper in bottom of pan and spray nonstick cooking spray sparingly on the sides.)

When well pressed in, make an indentation with wooden spoon down center.

Bake 30 minutes. Take out and push down again. Bake 15 minutes more. Press down again and bake for another 15 minutes. Cool on a wire rack. Wrapped well and frozen, bars last a long time.

Cut same day as baked. To cut, cut into slices, then cut through center. You will need a sharp knife.

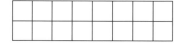

RICH BUTTERSCOTCH BARS

Dairy

1 (10 to 11 ounce) package
   butterscotch chips

8 tablespoons (1 stick) butter
   (no substitutes)

2 cups graham cracker crumbs
   (about 32 squares)

1 (8 ounce) package cream
   cheese, softened

1 (14 ounce) can sweetened
   condensed milk

1 egg

1 teaspoon vanilla extract

1 cups chopped pecans

This is a very rich and sweet dessert. Serve in small slices.

Preheat oven to 325 degrees.

In a large microwave-safe bowl, heat butterscotch chips and butter on high for 1½ to 2 minutes or until melted, stirring every 30 seconds until smooth. Add cracker crumbs. Set aside ⅔ cup of mixture and press the remaining crumb mixture into a greased 13x9x2-inch-baking pan.

In a small mixing bowl, beat cream cheese until smooth. Add the milk, egg and vanilla and mix well. Stir in pecans. Pour over the crust. Sprinkle with reserved crumb mixture.

Bake 30 to 35 minutes or until a toothpick inserted near the center comes out clean. Cool on a wire rack. Store in refrigerator.

Makes 3 dozen

SAVANNAH ALMOND COOKIES

Pareve

"I got this recipe from my friends in Savannah, so that's how it got its name. They are truly delicious. Enjoy. They are easy to make and are pareve."

1 cup sugar

2½ cups sliced almonds

1 stick margarine, melted and
   cooled

1 teaspoon vanilla

5 tablespoons all-purpose flour

3 egg whites, not beaten

Preheat oven to 350 degrees.

Mix together all ingredients and drop by teaspoonfuls onto a parchment paper-lined baking sheet. Don't put cookies too close together because they spread.

Bake 10 minutes or until brown. Cookies freeze well.

Makes about 50-60 cookies

GRANDMA ROSE'S ROSH HASHANAH TAIGLACH

Pareve

"This is my favorite food of all time. It is sweet, crunchy, and absolutely delicious. What a great way to insure a very sweet new year!"

DOUGH

6 eggs	½ teaspoon baking powder
1 tablespoon oil	1½-3 cups flour (approximately)

SYRUP

2 pounds sugar (4 cups)	2½ cups water
1 pound honey	1 tablespoon dry ginger

Knead the dough ingredients together by hand to make a soft dough. Add extra flour to keep the dough from sticking to the work surface. Roll into index finger shapes. Tie each long cylinder of dough into a love knot.

After all the dough pieces have been made, prepare syrup. Combine sugar, honey and water in a pot. Bring to a boil. (It is OK for the dough love knots to sit out for a while.)

Drop each love knot into the boiling syrup. Boil, uncovered, over medium heat for 65 minutes or until the syrup thickens and the taiglach are medium brown. Be careful – these dough pieces are very fragile and delicate.

Add ginger to the pot and stir. Let cook 25 minutes or until ingredients are browner. Dilute syrup with 1½ cups boiling water. Stir to mix. (Syrup sizzles up at this point. Be careful not to burn yourself.) Turn off the stove and let taiglach cool for 30 minutes or more. Spoon into airtight jars. DO NOT REFRIGERATE.

If your taiglach turns out "too hard" then shorten the cooking time.

KIDS IN THE KITCHEN
HONORS ITS FUTURE CHEFS

Aaron Adler
David Adler
Noah Adler
Sara Beth Adler
Josh August
Noah August
Dora Berg
Elizabeth Berg
Samuel Berg
Samuel Leonard
Bernstein
Jocelyn Broth
Noah Broth
Sam Brown
Ateret Peleh Frank
Yanniv Tzvriel Frank
Andrew Fried
Lauren Fried
The Green Children
Kennedy Helfand
Danielle Herman
Steven Herman
Hallie Hurwitz
Jared Hurwitz
Lindsay Hurwitz
Shana Rose Kaplan
Sarah Leah Katz
Adam Kerzner
Golan Klotzman

Bettie Kruger
Joey Kruger
Sam Kruger

Julia Rose Lax Garber
Ryan Samuel Levin
Shayna Raleigh Levin
The Low Children
The Lucas Children
Benjamin Z. Mendelson
Maxwell H. Mendelson
Erin Frieda Miller
Austin Reif
Erika Reif
The Schwartz Children
Allison Sellman
Emily Sellman
Jennifer Sellman
Henry Sholk
Seth Sholk
Molly Sugarman
Kimberly
Summerfield
Stephanie
Summerfield
The Weiner Children
Emma Wions
Samantha Wions
Noam Yaffe
Yaniv Yaffe
Evan Yerman
PJ Yerman
Lexi Zimmerman

KIDS IN THE KITCHEN

"Nothin' says lovin' like something from the oven..."™ Whether it's rolling out hamentashen for Purim or braiding challah for Shabbat, stuffing the Thanksgiving turkey or decorating the cookies for Mother's Day, these early experiences in the kitchen are the most precious gifts we can share with our children.

The kitchen is where our kids have fun while they learn to measure ingredients, calculate fractions and read temperatures. It is a safe and magical place, where they learn that it's okay to make a mistake. They learn that baking is a creative endeavor, that cooking is a labor of love and the delicacies that are fashioned in our kitchens enhance the way we share our love with family and friends.

It all begins with those small eager hands and curious faces yearning to experience the ingredients of our unique family recipes for the first time and continues on as we imprint those powerful memories from generation to generation.

TOFFEE BARS

Pareve

1 cup (2 sticks) pareve
    margarine, softened
1 cup brown sugar
1 teaspoon vanilla

2 cups sifted flour
6 ounces pareve chocolate chips
1 cup chopped walnuts

Preheat oven to 350 degrees.

Cream margarine, brown sugar and vanilla. Add flour and mix well. Stir in chocolate chips and chopped walnuts.

Pressed into an ungreased 15½x10½x1½-inch jelly-roll pan. Use hands as mixture is very dry and crumbly. Bake 25 minutes.

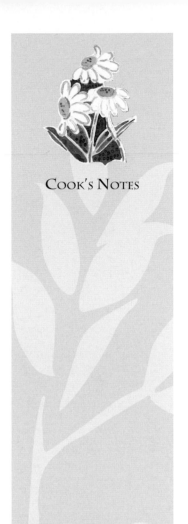

COOK'S NOTES

RAINBOW CHIP OAT BARS

Pareve / Dairy

1 package Super-Moist party
    cake rainbow chip cake mix,
    or chocolate cake mix or
    yellow cake mix with
    rainbow sprinkles
1 cup quick-cooking oats

½ cup vegetable oil
⅓ cup water
2 eggs
1 (6 ounce) package semi-sweet
    chocolate chips (1 cup)

Preheat oven to 350 degrees.

Mix dry cake mix, oats, oil, water and eggs in large bowl, using a spoon. Spread batter in a greased 13x9x2-inch baking pan.

Bake 20 to 25 minutes or until light golden brown. Sprinkle chocolate chips over hot bars in pan. Let stand 5 minutes or until chips are softened. Spread softened chocolate evenly over bars.

Cool completely. Cut into 2x1½-inch bars.

Makes 32 bars

PRETZEL KISSES

Dairy

1 (11 ounce) bag round pretzels, or if not available, any mini-size pretzel

1 bag chocolate kisses candy
1 bag M & M's®

Preheat oven to 300 degrees.

Put pretzels on a baking sheet. Place a chocolate kiss in the center of each pretzel. (Chocolate-peanut butter cups work, too!)

Bake 3 minutes. Take out of oven and put one M & M's® in the center and gently press down. Bring to room temperature before removing from baking sheet using a spatula. Refrigerate or freeze at least 20 minutes or until chocolate hardens.

CHOCOLATE CRACKER COOKIES

Dairy

1 (16 ounce) box unsalted tops saltine crackers
12 tablespoons (1½ sticks) margarine, melted

¾ cup sugar
6 ounces chocolate kisses candy
6 ounces chocolate chips

Preheat oven to 400 degrees.

Cover a 10½x15-inch jelly-roll pan with aluminum foil. Arrange a single layer of saltine crackers side by side to cover the pan. Mix margarine and sugar and pour over crackers.

Bake 5 minutes. Turn off oven; remove baking pan. Place chocolate kisses and chocolate chips on top of crackers. Put back into warm oven until chocolate is melted.

Remove from oven and place baking sheet in the freezer until chocolate is frozen. Cut into pieces and enjoy!

10 Minute Sugar Cookies

Dairy

"Here is a recipe that is simple enough to make with the children. And since it is one of Grandma Rose's recipes it's sure to be delicious as well. This recipe was found in my mother's recipe box on a real, honest to goodness recipe card. Crispy, yummy, wonderful."

Cook's Notes

8 tablespoons (1 stick) butter, softened

1 cup sugar

1 egg

1 tablespoon milk

¼ teaspoon vanilla extract

2 cups flour

2 teaspoons baking powder

Granulated sugar, cinnamon sugar or colored sugar for decorating

Cream together butter and sugar. In a separate bowl, beat egg and mix in milk and vanilla. Sift flour with baking powder. Add milk mixture and 1 cup dry ingredients to creamed mixture. Mix well. Blend in remaining dry ingredients. Chill dough in refrigerator for 3 to 4 hours, or in freezer for about 30 minutes.

Preheat oven to 375 degrees.

Roll the dough out on a floured wooden board. Cut with cookie cutters into shapes. Decorate as desired with sugar, cinnamon sugar or colored sugar. Place on a greased baking sheet.

Bake 8 to 10 minutes. Cookies are ready when they are slightly browned.

MRS. HOCHHEIMER'S CHOCOLATE STICKY APPLES

Dairy

"Mrs. Hochheimer sold sticky apples after school to my mother and her friends at Baltimore's famous Forest Park High School. My Mom begged Mrs. Hochheimer for this recipe and here it is for all of us to enjoy forever!"

This recipe is a Winner!

¾ cup dark corn syrup

¼ cup light corn syrup

1 cup granulated sugar

1 teaspoon real butter

4 (1 ounce) squares unsweetened chocolate

1 teaspoon vanilla

9 medium apples (We prefer tart and crisp to contrast the sweet topping)

9 popsicle sticks (you can get these at any craft store)

Adult to do: In a medium pot, mix together both corn syrups and sugar and heat. When sugar is melted, add the butter, then the chocolate. Cook over low to medium-low heat for at least 15 minutes or until mixture is completely smooth and no longer granulated. Stir in vanilla.

Adult to supervise well: Wipe each apple dry and put a popsicle stick in the core end. While keeping the pot on the stove, dunk each apple into the chocolate mixture until the apple is completely covered. Place apples on a greased baking sheet or a greased wax paper-lined plate. Keep apples separated so they don't stick together. The chocolate should harden in the air.

These apples will keep in the refrigerator for about 3 days. Enjoy!

Nana Ruthie's Brownies

Dairy / Pareve

4 (1 ounce) squares unsweetened
    chocolate
1 cup (2 sticks) butter or pareve
    margarine
Pinch of salt

2 teaspoons vanilla
2 cups sugar
4 eggs
1 cup flour

Preheat oven to 325 degrees.

Melt chocolate and butter in pan. Take off heat and add pinch of salt
and vanilla. Mix in sugar, one cup at a time. Beat in eggs, one at a time.
Add flour and mix well.

Pour batter into a greased and lightly-floured 13x9x2-inch baking
pan. Bake 25 to 30 minutes. The brownies should stick slightly to an
inserted knife. Let cool 30 minutes.

Easiest Ever Hamantashen

Dairy / Pareve

1 (18 ounce) box yellow cake
    mix
1 cup flour

2 eggs
2 tablespoons water
Fillings of your choice

Preheat oven to 375 degrees.

Combine all ingredients in a mixer and mix until blended. Roll out dough
to ⅛-inch thickness and cut into 2½- to 3-inch circles. Put 1 teaspoon filling
in center of each circle. Moisten edges with water and fold edges on three
sides to form a triangle. Place on a greased baking sheet.

Bake 10 minutes or until golden brown.

COOK'S NOTES

KIDS IN THE KITCHEN

CHOCOLATE SNOWBALL

Dairy /

This recipe came from my Mom's old family friend's mother, who gave it to my Mom's mother, who gave it to Mom. That's a "hand-me-up" snowball. Mom used to make this in an aluminum baking pan and keep it in the freezer. It's fabulous.

¾ cup cocoa

1 cup sugar

8 cups whole milk

Mix together all ingredients and put in a 13x9x2-inch aluminum baking pan. Place in freezer. Stir every hour to keep the mixture blended. It will eventually freeze.

When ready to serve, stir to break up. Serve with vanilla ice cream.

In cities outside of Baltimore, a snowball is referred to as a "sno-cone" or "shaved ice". In the hot, humid Baltimore summers, teenagers are found working snowball stands in every neighborhood.

CHOCOLATE LOVER'S CAKE

Dairy

Great, quick and easy, if a "chocolate quickie" is needed.

1 (18 ounce) box chocolate cake mix

1 (3 ounce) package instant chocolate pudding mix

1 (8 ounce) container sour cream

½ cup oil

½ cup water

4 eggs

1½ cups chocolate chips

Powdered sugar

Preheat oven to 350 degrees.

Beat together cake mix, pudding mix, sour cream, oil, water and eggs. Mix in chocolate chips.

Bake in a greased tube pan for 1 hour. When cooled, sprinkle powdered sugar on top.

Gar"licky" Pretzels

Dairy

1 package dry ranch dressing
  mix
½ cup olive oil
¼ teaspoon garlic powder

¼ teaspoon powdered dill
2 bags no salt beer-type pretzels,
  broken into about 4 pieces
  each (use no-salt sour dough)

Preheat oven to 350 degrees.

Combine all ingredients in a large zip lock bag. Shake bag well. Spread pretzels on a baking sheet sprayed with nonstick cooking spray.

Bake 10 minutes. Flip over with a spatula and bake another 5 minutes. Cool and serve.

Crispy Chicken Strips

Meat /

1½ pounds boneless chicken
  breasts, cut into strips or
  nuggets

1 (12 ounce) bag potato chips
1 large egg, beaten

Preheat oven to 400 degrees. Cover a baking sheet with foil and spray with cooking spray.

Crush potato chips until fine with a rolling pin and place in a shallow dish.

Dip chicken into egg, then roll in chips until covered. Place on prepared baking sheet.

Bake 15 minutes. Turn and bake about 15 minutes longer or until chicken is brown.

Serve with dipping sauce of choice.

Serves 4

COOK'S NOTES

1-2-3 Carrot Pudding

Pareve /

2 (16 ounce) cans sliced carrots, drained

4 eggs

2 teaspoons baking powder

1 cup flour or matzah meal

½ teaspoon salt

8 tablespoons (1 stick) pareve margarine, cubed

¾ cup sugar (combination of brown and white)

1 tablespoon hot water

Preheat oven to 350 degrees.

Beat carrots and eggs in mixer. Add baking powder, flour or matzah meal, salt, margarine, sugar and hot water. Mix well and place in greased 1-quart casserole dish. Bake 1 hour. Serve hot.

Serves 6

Easy Corn Casserole

Dairy

1 egg or ¼ cup egg substitute

4 tablespoons (½ stick) butter, melted

1 (8¼ ounce) can whole corn, drained

1 (8¼ ounce) can cream style corn

1 (8½ ounce) package corn muffin mix

1 (8 ounce) carton plain yogurt

Preheat oven to 350 degrees.

Combine all ingredients in a medium bowl and stir well. Pour into a well-greased 8-inch square baking dish. (Can double recipe and use a 9x13-inch pan.)

Bake 45 minutes or until set.

Serves 8

MENUS
FOR
JEWISH HOLIDAYS
AND
AMERICAN CELEBRATIONS

MENUS

MENUS ARE
OUR LEGACY

Memories of food are what holidays are all about.
From Rosh Hashanah to July 4th and everything in between, our holiday
and daily menus define our experiences, uniting families and friends by
assimilating our favorite tastes with their comforting aromas. These
foods dating back to our ancestors have been captured from the
past and brought to the forefront to fulfill our desire for
our customs and legacies to live on.

For Jews around the world, Shabbat, the day of rest,
the center point of our week, speaks to our identity, our
culture, and our tradition-and it does so through food.
And for Jews in America, Thanksgiving and other
national holidays do that as well.

Enjoy these sumptuous and extensive menus as they
evoke the treasured memories of your childhood, while
creating new traditions and experiences that
you will pass on to your families and friends.

WINTER SHABBAT DINNER

*Shabbat dinner brings the family together for a beautiful, relaxing,
uplifting meal of favorite foods, special blessings, and cheerful conversation.*

Traditional Challah…page 46

Herzog Late Harvest White Riesling

Spring Greens with Pears…page 86

Ahuva's Acorn Squash Soup…page 59

Cranberry Chicken…page 111

Green Beans and Mushrooms Gremolata…page 207

Grandma Rose's Candied Sweet Potatoes…page 218

Debbye's Jewish Apple Cake…page 235

SUMMER SHABBAT LUNCH

A delightful meal of "make ahead" dishes that honors the Jewish day of rest.

Traditional Challah…page 46

Herzog Special Reserve Edna Valley Syrah

Chilled Melon Wedges

Herring Salad…page 98

Bubbie's Original Chopped Liver…page 31

Ahuva's Cholent…page 134

Chef Diane's Persian Orzo Salad with Apricots and Almonds…page 92

Broccoli Surprise Salad…page 96

Marinated Pea Salad…page 94

Pistachio-Orange Biscotti…page 261

Arlene's Good Old-Fashioned Strudel…page 269

TRADITIONAL ROSH HASHANAH DINNER

Rosh Hashanah, the Jewish New Year, celebrates the beginning of the world. The table is set with foods that represent the wholeness, prosperity, and sweetness sought in the coming year.

Traditional Challah …page 46

Herzog Special Reserve Russian River Chardonnay

Apples and Honey

Helen's Traditional Gefilte Fish…page 158

Mixed Green Salad with Nectarines (or Apples)…page 86

Bubbie Nellye's Traditional Chicken Soup…page 62, with Matzah Ball Floaters…page 61

Roasted Sabra Chicken…page 118

Grandma Bessie's Traditional Beef Tzimmes…page 133

Roasted Broccoli…page 204

Vegetable Kugel…page 188

Carrots Vichy…page 206

Bubby Attman's Chocolate Chip Honey Cake…page 231

CHOL HAMOED SUKKOT DINNER

Sukkot is an autumn harvest celebration. Family and friends gather together in the festive outdoor sukkah shelter to enjoy the tastes of seasonal favorites and traditional holiday foods.

Hot Apple Cider with Mulling Spices
Hot Toddy for a Crowd...page 43
Herzog Late Harvest Chenin Blanc
Shiitake Mushroom Barley Soup...page 74
Honey Orange Chicken...page 112
Unstuffed Cabbage and Meatballs...page 144
Wilted Spinach...page 210
Acorn Squash Soufflé...page 220
Grandma Sally's Pumpkin Chocolate Chip Cake...page 232
Ginger Crisps...page 268

CHANUKAH DINNER PARTY

So much more than gift giving, Chanukah brings family and friends together to share a delightful winter dinner, which of course includes eating the symbolic latkes.

Linda's Eggplant Dip…page 26

Baron Herzog Sauvignon Blanc

Peasant Pea Soup…page 75

Sweet & Sour Brisket…page 129

Lemon Chicken with Pine Nuts…page 114

Ratatouille…page 210

Potato Latkes with Applesauce…page 225

Mandel Bread…page 259

Wende's Apple-Pear Crumble…page 266

PURIM MISHLOACH MANOT GIFT BAGS

Purim is a minor holiday that is highly treasured in the Jewish tradition.
"Mishloach Manot" (sending gifts) is a custom of sending money, food or delicacies
to at least two friends, neighbors, relatives and the needy.
This custom is an expression of the joy felt on this holiday.

Baked Trail Mix…page 37

"Cinn-ful" Pecans…page 38

Sweet Dorm Delight…page 38

Delectable Date-Nut Bars…page 274

Easiest Ever Hamantashen…page 283

Baron Herzog Black Muscat

YOM HA'ATZMAUT CELEBRATION DINNER

*Commemorating the day Israel became a state, Jews worldwide
celebrate Israel's independence and the spirit of the Jewish people.*

Baron Herzog Merlot
Chummus...page 26, with Herb-Toasted Pita Crisps...page 23
Israeli Coffee Chicken...page 114
Sautéed Sugar Snap Peas and Asparagus...page 204
Israeli Salad...page 84
Zippy's Exceptional Jerusalem Kugel...page 181
Zippy's Famous Chocolate Mousse...page 246

GOURMET SHAVUOT DINNER

Shavuot signifies the giving of the Torah. The Torah, which nourishes our spirit, is often likened to milk and honey. Traditionally we eat dairy, fruit and honey on this holiday.

Baron Herzog Rosé of Cabernet Sauvignon
My Daughter's Sweet Mini Blinis...page 25
Spring Vegetable Soup...page 77
Salad with Fresh Herbs and Frico...page 90
Salmon with Maple Balsamic Glaze...page 169
Spinach Mushroom Onion Quiche...page 192
Roasted Asparagus with Bell Pepper Sauce...page 203
Wild Rice Pancakes with Mushrooms...page 229
French Quarter Ice Cream Torte...page 255
Vanilla Cheesecake with Berries...page 251

SPECIAL MOTHERS' DAY BRUNCH

*In the spirit of our love for all mothers, this beautiful meal
is a tribute to one of America's best-loved holidays!*

Mimosas and Bloody Marys

Layered Pesto Cheesecake...page 28

Baron Herzog White Zinfandel

Assorted Bagels, cream cheeses, tomatoes, onions and lox

Berry-Baked or Outrageous French Toast...page 56

Cheese and Mushroom Brunch Eggs...page 190

"Absolutely To Die For" Tomato Pie...page 213

Strawberry Brie Salad...page 88

Fresh Fruit Platter with Fruit Sauce...page 257

Anne's Coffee Cake...page 238

AMERICAN SUMMER BAR-B-QUE

The all-American kosher kitchen now stretches to the backyard barbeque and picnic table.
Enjoy this cool summer fare whenever a festive outdoor meal is in order.

Apricot Brandy Slush…page 39

Olive Tapenade on Pita…page 35

Gazpacho…page 78

Mixed Green Salad with Nectarines…page 86

Herzog Special Reserve Napa Valley Cabernet Sauvignon

Hot dogs, hamburgers on grill

Charcoaled Marinated Chicken Breasts…page 106

All-American Cole Slaw…page 95

Corn Salad with Vidalia Onions…page 97

Peach Crunch…page 267

FAMILY THANKSGIVING FEAST

*We celebrate giving thanks for our bountiful blessings year-round.
Thanksgiving provides us an additional opportunity to come together as a family
and experience the traditional recipes we treasure from generation to generation.*

SUPER BOWL PARTY

Try these crowd-pleasing favorites while cheering for your home team.

Tio Pepe Sangría...page 44

Colorful Corn Salsa...page 36

Spicy Bean Dip...page 37

Baron Herzog Chardonnay

Apricot Glazed Bologna "Casserole"...page 34

Mark's Meltdown Chili...page 139

Freddie's Lazy Texas Brisket with Tangy Sauce...page 131

Crispy Onion Baked Potatoes...page 216

Green Beans with Roasted Onions...page 209

Chocolate and White Intrigue Cake...page 245

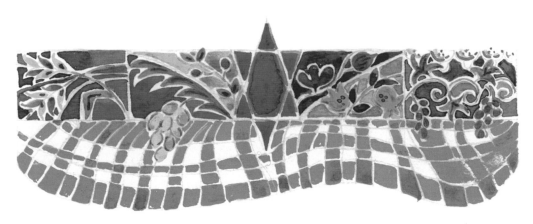

SUBSTITUTIONS

DAIRY TO PAREVE SUBSTITUTIONS

Keeping kosher requires some adjustments in choice of ingredients at times. Substitutions are becoming much easier in recent times due to the introduction and greater variety in non-dairy and vegetable-based products.

Pareve is a category of foods that are neither meat nor dairy and contain no meat or dairy derivatives. Examples of pareve foods include eggs, fish, fruit, vegetables, grains, natural juices, coffee and tea.

Examples of substitutions include:

Ingredient	Substitute
Butter	Pareve Margarine
Chicken or Meat broth	Vegetable broth, powdered vegetable stock mix, pareve powdered equivalent, or organic pareve broth
Skim, 1% and 2% milk	Rice milk, non-fat or low fat soy milk
Whole and 2% milk	Soymilk
Whipped cream	Frozen whipped non-dairy topping or liquid non-dairy cream-whipped

PASSOVER SUBSTITUTIONS

Many items are not available for Passover, so here is a list of what you can substitute for the original ingredient in your daily recipes. All items used must be labeled KOSHER FOR PASSOVER

1 ounce unsweetened baking chocolate	3 tablespoons unsweetened cocoa powder plus 1 tablespoon oil or melted margarine
6 ounces semi-sweet chocolate	6 tablespoons unsweetened cocoa powder plus ¼ cup oil and 7 tablespoons granulated sugar
4 ounces sweet chocolate German type	3 tablespoons unsweetened cocoa powder plus 2⅔ tablespoons oil and 4½ tablespoons granulated sugar
1 cup confectioners' sugar	1 cup granulated sugar (minus 1 tablespoon) plus 1 tablespoon potato starch — pulsed in a blender
1 cup corn syrup	1¼ cups granulated sugar plus ⅓ cup water, boiled until syrupy
1 cup vanilla sugar	1 cup granulated sugar with 1 split vanilla bean left for 24 hours in a tightly covered jar
1 tablespoon flour	½ tablespoon potato starch
1 tablespoon cornstarch	1 tablespoon potato starch
1 teaspoon baking powder	¼ teaspoon baking soda plus ½ teaspoon cream of tartar. If keeping for a while, add ¼ teaspoon potato starch.
1 cup graham cracker crumbs	1 cup matzah meal plus 2 tablespoons of cinnamon and sugar
1 cup bread crumbs	1 cup matzah meal
1 cup milk (if needed to convert a dairy dish to a pareve dish on Passover (for baking)	1 cup water plus 2 tablespoons margarine, or ½ cup fruit juice plus ½ cup water, or 1 cup almond milk (blend ⅓ cup sliced blanched almonds with 1 cup water until smooth)

METRIC CONVERSIONS

Weight equivalents

These are not exact weight equivalents, but have been rounded up or down slightly to make measuring easier.

American	Metric	American	Metric	American	Metric
¼ ounce	7 grams	8 ounces (½ pound)	225 grams	16 ounces (1 pound)	450 grams
½ ounce	15 grams	9 ounces	250 grams	1 pound 2 ounces	500 grams
1 ounce	30 grams	10 ounces	300 grams	1½ pounds	750 grams
2 ounces	60 grams	11 ounces	325 grams	2 pounds	900 grams
3 ounces	90 grams	12 ounces	350 grams	2¼ pounds	1 kilogram
4 ounces	115 grams	13 ounces	375 grams	3 pounds	1.4 kilgrams
5 ounces	150 grams	14 ounces	400 grams	4 pounds	1.8 kilograms
6 ounces	175 grams	15 ounces	425 grams	4½ pounds	2 kilograms
7 ounces	200 grams				

Volume equivalents

These are not exact volume equivalents, but have been rounded up or down slightly to make measuring easier.

American	Metric
¼ teaspoon	1.25 milliliters
½ teaspoon	2.5 milliliters
1 teaspoon	5 milliliters
½ tablespoon (1½ teaspoons)	7.5 milliliters
1 tablespoon (3 teaspoons)	15 milliliters
¼ cup (4 tablespoons)	60 milliliters
⅓ cup (5 tablespoons)	75 milliliters
½ cup (8 tablespoons)	125 milliliters
⅔ cup (10 tablespoons)	150 milliliters
¾ cup (12 tablespoons)	175 milliliters
1 cup (16 tablespoons)	250 milliliters
1¼ cups	300 milliliters
1½ cups	350 milliliters
1 pint (2 cups)	500 milliliters
2½ cups	625 milliliters
1 quart (4 cups)	1 litre

Oven Temperature equivalents

Oven	°Fahrenheit	°Celsius	Gas Mark
very cool	250–275	130–140	½–1
cool	300	150	2
warm	325	170	3
moderate	350	180	4
moderately hot	375	190	5
moderately hot	400	200	6
hot	425	220	7
very hot	450	230	8
very hot	475	250	9

KOSHER FOR PASSOVER INDEX

INDEX

INDEX

W

Y

Z

Zucchini (see Squash)

AMERICA COOKS KOSHER

℅ Beth Tfiloh Congregation and Beth Tfiloh Dahan Community School
3300 Old Court Road, Baltimore, MD 21208
410-486-1900,   www.bethtfiloh.com/cookbook

Please ship *America Cooks Kosher* to:

Name _____

Address_____ City_____ State_____ Zip_____

Phone_____ E-mail _____

Enclosed please find my **CHECK** made payable to **Beth Tfiloh** for_____ **AMERICA COOKS KOSHER** cookbooks.

Suggested Retail Price	$29.95 each	Quantity_____	$ _____
Sales Tax *(Maryland residents add 5%)*	$1.50 per book		$ _____
Shipping and Handling *(if applicable)*	$5.00 per first book		
	$3.00 each additional book		$ _____
		TOTAL ENCLOSED	$ _____

Or CHARGE to: *(circle one)*   Visa   MasterCard   Expiration Date_____

Account Number_____ Signature _____

All proceeds will nourish all of the ever-expanding Beth Tfiloh educational programs for children and adults.
Thank you for your support!

- -

AMERICA COOKS KOSHER

℅ Beth Tfiloh Congregation and Beth Tfiloh Dahan Community School
3300 Old Court Road, Baltimore, MD 21208
410-486-1900,   www.bethtfiloh.com/cookbook

Please ship *America Cooks Kosher* to:

Name _____

Address_____ City_____ State_____ Zip_____

Phone_____ E-mail _____

Enclosed please find my **CHECK** made payable to **Beth Tfiloh** for_____ **AMERICA COOKS KOSHER** cookbooks.

Suggested Retail Price	$29.95 each	Quantity_____	$ _____
Sales Tax *(Maryland residents add 5%)*	$1.50 per book		$ _____
Shipping and Handling *(if applicable)*	$5.00 per first book		
	$3.00 each additional book		$ _____
		TOTAL ENCLOSED	$ _____

Or CHARGE to: *(circle one)*   Visa   MasterCard   Expiration Date_____

Account Number_____ Signature _____

All proceeds will nourish all of the ever-expanding Beth Tfiloh educational programs for children and adults.
Thank you for your support!

AMERICA COOKS KOSHER

℅ Beth Tfiloh Congregation and Beth Tfiloh Dahan Community School
3300 Old Court Road, Baltimore, MD 21208
410-486-1900, www.bethtfiloh.com/cookbook

Please ship *America Cooks Kosher* to:

Name _____

Address_____ City_____ State_____ Zip_____

Phone_____ E-mail _____

Enclosed please find my **CHECK** made payable to **Beth Tfiloh** for_____ **AMERICA COOKS KOSHER** cookbooks.

Suggested Retail Price $29.95 each   Quantity_____ $ _____

Sales Tax *(Maryland residents add 5%)* $1.50 per book $ _____

Shipping and Handling *(if applicable)* $5.00 per first book

                           $3.00 each additional book $ _____

                                      TOTAL ENCLOSED $ _____

Or CHARGE to: *(circle one)*   Visa   MasterCard   Expiration Date_____

Account Number_____ Signature _____

All proceeds will nourish all of the ever-expanding Beth Tfiloh educational programs for children and adults.
Thank you for your support!

- -

AMERICA COOKS KOSHER

℅ Beth Tfiloh Congregation and Beth Tfiloh Dahan Community School
3300 Old Court Road, Baltimore, MD 21208
410-486-1900, www.bethtfiloh.com/cookbook

Please ship *America Cooks Kosher* to:

Name _____

Address_____ City_____ State_____ Zip_____

Phone_____ E-mail _____

Enclosed please find my **CHECK** made payable to **Beth Tfiloh** for_____ **AMERICA COOKS KOSHER** cookbooks.

Suggested Retail Price $29.95 each   Quantity_____ $ _____

Sales Tax *(Maryland residents add 5%)* $1.50 per book $ _____

Shipping and Handling *(if applicable)* $5.00 per first book

                           $3.00 each additional book $ _____

                                      TOTAL ENCLOSED $ _____

Or CHARGE to: *(circle one)*   Visa   MasterCard   Expiration Date_____

Account Number_____ Signature _____

All proceeds will nourish all of the ever-expanding Beth Tfiloh educational programs for children and adults.
Thank you for your support!